AF607963

FORMALISTS AGAINST IMPERIALISM

ANNA AYDINYAN

FORMALISTS AGAINST IMPERIALISM

THE DEATH OF VAZIR-MUKHTAR AND RUSSIAN ORIENTALISM

UNIVERSITY OF TORONTO PRESS
Toronto Buffalo London

Toronto Buffalo London
utorontopress.com

ISBN 978-1-4875-4385-3 (cloth) ISBN 978-1-4875-4386-0 (EPUB)
ISBN 978-1-4875-4387-7 (PDF)

Library and Archives Canada Cataloguing in Publication

Title: Formalists against imperialism : the Death of Vazir-Mukhtar and Russian orientalism / Anna Aydinyan.
Names: Aydinyan, Anna, author.
Description: Includes bibliographical references and index.
Identifiers: Canadiana (print) 20220166552 | Canadiana (ebook) 20220166757 | ISBN 9781487543853 (cloth) | ISBN 9781487543860 (EPUB) | ISBN 9781487543877 (PDF)
Subjects: LCSH: Tynīanov, ĪU. N. (ĪUriĭ Nikolaevich), 1894–1943. Smert′ Vazir-Mukhtara. | LCSH: Orientalism in literature. | LCSH: Formalism (Literary analysis) | LCSH: Orientalism – Russia – History. | LCSH: Russia – Civilization.
Classification: LCC PG3476.T9 Z54 2022 | DDC 891.73/42 – dc23

We wish to acknowledge the land on which the University of Toronto Press operates. This land is the traditional territory of the Wendat, the Anishnaabeg, the Haudenosaunee, the Métis, and the Mississaugas of the Credit First Nation.

University of Toronto Press acknowledges the financial support of the Government of Canada, the Canada Council for the Arts, and the Ontario Arts Council, an agency of the Government of Ontario, for its publishing activities.

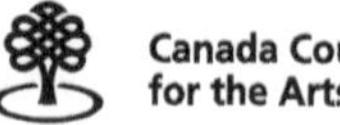

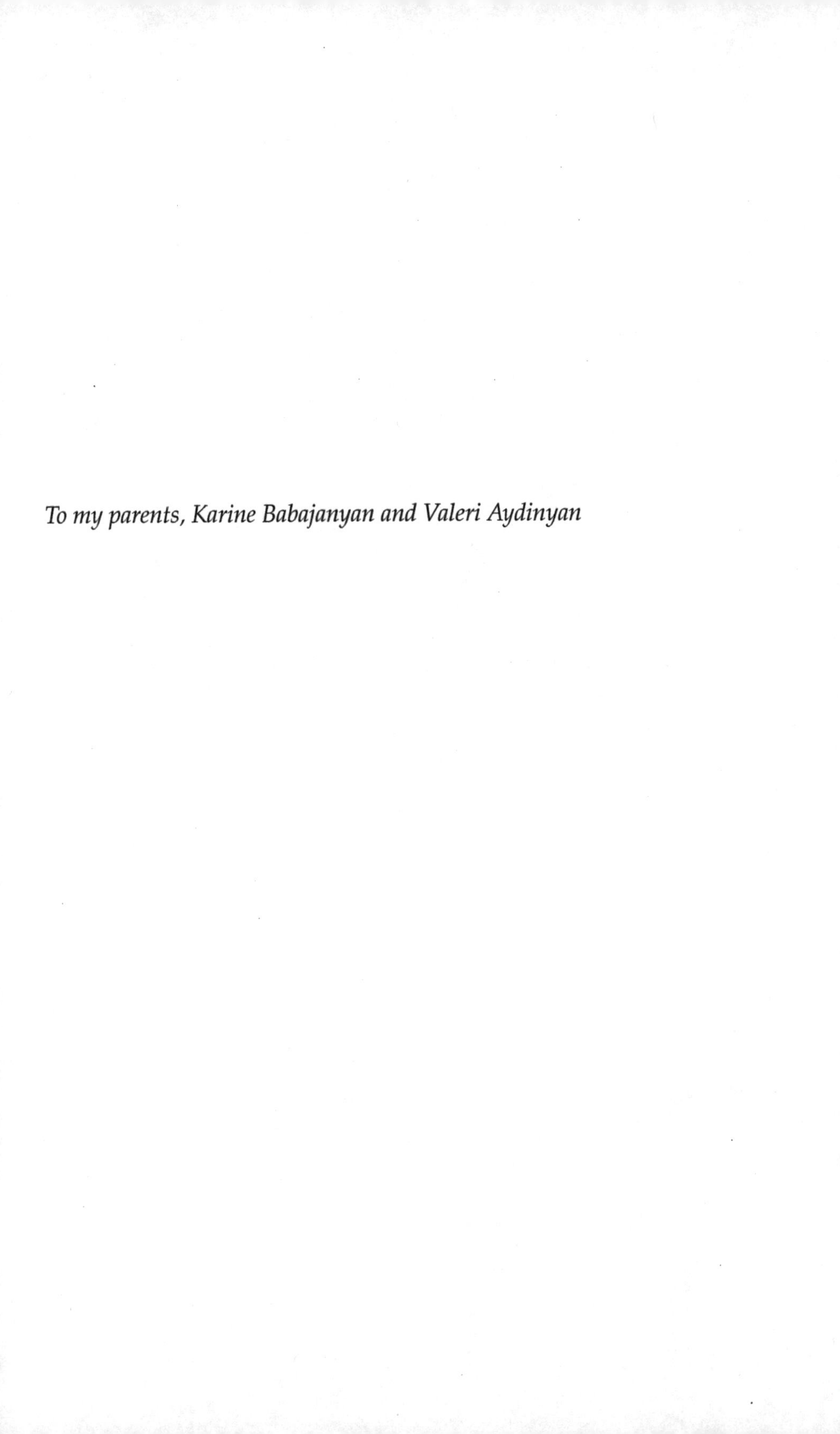

To my parents, Karine Babajanyan and Valeri Aydinyan

Contents

Acknowledgments

I started this book as my dissertation project at Yale Graduate School, but substantially revised it and added five more chapters. I am deeply grateful to my advisor, Katerina Clark, for encouraging me to continue working on it and eventually submitting it for publication. My other dissertation advisor, Abbas Amanat, guided me through my explorations of the history of Russian-Iranian relations. While still in graduate school, I received suggestions from a number of my professors, who at different times read and commented on my work. Among them are Vladimir Alexandrov, John MacKay, Bella Grigoryan, Harsha Ram, Kate Holland, and Ilya Kliger. My friend and classmate Rossen Djagalov has the gift of bringing people together; he not only gave me invaluable advice but also connected me with those who could help me.

My project received its second boost at the international workshop "Winning and Losing the Great Game: Literature, Art, and Diplomacy between Russia and Iran," held at the Ohio State University in 2014. I am especially grateful to Angela Brintlinger, one of the organizers of the workshop, for her vital suggestions on my work. I am also grateful to the other participants of this fruitful collaboration, among them Firuza Melville, George Bournoutian, Elena Andreeva, and Catherine O'Neil, as well as colleagues with whom I met at numerous other conferences, especially Mark Lipovetsky, Lyudmila Parts, Edyta Bojanowska, and Juliette Stapanian-Apkarian.

I was able to expand my section on Alexander Chavchavadze thanks to the Faculty Research Grant from Kenyon College that I received in 2016. The grant funded my work in the libraries and archives of Georgia, whose staff was truly supportive. My Kenyon colleagues Eliza Ablovatski, Nurten Kilic, James McGavran, and Maria Mendonca read my manuscript and gave me important feedback.

It was a great pleasure to work with my editor, Stephen Shapiro, in preparing this book for publication. The suggestions of my anonymous readers were extremely helpful, and I incorporated most of them in my final revision. Sam Brawand did a wonderful job in copy-editing and formatting my manuscript; at UTP, Christine Robertson ably steered the project to completion and Terry Teskey contributed impressive copy-editing.

I am very grateful to my husband, Randall Hardnock, for acting as my first copy-editor and reading the same passages over and over again without tiring. My sister Yelena Aydinyan helped me enormously by finding and copying for me books at the libraries of Yerevan, Armenia. I am also grateful to my parents, who ignited my love for literature and cultural history, and to my inquisitive children, who I hope will someday read this book.

While writing this book I was also thinking of my grandparents and great-grandparents, whose families were affected by the historical events discussed in this book. Growing up in Armenia gave me the initial impetus to start my explorations. I am indebted to the entire South Caucasus, in this book referred to as Transcaucasia. I hope that this beautiful and culturally unique mountainous land overcomes the troubling legacies of colonialism and continues to flourish in peace and prosperity.

A Note on Translations and Transliteration

Unless otherwise noted, translations from Russian and transliterations are mine. I use the most common spellings of the Russian names in my text ("Yury," "Shklovsky," etc.), but in endnotes follow the *Chicago Manual of Style* transliteration guide where needed for the original sources ("Iurii," "Shklovskii").

All translations from Persian are mine. For a number of historical references, I consulted the long-awaited annotated English translation of the diary by George Bournoutian, with accompanying excerpts from Russian sources: George A. Bournoutian, *From Tabriz to St. Petersburg: Iran's Mission of Apology to Russia in 1829* (Costa Mesa: Mazda, 2014). Tynianov's sources most likely included the notes of Count Paul Sukhtelen, who was assigned as the host of the Iranian delegation, edited by M.G. Rozanov, "Persidskoe posol'stvo v Rossii, 1829 goda (po bumagam Grafa P. P. Sukhtelena)," in *Russkii arkhiv*, vol. 27/1 (Moscow, 1889); as well as the study of A.P. Berzhe, "Khosrov-Mirza, 1813–1875," *Russkaia starina*, vol. 25 (St. Petersburg, 1879), 333–50.

Finally, I would like to explain the usage of geographical names. "Iran" is the name that the residents of the country historically used, while foreigners referred to it as Persia. I will use the name "Iran" in my text unless I represent the points of view of the Russian and early Soviet historical figures or fictional characters who would have used "Persia." To reflect the historical context I will at times refer to the capital of Georgia, Tbilisi, by the name "Tiflis," its Persian pronunciation, adopted by other countries including the Russian Empire and the Soviet Union before 1936. The word "Transcaucasia" implies an imperial point of view on the region located beyond the Caucasus if one looks at it from the Russian side. Since the collapse of the Soviet Union, the residents of the region refer to it as "South Caucasus." However, to preserve the context of the historical discourse on the colonial management of this land I will refer to it by its imperial name. In using the word "tribes" to describe the Caucasian peoples while discussing Russian poetry, I underscore the Eurocentric and colonialist views of the nineteenth century, as well as Tynianov's parody of their Eurocentrism. The word "gypsy" appears in citations or in quotation marks, and refers to the fictional character of Velimir Khlebnikov's poem and not a real person of Romani origin.

FORMALISTS AGAINST IMPERIALISM

Introduction

Long before Edward Said coined the term "Orientalism" and it became indispensable in postcolonial studies, Yury Tynianov (1894–1943) exposed in his novel *Smert' Vazir-Mukhtara* (*The Death of the Vazir-Mukhtar*) the phenomenon of Russian literary and cultural Orientalism through his parody of the nineteenth-century literary and non-literary text. Current analysis of the novel, as well as related works by Russian formalists and futurists, brings together for the first time the usually separated fields of postcolonial studies and the Russian literary theory of late formalism, with its preoccupation with the centre and periphery. It reveals that Tynianov and his fellow formalist, Viktor Shklovsky (1893–1984), were keenly interested in the problems of Russian imperialism. Their artistic foresight into the phenomenon that much later received the name of Orientalism is the missing link in the genealogy of postcolonial thought.

The Death of Vazir Mukhtar was published in 1929 as part of a series of cultural events commemorating the one hundredth anniversary of the death of Alexander Griboedov (1795–1829).[1] Griboedov was best known as the author of an 1825 comedy in verse, *Gore ot uma* (*Woe from Wit*),[2] and was also a diplomat in Iran and a long-term administrator in the Caucasus. Tynianov's novel is based on the last year of Griboedov's life and his violent death in Teheran on 11 February 1829. Having always enjoyed a wide readership in Russia, and further promoted by its 2010 television adaptation,[3] the novel still shapes ideas on Russia's historical relationships with Iran and the South Caucasus in popular imagination.

The historical events that the book discusses can be summarized as follows.[4] Griboedov played an important part in negotiating the Treaty of Turkmenchay at the end of the Russo-Persian War of 1826–8, and was responsible for enforcing it as the head of the Russian mission in Iran. In Teheran in January 1829, an angry mob destroyed the mission, killing all the delegates and employees, including Griboedov. In order to apologize for what had happened and to preserve a peaceful relationship with Russia, the Iranian government sent a delegation to Petersburg led by the shah's grandson Prince Khosrow Mirza. Shortly before his death Griboedov, in collaboration with Peter Zaveleisky (1800–1843), had submitted to the government officials a proposal for establishing a Russian Transcaucasian agricultural manufacturing and trading company. At the time, Zaveleisky was the manager of the treasury expedition collecting statistical information on the economy and resources of Transcaucasia, and was soon to be appointed the civilian governor of Tiflis.[5] It was an ambitious project with the goals of modernizing and "civilizing" the newly acquired region with the help of a state-sponsored monopolistic company that would use forced labour. Tynianov's *The Death of Vazir-Mukhtar* gives special importance to the proposal as the main project that preoccupied his protagonist's life before his premature death.[6]

Important scholarly work dedicated to *The Death of Vazir-Mukhtar* explores the ways in which Tynianov uses history to highlight the political upheavals of his own time,[7] the themes of autocracy and the Decembrist revolt in the novel,[8] its unique cinematic writing style, and its connection with the theory of formalism.[9] The present study, however, argues that Orientalism, in its connection to the imperial project, is the main topic of the novel. Through his parody of the Russian texts about the "Orient," Tynianov essentially outlines the main arguments of the studies in Russian Orientalism that appear half a century later.

While Tynianov's fiction is far from the thorough analytical studies of Russian empire-building projects conducted by contemporary scholars,[10] it provides an insightful, intuitive outline of its most important phenomena. In the novel, literary Orientalism plays an important part in exciting people's interest, in shaping their views of Russia's new colonial acquisitions, and in influencing the policies of their management. Tynianov shares with his friend, the formalist Shklovsky, his special interest in Russia's relationship with its "Orient." They both denounce the imperial legacy and ponder the new principles on which, after the Revolution, the former empire could be transformed without the practice of colonial domination.

Tynianov's anticolonial views coincide with the prevailing ideological trends of the Soviet 1920s, when imperialism ("the highest stage of capitalism," in Vladimir Lenin's [1870–1924] memorable words) was to be denounced and confronted.[11] Yet Tynianov's attitude towards imperialism comes not from political conformism, but from a personal conviction to which it owes its originality. This conviction bears the influences of the larger cultural history of re-evaluating views of the relationship between East and West, and of a general disapproval of colonialism that developed in the Russian Empire by the end of the nineteenth century and was radicalized after the First World War and the revolutions of 1917–23.

Vera Tolz in her 2011 *Russia's Own Orient* argues that the first systematic outline of the phenomenon of Orientalism in Russia was introduced by Russian Orientalists themselves.[12] The school of Oriental studies, developed in the second half of the 1880s by Baron Viktor Romanovich Rozen (1849–1908) and his disciples, continued its work during the Soviet times and gradually developed the view of Oriental studies as a form of knowledge that the imperial power used to subdue the Orient.

In the late imperial period, the school still viewed the connection between the imperial project and the field of Oriental studies as a positive force that helped the "civilizing mission" of the Russian Empire in its eastern and southern provinces. However, after Russia's defeat in the Russo-Japanese War of 1904–5, and especially after First World War, their evaluation of European Oriental studies as a tool used to colonize the Orient became increasingly negative. They criticized their European, and sometimes Russian, colleagues for Eurocentrism, and questioned the Orientalist notions of East and West as "self-evident categories," describing them as "geographical, cultural and political constructs" and tracing the changes they have undergone throughout history.[13]

During Soviet times, they were striving to create a "new type of scholarship … free from Western European prejudices against the 'East' and from the corrupting influences of imperialism." They also participated in a nation-building process for the small minorities of the former Russian Empire.[14] Their motivation, Tolz argues, was not "political opportunism," but rather their re-evaluation of their own belief in Europe's "civilizing mission" in the aftermath of the First World War.[15]

Even though Edward Said (1935–2003) was not directly familiar with their works, Tolz suggests that he could have been acquainted with their ideas indirectly through "several Arab authors, who in the early 1960s had initiated a major critique of Western Oriental Studies from a perspective which was at the same time Marxist and post-colonial nationalist."[16] Some of these authors, most importantly the Egyptian communist Anouar Abdel-Malek (1924–2012), whom Said extensively cites in his 1979 *Orientalism*, were conversant with the Soviet literature.

At the same time, the ideas of the scholars of Rozen's school took shape in the intellectual and cultural environment of Orientophilia (*vostokofil'stvo*) of the Russian fin-de-siècle. Their works were widely read by the cultural elites of both the late imperial and early Soviet times.[17] While Tolz does not discuss particular cases in which Rozen's school exerted influence on Russian literature and literary studies, the presence of certain ideas developed by its scholars in Tynianov's novel suggests that it was highly probable he was either directly or indirectly familiar with their work.

Reading Tynianov's novel, one cannot miss the vastly different perceptions of the "East" and the moral evaluations of colonialism held by the characters of the novel, set in the late 1820s, as opposed to its narrator. Characters and narrator are separated by a century and such historical events as the emancipation of serfs, the Russo-Japanese War, the First World War, the revolutions of 1905 and 1917, and the disintegration of the Russian Empire and its consolidation by the Bolsheviks.

Among the texts Tynianov parodies is Griboedov and Zaveleisky's own proposal to establish a Russian Transcaucasian Company. That project in many instances rearticulates the ideas and the practical suggestions of *A Philosophical and Political History of the Settlements and Trade of the Europeans in the East and West Indies* (1770), by Abbé Guillaume-Thomas-François Raynal (1713–1796). This book was Raynal's collaboration with Denis Diderot (1713–1784) and other French Enlightenment thinkers. It was well known to the Russian intellectual and administrative elite since the reign of Catherine the Great (r. 1762–96) for its "discussion of Russia's potential role in East-West trade" that influenced the strategies of Russian imperial expansion.[18]

This work places the proposal for a Russian Transcaucasian Company in the context of comparative colonialisms, analysing the Russian imperial project alongside its French and British counterparts. It examines the surviving fragments of Griboedov and Zaveleisky's proposal together with the comments of its main critic, General Mikhail Zhukovsky, as a particular example of a wider discourse on the development of the Russian Empire and on the best methods of colonial management. It reveals the legacy of the thinkers of the European Enlightenment in the political, economic, and cultural development of the Russian Empire – a legacy that Tynianov juxtaposes in his novel with the romantic nationalism of Griboedov's time.

The novel especially underscores the role of romantic nationalism of Griboedov's generation in the imperial projects and in the legacy of the ideas of the Enlightenment in the cultural and political discourse of the nineteenth and the twentieth centuries. According to Tynianov, the revolutionary ardour of the 1920s, with its ideals of internationalism and of aversion to imperialism, is the true successor of the Enlightenment, to which it offers its hand "over the head of the XIX century."[19] Tynianov's allusions to the book of his friend and fellow formalist Victor Shklovsky, *A Sentimental Journey: Memoirs 1917–1922*, reveal the latter's loyalty to the humanistic ideals, moral universalism, and sensible rationalism of the Enlightenment.

At the same time, Tynianov sees many parallels between the late 1920s – with their increasingly authoritarian political atmosphere, regained centrist control over colonial peripheries, and steady loss of political freedoms – and the despotic nationalist imperialism of Nicholas I's reign. In the prologue to his book, the Decembrist revolt of 1825 appears as the moment of rupture in Russia's political life, when time breaks in two and the 1830s arrive prematurely in the middle of the 1820s. This is an allusion to the changes in the political course after Lenin's death, as well as Joseph Stalin's (1878–1953) idea of the late 1920s as the time of the "great break [*velikii perelom*],"[20] and a foreboding of the oppressions of the 1930s. Stalin's article "God velikogo pereloma: k XII godovshchine Oktiabria" ("The Year of the Great Turning Point: For the XII Anniversary of October")[21] appeared in the newspaper *Pravda* in 1929, the same year *The Death of Vazir-Mukhtar* was published as a book, and Tynianov was most probably alluding to the ideas in circulation rather than this particular article. As an intellectual who has to compromise with the oppressive regime, Tynianov identifies with his protagonist Griboedov, who joined the program of imperial domination, and even more so with the great mouthpiece of romantic nationalism, his beloved poet Alexander Pushkin (1799–1837).

Pushkin's works serve as the major original texts for Tynianov's parodies that explore the interconnection between literary Orientalism and imperialism. The many parodic allusions to Pushkin's early "Southern" poem "The Fountain of Bakhchisaray" expose the tropes of imperialism as the dominance of a wilful masculine power over the feeble feminine colonial essence. Using Pushkin's unflattering characterization of a eunuch as a hook, Tynianov explores the conflict between individual freedom and the confinement of a harem as a metaphor for a despotic state. In this exploration, Tynianov follows the precedent established by Charles de Secondat Baron de Montesquieu (1699–1755) in his "Persian Letters."

Tynianov's parody of Pushkin's mature "rigorous prose," his *Journey to Arzrum*, treats it as an intermediate between the *Journeys* of the eighteenth-century Enlightenment writer Alexander Radishchev (1749–1802) and the twentieth-century avant-garde, intellectual Shklovsky, making it the focal point of the discourse on imperialism and colonial policies. In his novel, Tynianov also includes the voices of his other contemporaries, the futurist poets, within the dialogue about the legacy of the Russian Empire. Unlike Tynianov and Shklovsky, who recognized the connections between the civilizing mission of colonization and the desire to spread the revolution of 1917 to the Russian "Orient" and beyond, the futurists expressed unequivocal enthusiasm for exporting the revolution to Iran. In a parodic form, Tynianov juxtaposes their enthusiasm with Griboedov's colonial aspirations.

In order to break the overwhelmingly Euro- or Russo-centric perspective on the Russo-Persian War and its aftermath, this book introduces Iranian and Armenian sources. They include extensive travel notes by a member of Prince Khosrow Mirza's delegation to Petersburg in 1829, Mirza Mostafa Afshar, and several texts by the Armenian pedagogue Khachatur Abovian (1809–c. 1848), a native of the land lost by Iran and acquired by Russia during the war. Abovian's ideas on colonialism and economic development of Transcaucasia are compared with those of Griboedov.

Chapter 7 of this study examines how Tynianov represented the 1829 visit of the Iranian prince Khosrow Mirza, who arrived in Petersburg to convey the shah's apologies for the massacre of Griboedov and the rest of the Russian mission. I compare Tynianov's interpretation with an account of the same event given by Mirza Mostafa Afshar, the personal secretary of Mirza Mas`ud, an important member of the prince's delegation. The comparison reveals different views on the legacy of Peter the Great's (r. 1682–1725) modernizing and Westernizing project, the Iranians' hopeful desire to emulate it in order to create an independent and advanced state free from the encroachments of colonizers, and Tynianov's weary disillusionment with radical state-initiated transformations.

Scholarly Orientalism, another important component of the imperialist rhetoric, appears in the novel as amateur pseudo-intellectual gibberish, and Orientalist scholars as pretentious buffoons. The main protagonist of the novel, Griboedov, is a many-faceted man who reveals to the reader different aspects of his complex personality. He is alternately an owner of a harem or a eunuch, an Orientalist scholar or a greedy colonialist entrepreneur, Napoleon or a Russian serf owner. All these facets of the protagonist's character help the novelist to put together the mosaic of Russian cultural Orientalism of the nineteenth century in its connection to the grand empire-building project, which he judges using the moral guidance of the Enlightenment and the historical perspective of his own time.

Last but not least, Tynianov's novel bears comparison to his contemporary Rudyard Kipling's (1865–1936) spy novel *Kim*, and indeed to the spy novel genre. Even though Kipling's novel is set in what is now India and Pakistan and Tynianov's in Russia, the Caucasus, and Iran, both highlight the whimsical and amusing symbiosis of tradition and modernity, superstition and scientific inquiry in the colonized regions. While Kipling uncritically celebrates the advancements of modernization and prosperity brought by the imperial power, Tynianov denounces the predatory nature of imperialism. The main protagonists of both novels embrace their role in the Great Game, the Russo-British diplomatic rivalry in Persia, Central Asia, and Afghanistan; only *The Death of Vazir-Mukhtar,* however, ends tragically for most of the participants.

Chapter One

Colonial Management of Transcaucasia and the Ideas of the European Enlightenment

In the last year of his life Griboedov, together with Zaveleisky, developed a project for the establishment of the Russian Transcaucasian Company, an agricultural, manufacturing, and trading business. The company promised to play a key part in the economic and cultural development of Transcaucasia, in facilitating the rapprochement between the core of the empire and its newly acquired Transcaucasian provinces, and in increasing the state revenues.

Griboedov and Zaveleisky's project plays a crucial role in Tynianov's novel and its criticism of Russian colonialism through contrasting the attitudes and ideas of the late Enlightment and the romantic nationalism of the nineteenth century that paradoxically coexist in the proposal. Unfortunately, this important project is very poorly studied. Most of the scholarly research on Griboedov's life and work is dedicated to his famous play in verse *Woe from Wit*, to his relationship with the Decembrists and their movement, and to his diplomatic career in Iran. Almost every scholar of Griboedov briefly mentions the Russian Transcaucasian project in their work, and suggests some evaluation of its merits using different criteria. Thus, according to Militsa Nechkina and Aleksandr Lebedev the project was economically and culturally progressive, and if implemented would have benefited Transcaucasia by launching its industrialization and capitalist development, and ensuring the gradual replacement of serf labour with the labour of hired workers. Against the historic background of feudal relationships, these scholars evaluated such results as a definite step forward.[1] By contrast, Nikolai Piksanov harshly criticized the project as an oppressive and imperialistic attempt to exploit both the local population of Transcaucasia and the Russian peasants, whom the authors of the project were planning to buy from the serf owners in Russia proper and resettle them on the lands of the company.[2]

Maria Rozhkova criticized the project from the opposite point of view, as one that would impede the development of capitalism in the core of the Russian Empire, by promoting the economic independence of Transcaucasia. It would prevent the region from serving as the provider of the raw materials needed for the growing Russian industries, such as the cotton industry, and from becoming the market for the products of Russian manufacture.[3] Natan Eidelman gave the most comprehensive overview of the project and rightly noticed that the main point of disagreement between the authors of the project, Griboedov and Zaveleisky, and the author of the detailed critical comments on the project, General Zhukovsky, was their different views on monopolies, privileges, and state protectionism.[4]

However, none of these scholars was able to inscribe this debate within the broader discourse on global colonialism and imperial domination, the topics that are crucial for understanding Tynianov's novel. This book contributes to the study of comparative colonialisms and one of the few works that places Russian colonialism alongside its more famous French and British counterparts.[5]

Among the most important underlying themes of *The Death of Vazir-Mukhtar* is the comparison between the attitudes of the Enlightenment and the subsequent romantic nationalism regarding imperial expansion and colonial management. Griboedov's project to establish the Russian Transcaucasian Company appears in the novel as the poet's most cherished enterprise that, at times, eclipses his love for writing. The author harshly judges his protagonist as an intellectual who betrays his principles by opportunistically jumping on the bandwagon of the empire-building project. In order to evaluate this judgment, it is necessary to reconstruct the historical background in which Griboedov developed his project, using information that was not available to Tynianov.

This chapter complements and clarifies the rest of this book by analysing the ideological discourse that Griboedov and Peter Zaveleisky's proposal ignited, revealing its historical background and its European connections. This discourse encompasses such topics as colonialism and social justice, monopolies and free trade, slavery and serfdom, the protection of intellectual property, among others. While some of these topics appear in Tynianov's novelistic study, others, equally important, do not. By providing the two views of the same discourse, one through Tynianov's novel and the other through my own research, this book creates a more comprehensive representation of Russian Orientalism and its ideas on colonial management in the aftermath of the Russo-Persian War of 1826–8.

In his novel, Tynianov notices the affinity between Griboedov's project of the Russian Transcaucasian Company and the proposals of Guillaume Thomas Raynal and Denis Diderot about the new ways of colonization that would be mutually beneficial for both colonizers and local residents, and that would bring them closer together. However, although Tynianov's novelistic study subtly reveals the author's findings through literary devices, it does not explicitly analyse the similarities between Griboedov and Raynal's arguments. The novel prompts the reader to do the further research.

While it is important to place Griboedov's project of colonial management of Transcaucasia in the context of Russian and European imperial discourses, it is equally important to compare it to how the natives of that newly acquired region viewed the economic and cultural development of their land. This chapter concludes with an analysis of the views of the Transcaucasian resident, writer, and pedagogue Khachatur Abovian on such topics as the colonization of the Americas, economic and cultural development of Armenia, and educational reforms that would support modernization of Transcaucasia. While critical of the dark sides of imperialism, Abovian, who did not have the perspective of Tynianov's historical hindsight, was more accepting of the Russian presence in the Caucasus, seeing a temporary union with Russia as a path to the political independence of Armenia.

Transcaucasia as a Colony in Griboedov's Project

> Bozhe! Kak eto ne brosalos' ranee v glaza: Zakavkaz'e – eto ved' koloniia![6]
>
> – Tynianov, *Smert' Vazir-Mukhtara*

> (God! How come it did not strike him before: Transcaucasia, you know, is a colony!)

In 1828, Griboedov, who at the time served as Russian minister plenipotentiary in Iran, and Zaveleisky, soon to be the civilian governor of Tiflis, co-authored the project of the Russian Transcaucasian Company. The text of the proposal that they wrote together in Tbilisi is lost with the exception of two surviving pieces: "Zapiska ob uchrezhdenii rossiiskoi zakavkazskoi kompanii" ("A Note on the Founding of the Russian Transcaucasian Company") and "Vstuplenie k proektu ustava" ("Introduction to the Project of the Charter").[7] However, General Mikhail Zhukovsky's "Zamechaniia na zapisku ob ustroistve zemledel'cheskoi, manufakturnoi i torgovoi kompanii" ("Comments on the Note about the Founding of the Agricultural, Manufacturing, and Trading Company"), a document criticizing the project on economic and ethical grounds, gives us insights into the main points of the project.[8]

The project asked the government of Emperor Nicholas I (r. 1825–55) to grant their company monopolies and privileges similar to those enjoyed by the British East India Company at its inception. At the time Griboedov and Zaveleisky made the request, the British East India Company was already stripped of almost all of its privileges; the ideas of free trade and free enterprise were becoming more popular, and the project attracted criticism for being based on an outdated mercantilist ideology. The authors of the project were seeking governmental assistance in founding a chartered company in Transcaucasia. In return, they promised to promote the economic and cultural development of the region and to produce high revenues for the empire's treasury. Their critics, however, thought that the authors' plans to monopolize trade and production in Transcaucasia would benefit neither the empire nor the region, while also undermining the principles of social justice.

Together, the project itself and Zhukovsky's criticism read as an ongoing polemic about the proper management of the colonies, in which the two sides follow separate threads of thought stemming from the European thinkers of the eighteenth century. Zhukovsky criticizes the authors of the project from the viewpoint of a supporter of free trade and free enterprise, whose negative opinion on monopolies and chartered companies is shaped by the ideas of Adam Smith.[9] As Muriel Atkin notes, Griboedov's and Zaveleisky's positions are close to that of the French Enlighteners, Raynal, Diderot, and other contributors to *A Philosophical and Political History of the Settlements and Trade of the Europeans in the East and West Indies*,[10] whose "discussion of Russia's potential role in East-West trade constituted a brief for imperial expansion."[11]

Diderot, just like Smith, denounced many colonial practices, among them the founding of exclusive chartered companies, as being both economically ineffective and oppressive towards the inhabitants of the colonies. Yet at the same time Raynal and his collaborators occasionally demonstrated enthusiasm for colonial trade as a stimulator of industrial development worldwide, and they also showed admiration for British successes in this type of endeavour. They encouraged their own country not to give up on its involvement with the colonies, but rather to seek new mutually beneficial ways of collaborating with them. In some passages of his *History*, Raynal actually argues in favour of big trading companies, while Diderot goes further to specify certain circumstances where, in his opinion, successful trade requires the existence of a monopoly.

The authors of the project for the Russian Transcaucasian Company share the French thinkers' desire for their own country to compete successfully with the British. As Raynal writes, national pride has long been recognized as one of the important features of Griboedov's personality, and it contributed to his ambition to become an entrepreneur who knows "the art of making all other nations tributary to his own."[12] At the same time, just like the French Enlighteners, he believed in the possibility of a mutually beneficial collaboration between the mother country and the colony.[13]

No One's Land

> A potom shli podozritel'nye sultaniaty i khanstva, ne to persidskie, ne to turetskie, ne to nich'i.[14]
>
> – Yury Tynianov

> (And then there were suspicious sultanates and khanates, either Persian or Turkish, or no one's.)

In their project, Griboedov and Zaveleisky retroactively justify the colonial appropriation of land by claiming that the local population was not able to take advantage of its natural resources. One of the two surviving documents of the project, the "note on the founding of the Russian Transcaucasian Company," opens with the following assertion: "Upon careful examination of Transcaucasian lands anyone will become convinced that there, nature prepared everything for man; but people hitherto did not make use of nature."[15] In the other surviving document, "introduction to the project of the charter," the authors expand this statement by describing the bountiful nature of Transcaucasia. According to them, "the natural resources of Transcaucasia are so varied and so abundant" that the only remaining action is to decide which of those resources one should explore.[16] They go on to claim that greedy, shortsighted, and corrupt entrepreneurs and inept producers have not been able to benefit from that bounty. Raynal, in his *A History of the Two Indies*, provides a similar account of colonized lands and their populations:

> Nature had provided for the happiness of the Malays ... land lavish in its supply of delicious fruit, enough to provide for uncivilized man, but capable of the cultivation of all the production needed for the society ... Nature had done all for the Malays; but society had done them every possible injury.[17]

Behind these statements is a justification of the appropriation of wasted natural resources and the idea of legitimate ownership based on *improvement* of the land, expressed by such Enlighteners as John Locke and Emmerich de Vattel.[18] Griboedov and Zaveleisky were not the first of their Russian contemporaries to exploit this notion. Thus, Decembrist Pavel Pestel, in his major outline of reforms that the provisional government was supposed to undertake in the event of a successful uprising, argued in favour of subjugating the Northern Caucasus because, among other considerations, it was important to use its natural resources efficiently:[19]

> The land they inhabit from time immemorial is known as a blessed country, where all the products of nature could reward human labor with abundance, and which once flourished and prospered, it is now desolate and is of benefit to no one, because semi-savage peoples own this beautiful country.[20]

Claiming that they are able to reap the benefits of otherwise wasted natural resources, Griboedov and Zaveleisky admit that the lands they request should be returned to their original state if after fifteen years at least a quarter of them are not effectively used for growing cotton and other cash crops. A similar policy, according to Smith in his *An Inquiry into the Nature and Causes of the Wealth of Nations*, contributed to the rapid economic development of the North American colonies, where a law stated that if the owner of the land does not "improve" at least a certain part of it, the land becomes grantable to another person.[21]

To make the idea of wasted resources apply to Transcaucasia, Griboedov and Zaveleisky exaggerated the bounty of the land and understated the work invested in it. Thus, they argued, grapes grew in the region without requiring any care. These naturally growing grapes were of such high quality that, paradoxically, even though the local population did not know how to properly make wine, the wine they made was almost as good as French wines.[22]

The tsarist General Zhukovsky takes upon himself the task of rehabilitating the local population: "One cannot say that no basis has been established there by industriousness and activity. On the contrary, there are already agriculture, winemaking and gardening, crafts and trade, government and sciences."[23] He argues that the people of Transcaucasia already possess all those qualities that the authors of the project enumerate as prerequisites to building a strong and enduring state:

> Who could say that Georgians and other inhabitants of the Transcaucasian provinces do not have enough means for sustenance, clothing, housing

adapted to the climate, and income to the extent of the conveniences and pleasures of their lives? Consequently, they also have those virtues, which are the bases of the strength and durability of a state.[24]

According to Diderot, the very idea of ownership based on "mixing one's labour with the land" is wrong. Within a country, he argues, "an individual should be allowed to leave his land uncultivated, if that suits him," and the government's interference in this case would result in circumscribing property rights and liberty.[25] On a global scale, Diderot points out that basing ownership on the European idea of land use results in declaring the land, which does not belong to any European power, as "no one's land." That is exactly how Griboedov and Zaveleisky refer to the lands they are planning to acquire in Transcaucasia with an intention to "improve" them through their care and labour. Their future company, with its development and cultivation, its enterprises and buildings, and the very "instruments" and "hands" used to create it all, "will give value to those plots that in their wild state were abandoned in neglect as if they did not belong to anyone."[26]

Diderot believed that "an entirely uninhabited land is the only one that may be appropriated" and "its first properly attested discovery constituted a legitimate taking of possession."[27] In his view, "conquest is not more binding than theft," and he recognizes the right of colonized peoples to fight for their liberty.[28] Furthermore, he argues, "the authority of one nation over another can only be based on ... general consent, or conditions which have been proposed and accepted."[29] However, as he specifies, "the consent of forefathers cannot commit their descendants; and there are no conditions, which do not exclude the sacrifice of liberty."[30] These last remarks apply very well to the situation in Georgia.

For many Russians, the protection of their fellow Christians served as a moral justification for their country's involvement in the Caucasus and Transcaucasia. They especially cherished the idea that Georgia was not conquered but voluntarily joined Russia, a point of view that persisted throughout Russian history of the nineteenth and twentieth centuries. In their project, Griboedov and Zaveleisky do not forget to specify that, while other parts of Transcaucasia were acquired through conquest, Georgia had asked for the patronage of Russian sovereigns:

Russians, stepping over the Caucasus, were first and foremost concerned about standing with firm foot in Georgia, which herself asked for the patronage of our sovereigns, as well as in khanates, acquired with the help of the emperor's arms.[31]

The necessity to "stand with firm foot" in Georgia, which had itself asked for patronage, means not only to protect it from the rival powers of Iran and Turkey and encroachments of the Northern Caucasian tribes, but also to overcome strong resistance within Georgia itself. The formula of voluntary joining did not quite reflect the complexities of the history of Russia's annexation of Georgia, which resulted in the abolition of both the Georgian dynasty and, subsequently, the autonomy of its church. This, together with the restructuring of the entire society and the introduction of the new rule without much regard for Georgian culture, led to resentment in almost every social class in Georgia. A series of insurrections followed.[32] A conspiracy aimed at the restoration of the Georgian monarchy, in which Griboedov's father-in-law Prince Alexander Chavchavadze (1786–1846) was indirectly involved, was brewing right around the time that Griboedov was writing his project.

While never questioning the legitimacy of Russian power in Transcaucasia, the authors of the project do acknowledge the inevitability of the resentment it generated in the local population. They outline the major causes of "mutinies" that have taken place "within the newly acquired provinces," which include the introduction of new order and new social structures, and "exacting authorities, who wished for speedy execution, obedience," admitting that those are the sorts of "changes no people submit to voluntarily."[33] In principle, the authors of the project subscribed to Smith's argument that colonies will always resist imperial domination and to his reminder of the price to be paid in forcing that submission:

> It is not very probable that they will ever voluntarily submit to us; and we ought to consider, that the blood which must be shed in forcing them to do so, is, every drop of it, the blood either of those who are, or of those whom we wish to have for our fellow-citizens.[34]

Smith argues that imperial domination is not only ruinous for the economy of the colonies but also, in the long run, disadvantageous for the mother country. Yet he does not entertain the illusion that understanding these disadvantages would prompt mother countries to renounce their colonies. Smith identifies the main obstacles for such renouncement, which in his opinion would be best for every party, as national pride and the gains of the governing and commercial elite made at the expense of their fellow citizens.[35]

Sceptical that Great Britain would ever give up its North American colonies, Smith suggests as a remedy that American voters and taxpayers get representation in the British Parliament in the hope that it would give them a sense of belonging to the empire and control over the decisions made by its government. Using a somewhat similar approach, the authors of the project argue that including Transcaucasian stockholders in their company would make the natives feel they had some control over the economic and political development of their land.[36]

They also make clear that the major reason the people of Transcaucasia did not take advantage of their natural resources was the war itself:

> A Transcaucasian resident did not have time to think about the improvement of his farm; his house, household utensils, harness, cart, cattle, and almost all his real estate could at any time be requested for public needs during the advancement of the troops.[37]

Diderot and Raynal expressed a similar notion of war as not only morally wrong but also economically ruinous, "for pillage, fire and the sword nourish neither the soil nor men."[38] Colonial war, in their opinion, is disadvantageous for all parties involved, including the conquerors: "Even the victorious nations succumbed beneath the burden of their conquest, and seizing more territory than they could retain or cultivate, destroyed themselves, so to speak, in the destruction of the enemy."[39] Moreover, the *History* contains direct advice to Russia to be "cautious of exposing the lives of its subjects" and to "renounce the rage of conquest, to apply solely to the arts of peace."[40] "The desire of increasing a territory already too extensive" would hinder its ability to "form a close and compact state, or become an enlightened and flourishing nation."[41]

This idea of limiting expansion and instead concentrating on the development of existing territories had its supporters among Griboedov's contemporaries. Thus, the Decembrist Pestel wrote in his constitutional project, *Russkaia pravda* (*Russian Truth*), that "one should not be concerned with broadening the boundaries but care solely about bringing well-being to this vast domain."[42] At the same time, Pestel considered "good boundaries" an important condition for a safe and prosperous state. His idea of "good boundaries" included not only those parts of the Caucasus and Transcaucasia that belonged to Russia at the time of his writing, but also certain additional annexations, such as the Caucasian coast of the Black Sea, which at the time belonged to Turkey and which he claimed were vital for the empire.[43] These annexations, as well as retention of the Caucasian provinces already conquered by Russia, required forceful subjugation of the Caucasian peoples, which Pestel and many other "progressive representatives of Russian society" justified in terms of security and state interests.[44]

Just like Pestel, Griboedov was aware of the danger of seizing too much territory. At the time of the Erivan campaign, while still supporting the empire-building rhetoric in principle, he was already sceptical about the expediency of Russia's further acquisitions. In his travel notes on the Erivan campaign he writes about "the real friend of the people," Hadrian, the Roman emperor, who renounced the territories of Mesopotamia, Assyria, and Armenia conquered by his predecessor.[45] Yet in their "Note on the founding of the Russian Transcaucasian Company," Griboedov and Zaveleisky outline their own idea about "good boundaries" in a way similar to that of Pestel, and they make a "suggestion" about annexing the port of Batumi "from the side of Asiatic Turkey," which would bring their company "the utmost conveniences."[46]

The project of the Russian Transcaucasian Company thus reflects Griboedov's desire for a shift in empire-building policies from further acquisition of territories to making use of the empire's existing territories. It shows his ambition to prove that Russia is capable not only of retaining but also of cultivating the lands it has acquired and thus is their rightful owner. For Griboedov and Zaveleisky, the acquisition of Transcaucasia brings an opportunity for the Russian Empire to rise in economic power and political prestige, as well as the prospect of economic and cultural development for Transcaucasia.

Unlike the authors of the project, their critic General Zhukovsky argues that the aim of the conquest was purely strategic: to create safer borders and not to "civilize" the Caucasus while economically exploiting it.[47] Commenting on Griboedov and Zaveleisky's wish to change the general opinion in Russia that the acquisition of Transcaucasia was economically burdensome, Zhukovsky notices with indignation that it would be insulting to think that the great sacrifice of Russian blood was made for "some revenues and sugar plantations."[48] This comment resonates with an argument by Smith, who says only statesmen influenced by shopkeepers would try to "find some advantage in employing the blood and treasure of their fellow-citizens, to found and maintain such an empire."[49] It is also aligned with Raynal's assessment of "the benefits and harm Europe has received from the discovery of the New World," where he asks: "Are these frivolous benefits, so cruelly won, so unequally shared out, so ferociously disputed, worth one drop of the blood that has been and will be shed? Can they be compared to the life of a single human being?"[50]

While Zhukovsky, in this particular criticism, is primarily concerned with the lives of Russian soldiers, Raynal, starting with an assessment of the losses of the Europeans in the colonial enterprise, ends up reminding the reader of the value of the life of any human being. It is less obvious, though, whose benefits Griboedov had in mind when he was thinking about "the real friend of the people," the emperor Hadrian. Griboedov's suggestion to curtail conquests was supposed to benefit the Russian Empire, but his use of the word *liudi* (people, human beings) rather than *narod* (a people, the people) may imply his desire, as Raynal puts it, to rise "above the prejudices of national glory in order to consider the happiness of mankind."[51] Yet in most of Griboedov's personal correspondence the romantic nationalism of his generation outweighs the universal humanism of the eighteenth-century Enlightenment writers and thinkers. In his official letters, he does show concern for the well-being of the people of Transcaucasia, whom he sees as new subjects of the Russian Empire.[52] The authors of the project share with its critic, Zhukovsky, concerns about the residents of newly acquired territories.

A keen sense of national pride, characteristic of Griboedov and many Decembrists, among them Pestel, was an important motivational force behind the project of the Russian Transcaucasian Company.[53] The company was conceived in an attempt to compete with foreign, and primarily British, primacy in colonial trade and industrial development.[54] It should therefore come as no surprise that the ideas and aspirations of its authors closely resembled those of the *History of the Two Indies*, whose authors expressed "great, even envious, admiration"[55] for the successes of the British while trying to "rethink French colonial policy after the losses of the Seven Years' War."[56]

Thus, despite his statement that "an entirely uninhabited land is the only one that may be appropriated," Diderot does not resist the temptation to propose an alternative way of founding new colonies in lands already inhabited.[57] This alternative colonization would be founded on the principles of harmonious coexistence and beneficial collaboration between the old inhabitants and the newcomers. The only justifiable way for Europeans to explore new lands would be to send small groups of individual settlers, who would be ready to share their knowledge and skills with the local population, and work towards satisfaction of "mutual needs."[58] The best way to ensure peaceful and friendly collaboration, in Diderot's opinion, was intermarriage between locals and newcomers: "The men would have married the women of the country and the women the men. Consanguinity, the most pressing and strongest of bonds, would soon have made the newcomers and the natives of the land one single family."[59] These settlers would have a greater chance of succeeding than colonizers with "the lordly and domineering tone of superiors and usurpers."[60] They could pursue their own interests while at the same time enjoying the friendship and trust of the local people.

The project of the Russian Transcaucasian Company was concerned with making use of a region already acquired through military conquest. Yet in the "Introduction" to the project Griboedov and Zaveleisky declare one of their important goals to be the establishment of peaceful, mutually beneficial relations. Until that point, Griboedov and Zaveleisky maintain, the local people had thought of the Russians as proud and unapproachable because they knew them only as imperial officials, "vested with power imperious and strict."[61] The "Introduction" stresses the need to soften the divide between conquerors and conquered by encouraging the kind of personal interaction Diderot suggests.

Griboedov and Zaveleisky contend that the establishment of the company would create a common economic interest between its Russian and Transcaucasian participants, with the latter presumably constituting the majority of the stockholders.[62] Working in the same business would foster the practice of visiting each other's homes and travelling to each other's homelands. Socializing on a personal level would introduce some sense of equality between the peoples: "Peaceful, pleasant relations for one's own benefits, mutual services of all kinds, will establish certain equality between the members of one and the same society."[63] This, according to the authors of the project, would be the only way to overcome the divide between Russia and the Caucasus: "only thus will the prejudices that established sharp boundaries between us and our subject peoples disappear."[64] Although one could hardly expect the authors of a business proposal to mention intermarriage as one of the steps of their project, Griboedov's contemporaries viewed his own marriage to Princess Nina Chavchavadze as an example of "voluntary and mutually benefiting ... happy marital union" between Russia and Georgia.[65]

The influence of Diderot's arguments and rhetoric on the authors of the project creates an interesting example of transforming the genre of philosophical history into that of an economic and political proposal. The change of verb modes reflects this transformation. Diderot tries to imagine what would have been a better way of interacting with the world outside of Europe, what should have been done differently. Griboedov and Zaveleisky are trying to make a reality of Diderot's hypothetical alternative history. In their project, the conditional past turns into the future perfect. Without questioning the political legitimacy and economic advantages of the conquest, the authors of the project want to smooth over its moral damage, and consequently to repair the history.

History will repair itself, according to Smith, only when the colonized people become as powerful as the colonizers. Ideally, he explains, the Europeans' discovery of new lands and of new commercial routes should have benefited the entire world by allowing everyone to enjoy products that are not available in their own countries and by encouraging improvements in agriculture and manufacturing. Yet to the inhabitants of the colonized lands, all the benefits they could have received "have been sunk and lost in the dreadful misfortunes which they have occasioned."[66] These misfortunes, however, were possible only because at the time of the discoveries "the superiority of force happened to be so great on the side of the Europeans, that they were enabled to commit with impunity every sort of injustice."[67]

Smith is hopeful that someday the natives of the colonies "may grow stronger, or those of Europe may grow weaker," and the inhabitants of all parts of the world will "arrive at that equality of courage and force," which alone can stop injustice by "inspiring mutual fear" and making all independent nations respect each other's rights.[68] He believes that "nothing seems more likely to establish this equality of force, than that mutual communication of knowledge, and of all sorts of improvements, which an extensive commerce from all countries to all countries naturally, or rather necessarily, carries along with it."[69]

The British East India Company as Anachronistic Model for the Russian-Transcaucasian Company

> Bylo mirnoe sopernichestvo, ochen' vezhlivoe, Rossiia poluchila znachenie, chert voz'mi, – Anglii![70]
>
> – Yury Tynianov

> (It was a peaceful rivalry, a very polite one, Russia was gaining the importance of, damn it, England!)

The British respect for commerce, according to Raynal, allowed their country to get ahead of the world in their social and industrial achievements. They were the ones who "first considered commerce as the proper science and support of an enlightened, powerful, and even a virtuous people."[71] While both Diderot and Raynal denounced the cruelty of colonial exploitation and the detrimental role of monopolies in the development of industry and commerce, they did show their admiration for the British industrial and commercial achievements and considered their "art of making all other nations tributary" to their own worthy of emulation.[72] They admit that British commercial activity entailed "a constant desire of dominion, which implies that of enslaving other people."[73] However, they argue, those who conquer others by means of commerce rather than by war "necessarily introduce industry into the country, which they would not have subdued if it had been already industrious, or in which they would not maintain themselves, if they had not brought industry in along with them."[74]

Using similar reasoning, Griboedov and Zaveleisky attempted to achieve their double goal of "enrichment" of Transcaucasia and "veritable benefit" for the empire by building upon the experience of the British East India Company.[75] However, the British East India Company was an anachronistic model for the Russian Transcaucasian Company. Throughout the history of its existence, the activities of the British East India Company continuously changed in scope and in character. It began at the beginning of the seventeenth century as a company committed to peaceful trade and was granted a trading monopoly and privileges by the crown. By the beginning of the nineteenth century the company had transformed "from trader to sovereign."[76] Together with military, administrative, and economic control, the company assumed certain responsibilities to promote development and well-being in the territories under its control. At the same time, when the company achieved this "sovereignty" it lost its former monopoly and trading privileges.[77]

The authors of the project aimed to combine the features of the earlier and the later periods of the British East India Company. They requested that the Russian government grant them a trading monopoly and privileges similar to those the British East India Company had in its earlier period, and simultaneously proclaimed the economic and cultural development of the Transcaucasia to be one of their main goals, trying to assume *stewardship* over the region similar to that the British company in its later period held over India.

From the very beginning the Russian Transcaucasian Company was conceived as an agricultural, manufacturing, and trading company, and the monopolies and privileges they requested from the government were not only in the sphere of trade, but also in production. Griboedov and Zaveleisky especially emphasized the importance of export for the development of the region. They argued that the merchants of Tbilisi at that time were already successful in importing goods from Leipzig into Transcaucasia and in selling them in Iran. This trade, according to them, benefited only the merchants without changing the condition of the region's agricultural producers or stimulating the development of industry there.[78]

To overcome this situation, the Russian Transcaucasian Company would introduce new technologies in cultivating and processing the agricultural produce in the region. These new technologies would improve the quality of the produce and allow it to compete in Russian and European markets.[79] Transcaucasia would become a major supplier of "produce of the warm and the hot climates," such as wine, silk, cotton, and dyes.[80] Russia would thereby gain by producing within its own territory the goods that it had to import for high prices. It would also benefit from selling them to the Europeans, who, attracted by the proximity of Transcaucasia in comparison to their own overseas colonies, would "rush, racing each other" to its ports and markets.[81]

Griboedov and Zaveleisky's project is consistent with the main ideas of mercantilism, the economic theory that dominated European economic policies at the time the British East India Company was launched.[82] In accordance with this theory, which argues that the total wealth of a state increases with exports and decreases with imports, European countries of the time strove to maintain a positive balance of trade by producing domestic substitutes for imported goods and improving the quality of their own products in order to make them competitive on international markets.[83]

When possible, European countries avoided importing not only manufactured goods but also raw materials, and a country's self-sufficiency in procuring exotic raw materials was supposed to boost its people's national pride. Thus, according to Raynal, it was considered not only "more advantageous" but "more honorable" to "search" for luxury goods "across an immense ocean," that is, to establish one's own colonies rather than buying "from rivals."[84] The "exotic raw materials" derived by the British from their colonies were "perceived as indigenous to wider Britain."[85] In the case of the Russian Empire, this translated into an aspiration to produce in its own contiguous colonies and to offer for the European market "the colonial goods, in the same amount and of the same quality" that were previously searched for "in the other hemisphere."[86] Pride over possessing in one's own country the products of all climatic zones reveals itself in the text of Griboedov and Zaveleisky's project: "in Russia, in our beloved fatherland, all the roads to achieving the highest well-being are open to us. Its vast provinces contain all climates, all products, from the cold north to the blessed south."[87]

However, add the authors of the project, the recent wars and instability in Transcaucasia, as well as the uneven economic and cultural development of the Russian provinces, prevented the Russian Empire from reaping benefits from these southern regions. As a result, while Russia provides itself in full with the products of northern and temperate climates, it is "forced to borrow" the "products of warm and hot climates" from western and southern Europe and Central Asia.[88] They illustrate this claim with a table of annual imports of dies, pharmaceutical products, fruits, olive oil, wine, cotton, and silk, amounting to 119 million rubles.[89] The company would take upon itself the task of producing at least one-fourth of all these products domestically, which would save the empire money and allow its citizens to enjoy these goods without owing this opportunity to foreigners.[90]

If a country, while striving to reduce imports, cannot avoid buying certain products, according to the mercantilist economic theory it should prefer to buy them in a raw form. When exporting its own goods, however, it should offer them in processed, manufactured form to maximize profits. The authors of the project therefore stress the importance of processing agricultural produce in order to attract both domestic and foreign buyers. They regret that foreign ships stop at the shores of Mingrelia only to sell their own goods in a new market while finding local products not suitable for European use because of their "insignificance [*malovazhnost'*]" and "lack of perfection [*nesovershenstvo*]."[91]

It is possible to overcome this lack of perfection, Griboedov and Zaveleisky argue, by introducing new processing techniques. Thus, they describe a French silk-winding master, recently arrived in Tbilisi, who had proven that silk from the Transcaucasian region of Shamakha, if properly processed, is not inferior to silk from Italy. The authors hoped that the silk from Shamakha, while trading for three to five times less than foreign varieties on the Moscow market, would in due time be preferred to Italian silk and thereby increase its market value.[92]

Similar desires to match the technological achievements of rival countries, stimulated to a great degree by mercantilist ideas, played a large part in the development of manufacturing in European countries.[93] Thus, the endeavour to match the quality of Indian, Chinese, and Japanese commodities by imitating the skills and technologies of their producers was an important stage in the development of British industry, when imitation bordered on and led to invention.[94] According to Raynal, the "spirit of emulation" of the French and their ability to "greatly surpass their rivals" in manufacturing skills allowed them to make "a double profit" on "the materials" they received from their colonies and improve "the workmanship of the manufactures."[95]

This competition against foreign manufacturers took not only the positive form of outperforming them in production technologies and in the quality of finished products, but also relied on such artificial measures as banning imported goods or imposing high duties on their importation. Consistent with this mercantilist trend, Griboedov and Zaveleisky requested that

> if the company will be able to replace with any of its products foreign ones of the same kind that are being imported from abroad, then upon

notifying the government the importation of such products must be banned or the duty on their importation must be considerably increased.[96]

Commenting on this request, Zhukovsky argues that if the products of the company will be more expensive and of inferior quality than their foreign equivalents, by banning imports the company will put domestic consumers at a disadvantage.[97] His reasoning follows that of Smith, who argues that if a domestic product of equal quality is cheaper than its foreign equivalent then regulation is simply useless; if it is more expensive then it is hurtful.[98] Just as "it is the maxim of every prudent master of a family never to attempt to make at home what it will cost him more to make than to buy," the international division of labour can be beneficial for each of the trading sides.[99] However, Smith does mention that a short importation prohibition can be used as retaliation for a prohibition imposed by another country if there is a hope that such a policy will restore free trade between the two sides.[100]

Raynal is similarly critical of the mercantilist "presumption" that other nations' industries and trade can "flourish" only "at the expense" of one's own.[101] Yet, while denouncing mercantilist regulations in principle, he argues that one should not expect a country to drop them unilaterally. If all European countries, in their attempt "to dispense with foreign industry" and "liberate" themselves from "dependence," ban imports of English and French manufactured goods, then why should the latter two countries "open their ports to those who are, so to speak, forcing them to shut up shop?"[102] Failing to find an outlet for their products in Europe, they will strive to use their colonies as markets for their manufactured goods. Griboedov and Zaveleisky use a similar justification of their plans. The "excessive duties on Russian goods" imposed by foreign countries make it "anxiously search for new ways of selling its production." The residents of Transcaucasia, whose well-being, according to the authors, will greatly increase because of the activities of their company, will eagerly buy the Russian goods that they would not otherwise be able to afford.[103]

However, it was not Griboedov and Zaveleisky's intention to turn Transcaucasia simply into a supplier of raw material for Russia and the market for its manufactured goods. As an agricultural, manufacturing, and trading company, the Russian Transcaucasian Company took upon itself the role of a steward responsible for the economic development of the region. Its future leaders stressed that by processing the produce locally, rather than exporting it in a raw form, the company would bring industrial development to Transcaucasia. The need for new technologies would promote education in the region and create a large number of new professionals, a "mass of useful people."[104]

Their proposal implied that they envisioned for their company a beginning that in an important way differed from that of the British East India Company. The latter, starting as a mere trader interested in profits rather than in the economic development of the region it gradually brought under its control, caused de-industrialization of India by suppressing its manufacturing production.[105] Another difference, intended to benefit Transcaucasia, was that a big percentage of the company's future stockholders were supposed to be local landlords and merchants. The establishment of the company would thus stimulate cooperation between the company's Russian and Transcaucasian stockholders; common interest would promote rapprochement between the Russian and the Transcaucasian nations, and improve the "moral and political" climate in the region.[106]

Commenting on the authors' plans to open factories in Transcaucasia, Zhukovsky argues that they may benefit the local economy but will not contribute much to the well-being of the empire overall or eliminate poverty in Russia proper. He immediately adds that he does not mean to discourage new industrial enterprises in Transcaucasia, but they should be established "without extraordinary sacrifices of indigenous institutions and the general state laws and order."[107]

Zhukovsky's reluctance to endorse the project of economic reform in Transcaucasia, which Griboedov and Zaveleisky were trying to achieve through establishment of a new company, was often interpreted as his reactionary imperialist unwillingness to allow the peripheries of the empire to become strong and independent. Yet he was as concerned about the well-being of all sides involved as were the authors of the project. While Griboedov and Zaveleisky claimed that their company would bring economic benefits to both the empire and Transcaucasia, Zhukovsky doubted this and tried to prevent both sides from intentional and unintentional damage that he believed the founders of the company would inflict.

Besides suspecting "the gentlemen innovators" of promoting their own self-interest under the mask of care for the public well-being, Zhukovsky expected their future chartered company to develop according to the same pattern as its European predecessors, regardless of its authors' initial intentions. The critics of mercantilism and the supporters of free trade, the most convincing and influential of whom was Smith, shaped Zhukovsky's view of such companies. They argued that the "mercantile habits" of the British East India Company made its directors "incapable of considering themselves as sovereign" of their Indian domains "even after they have become such." As "a company of merchants," they strove to increase their mercantile profits by buying goods in India for the lowest possible prices and selling European goods there for the highest prices. Meanwhile, as a sovereign concerned with the economic development of India, they were supposed to do exactly the opposite. Hence, regardless of their initial intention, "almost necessarily, though perhaps insensibly" they tended to turn their colony into a supplier of cheaper raw material and a market for more expensive manufactured goods.[108]

While Griboedov and Zaveleisky look forward to growing "tropical" or, as they otherwise call them, "colonial" products[109] in Transcaucasia, Zhukovsky thinks it would be more prudent to establish enterprises not with "tropical plants" but "plain ones" with "certain improvements" in their quality.[110] He argues that by turning Transcaucasia into a supplier "of products of warm and hot climates," Russia will in turn have to provide it with grains.[111] In other words, as a grower of plantation and industrial crops for export, Transcaucasia will not have enough food crops for its subsistence. Zhukovsky was certainly aware of the situation in British East India, where, as both Smith and Raynal believed, the policies of the company greatly exacerbated the dreadful consequences of famines.[112] It should be mentioned, however, that in the late nineteenth century, British officials referred to the authority of Smith when they refrained from organizing famine relief in India that could have had saved many lives. They were influenced by Smith's conviction of the harm of governmental intervention in attempts to "remedy the inconvenience of dearth" and his belief in the ability of free trade to alleviate it.[113]

Zhukovsky's reservations about Griboedov and Zaveleisky's proposal stem not only from his doubts concerning the benefits the empire could receive from it, but also from his reluctance to view Transcaucasia as a colony for growing cash crops. He argues that cash crops enrich only those few who trade in them without improving the well-being of states and peoples: "One can ask those peoples, in whose lands expensive plants of luxury grow, whether they enjoy the well-being of educated peoples. Aren't they more oppressed by the greed of those who trade in the expensive products of their land?"[114]

Just like Smith and to a certain degree Raynal, Zhukovsky considers a chartered company of the kind that Griboedov and Zaveleisky are trying to establish to be "a stumbling block" in the development of the region, which they wanted to supervise.[115] He argues that just like a private person, the company will put its short-term commercial profits above the public benefits of either Russia or Transcaucasia, and its activities will not be compatible with its declared role of an agent of economic and cultural development of Transcaucasia. That role, in Zhukovsky's opinion, belongs to the government.[116]

Zhukovsky's view of the role of government coincides with that of Smith, who thought that its responsibility is to ensure safety and justice, as well as to support those "institutions" and "public works" that are "beneficial to the whole society" but not profitable enough to interest private undertakers.[117] As a supporter of free trade and free enterprise, Zhukovsky disapproved of government interference in production and commerce: "It would be strange to think that the government should supervise the house expenditures of every entrepreneur."[118] However, he stresses its role as the guarantor of equal rights for producers and entrepreneurs: "It depends on the government to promote the prosperity of the region, with the means that the government has at its disposal, such as laws, justice, and protection from internal and external enemies."[119]

At the time Zhukovsky was writing his comments on the project, in 1828, the tension between the British East India Company and the British state was very high. It was a transitional time, when the company "entered an age of social and economic planning"[120] regarding its involvement in India but was "no longer a free-standing and independent trading company."[121] It was undergoing gradual incorporation into the "state machinery of the empire," transforming into "a limb of the government," or "a department of state."[122] By that time, the company had been stripped of most of its privileges, support of free trade was prevailing in British society, and the attitude towards monopolies was negative.[123]

The text of the introduction to the project reveals that support for free trade in Russia was strong enough for Griboedov and Zaveleisky to feel the need to justify their request for privileges. In a nod to the prevailing winds, they concede that monopolies must be avoided whenever possible; nonetheless, the two maintain, they are vital at the very beginning of such a difficult undertaking as developing a territory where the economy is still in its "infancy."[124]

Support for free trade in Russia was not unanimous. Thus, among the Decembrists there were both supporters of free trade and those who argued it was necessary to protect Russia's commercial interests by means of monopolies. Griboedov's friend Kondraty Ryleev, a leader of the Northern Society of Decembrists, worked for a short period as a manager for the Russian-American Company; while employed there, he wrote a note arguing in favour of preserving the company's monopoly on procurement and trade in fur and fish in the territory under its authority.[125] Meanwhile, another leader of the Northern Society, Mikhail Lunin, named the establishment of free trade as one of the goals of the uprising.[126] Similarly, the head of the Southern Society, Pestel, in his constitutional outline of future reforms *Russkaia pravda*, stated that it was necessary to "make every effort in order to eliminate all those numerous obstacles and inconveniences that presently hamper the commerce so much and oppress the traders."[127] In his opinion, "the most unfortunate peoples [in the Russian Empire] are those who are under the government of the [Russian-]American Company. It oppresses them, plunders them, and not in the least does it care about their well-being."[128] For that reason, Pestel argues it is necessary to free these people from the governance of the company.[129]

Like Pestel, Zhukovsky supports free trade and suspects that the proposed company would economically exploit the residents of Transcaucasia. He also guards the interests of the state, claiming that the authors of the project are trying to "shackle" "not only Transcaucasians" but also the Russian government. He regards as "shackling" Griboedov and Zaveleisky's request to grant them privileges for fifty years, not only in those Transcaucasian provinces that belonged to the Russian Empire at the time, but also in those that might be annexed to it "from this side" in the future.[130]

The only particular case in which Zhukovsky thinks that granting privileges to the company would be justified is when the company helps the state to expand and consolidate its imperial power. The authors of the project requested for their future company the right to enter into relationships and to sign special commercial treaties with the "owners of Transcaucasian provinces" that are "only in indirect possession of Russia, or under its patronage."[131] Zhukovsky's opinion was that the company's attempt to explore provinces that were not yet completely subdued by the Russian state, by establishing commercial ties with them, could benefit the empire in the long run. Hence, "here among other mountaineer peoples who are not subject to Russia, it seems that the company could fairly seek exclusive rights of the kind similar companies enjoy from England in East India or from Russia on North-American Islands."[132] Zhukovsky, who aligned himself with the interests of the Russian state, thought that privileges should be granted in those places where Russian power does not have a strong hold, and where they can help to spread Russian economic and political influence. By contrast, in the territories, which already belonged to the empire, granting privileges to any company would, according to Zhukovsky, make no sense.[133] He supports his argument by referencing the pattern of development in the relationship between Britain and the British East

India Company: the British state granted the company its privileges at a point when the state was not able to acquire and maintain the colonies, and it tried to abridge them afterward. Eventually, after the company's demise in 1858, it handed over control of the territory it had appropriated to the British state.[134]

Zhukovsky justifies the augmentation of territories under Russian control in the Caucasus and Transcaucasia in terms of security rather than a preconceived imperative for expansion. In this he is similar to Pestel, who, while asserting the right of powerful states to absorb smaller nations that in his opinion do not stand a chance of surviving independently, specifies that it should only be done when "taking into consideration the establishment of security, and not some vain expansion of the state bounds."[135]

The specific circumstances under which Zhukovsky approves the granting of privileges are similar to those mentioned by Diderot, who justifies monopolies when the trader is in constant war with the inhabitants of the region. Zhukovsky sees privileges as fair among the hostile "mountaineers" but not in Georgia and other Transcaucasian provinces that are already "parts" of Russia's "body."[136] In the former case, the company receives privileges for its potential role in achieving collaboration through commercial ties, in overcoming the antagonism that military conquests created and attempts at pacification exacerbated. In the latter, the same privileges would not only be of no benefit to the empire and restrictive for the traders and industrialists of Russia, but unfair with respect to the residents of Transcaucasia, "people who already earned their rights and privileges incompatible with other privileges."[137]

Here again, as in a number of other important issues, Zhukovsky's ideal of the future empire was very similar to that of the Decembrist Pestel.[138] While neither questioned the legitimacy of Russia's power over other peoples, they both believed that in a unified Russian Empire the citizens of different nationalities should have equal rights, which included the rights of free trade and of free enterprise. They differed from Griboedov and Zaveleisky in viewing the Transcaucasian provinces not as a colony but as "in essence already parts of the body of Russia,"[139] the only real Russian colonies being, in Pestel's opinion, those in North America.[140] Hence, Zhukovsky judged that assisting Griboedov and Zaveleisky in their attempt to found a chartered company like the British East India Company or Russian-American Company was unjustified.

The British East India Company was in a very important way different from the company proposed by the authors of the project. It started as a trading company that did not have any goals in acquiring territories. Only over its 250 years of development did it become a territorial power that eventually transferred its authority to the British state. The company proposed by the authors of the project was supposed to take charge of the territories already conquered by the tsarist military forces, and the tsarist regime considered it an infringement on its own authority in the region. Yet in defending the interests of the autocratic state in Transcaucasia, Zhukovsky was also protecting that region from what he saw as social injustice and economic oppression. His unwillingness to have in Transcaucasia a chartered company that could potentially develop into *status in statu* reflected his desire to strengthen centralized imperial power there.[141] But an equally important motivation was his belief that if given the power, the alternative "government of merchants," as Smith puts it, would in its turn be "necessarily" "despotic" in its attempt to make people submit to its oppressive rules.[142]

Abovian's *Wounds of Armenia* and the Project of Modernizing Transcaucasia

The historical debate on the economic and cultural development of Transcaucasia would not be complete without consideration of the opinions of its residents. It is also important to know what they thought about the annexation of their homeland by Russia. *Verk' Hayastani* (*Wounds of Armenia*)[143] is a description of the events of the Russo-Persian War of 1826–8 given only a decade after it ended, by Khachatur Abovian, an Armenian pedagogue and a native of the land that was contested. In this novel, Abovian expressed the hopes of the nineteenth-century Armenian intelligentsia that the path to political independence for Armenia lay through a temporary union with Russia. Abovian also expressed his ideas on the economic and cultural development of Transcaucasia. Comparing them with Griboedov and Zaveleisky's proposal of invigorating the economy and social life of Transcaucasia in order to benefit both the colony and the empire would expand our field of view of the colonial discourse of the time. Abovian was a prolific writer, and the short account below is only a brief outline of his life and political, cultural, and economic thought.

Abovian was born in 1809 in the village of Kanaker, which had long since become part of the city of Yerevan. From the age of ten he studied at the Ejmiatsin monastery in preparation for ordination, and later at the Armenian Nersisian School in Tbilisi. In 1825, not long before the beginning of the Russian-Persian War of 1826–8, he heard rumours of a plan to move the entire population of Yerevan and its suburbs to

Iran. Trying to reach and help his parents and sibling, Abovian became stranded in the area of Gharakilisa (Vanadzor), witnessing the massacre of the Armenian village of Khlgharakilisa, which he describes in an account titled "Parskastani ev Rusastani mijev tsagats paterazmi nakhorein, mot 1825 t'vakanin" ("Around 1825, on the eve of the war between Persia and Russia").[144]

In 1826, Abovian graduated from the Nersisian School. On his way home, he witnessed the tragic events of the early Russo-Persian War, which he later wrote about in his novel. In 1828, after teaching for a year at the monastery of Sanain, Abovian returned to Ejmiatsin and soon became translator and secretary for the Armenian Catholicos, the head of the Armenian Apostolic Church. A year later he joined an expedition led by Friedrich Parrot, a naturalist and explorer from the University of Dorpat (now Tartu), climbing with him to the summit of Mount Ararat. Impressed by Abovian's inquisitiveness and aptitude, Parrot arranged for him to study at Dorpat with a scholarship provided by the Russian state.

Graduating from Dorpat in 1836, Abovian returned to Transcaucasia eager to participate in its cultural renaissance and economic modernization. He became superintendent of the Tbilisi county school, and at the same time opened his own private school, in which he hoped to educate teachers for a future network of progressive, secular educational institutions in Transcaucasia. Abovian espoused the ideas of universal literacy, the study of nature, learning through hands-on activities in workshops and experimental sites, teaching students self-governing skills, and educating girls together with boys. However, the Armenian clergy and the Russian administration in Transcaucasia thwarted his enthusiastic push for change and innovation. Abovian left Tbilisi to become superintendent of the Erivan county school, but did not obtain support there either. Having received his initial education and written his early poems in classical Armenian, Abovian, after returning from Dorpat, strove to introduce vernacular Armenian, both in literature and in education. He created new phonetic textbooks of Armenian and Russian languages, but the "combined efforts of Armenian obscurantists and Russian bureaucrats" banned them from use in Transcaucasian schools.[145]

While remaining a devout Christian throughout his life, Abovian criticized the Armenian clergy as self-serving and resistant to modernization, describing them satirically in his novel *Wounds of Armenia*. This criticism of the religious establishment appears in the writings of other representatives of the Transcaucasian intelligentsia. Thus Mirze Feteli Akhundov, one of the main fugures of the "Azerbaijani Enlightenment," "critiques religious figures, teachings and institutions" while advocating for "a reformation of Islam, which he calls 'Islamic Protestantism.'"[146] A complaint of the governor of Erivan county, Blavatsky, reveals an amusing episode that demonstrates Abovian's defiant liberal stance vis-à-vis the clergy and the governmental officials. The complaint states that the superintendent of the Erivan county school, Abovian, met the Armenian Catholicos Nerses wearing a "white, ugly unofficial [*particuliarnyi*] frock or a blouse." When admonished, Abovian replied that the governor had no right to dictate what he wore and, according to Blavatsky, showed off his outfit, "trying to be in front of everyone."[147]

Abovian explained his grievance against the clergy as stemming not only from their resistance to a more dynamic secular system of education in a vernacular language, but also from their creating obstacles to Armenians' move from identifying as an ecclesiastic community to thinking of themselves as a nation. Abovian's romantic nationalism took the form of primordialism, as he interpreted the Armenians' struggle for independence in terms of their desire to recover their ancient statehood, tracing it back to the Armenian kingdoms of the past. Moreover, he argued that glorifying Christian martyrdom and denouncing armed resistance does not help to raise brave soldiers who can defend their homes. At the same time, Abovian confirmed the role of Christianity as a major unifying force for his people. Armenians' resistance to the Persians and fighting on the side of the Russians reminded him of the battle of Avarayr, led in the fifth century by Vardan Mamikonian against the Sassanian Empire. Although the battle was lost, it secured the Armenians the right to profess their faith.

Starting in the eighteenth century, Armenian intellectuals saw fostering connections with Russia as their only hope for future independence.[148] Abovian expressed unequivocal support for Russian rule in Transcaucasia, although the Russification policies of Nicholas I exasperated him. His novel *Wounds of Armenia* is dedicated to the Armenians who fought against the Persian occupation and with the Russians. His protagonist, Aghasi, is a young villager from Kanaker who kills soldiers of the Persian sardar Hussein Khan when they attempt to kidnap his neighbour, a girl named Takuhi, the only daughter of her widowed mother. He then goes into hiding and joins a resistance group, but others pay the price for his actions: he brings the revenge of the sardar's brother, Hassan, down upon several Armenian villages.[149] The vulnerability of the villagers and their readiness to fight for their freedom, relying on the Russians as their allies, is the main theme of the book. Abovian subscribes to the justification of the Russian presence in Transcaucasia as expressed by the Russian imperial administrators, who argued that it would provide personal safety for Transcaucasia's peoples. While Europeans devastated the Americas, Russians, in his opinion, restored Transcaucasia. Of course, in order to do so they brought devastation to the North Caucasus.

Abovian articulates his stance on colonization in "Ameriku lis k'tsily" ("The Discovery of America"), one of the many pedagogical works he wrote for schoolchildren. He was critical of European historiography, considering it a history of the conquerors and elites that excludes conquered nations and common people. "Ameriku lis k'tsily" is a brief history of the age of exploration. To prevent his students from developing a Eurocentric worldview, Abovian begins by mentioning the role of the Arabic states in Spain and Portugal in spreading education and enlightenment in Europe, concluding that "in general the source of European enlightenment is Asia." That said, Abovian's stance towards colonization is very similar to that of Raynal and Diderot. While denouncing the atrocities committed against the natives and African slaves, he admires the inquisitiveness, courage, and adventurous spirit of the explorers. He attempts to shield such figures as Columbus and Cortéz, blaming the commission of atrocities on their crews, whom they were not able to control.[150]

Abovian's true hero is Bartolomé de las Casas, the sixteenth-century Dominican friar and historian, who revealed the atrocities committed against the native peoples of the Americas and vehemently fought for their liberation and human rights. Abovian refused to believe that las Casas, in order to protect the natives, suggested exploiting African slaves instead; such an honest person as las Casas, he suggests, could not be guilty of such an immorality. He maintains that the Europeans will be ashamed of the slave trade "forever and ever."[151]

In his description of the Caribbean and the Americas, Abovian recapitulated the idea of a bountiful land populated with happy and "lazy" natives who eat fruit, sleep in the trees or near springs, "run, play, laugh, call each other, chirp head to toe unclothed."[152] This, however, does not justify taking their land from them, according to Abovian, who disapproved of Columbus's appropriation of the island of Guanahani in the name of the Spanish crown on the pretext that pagans cannot own a country.[153] While opposing colonization and slavery in principle, Abovian, just like Raynal and Diderot, admired the economic success and political progress of the United States. He compared it with the development of Spanish colonies, in which the obsession over gold prevented new settlers from developing agriculture, manufacturing, and trade, and blamed the Spanish government for restricting the establishment of factories and mills in the colonies with the aim of selling them goods manufactured in Spain.[154]

Interestingly, in discussing the economic development of his own region, in his article "Hayastani ev hay zhoghovrdi tntesakan u kulturakan vichaki barelavelu ughineri masin" ("On Ways of Improving the Economic and Cultural Conditions of Armenia and Armenian People"), Abovian is cautious about introducing labour-intensive and technologically advanced manufacturing facilities, such as factories for processing silk. Internalizing the discourse about the "lazy native," he criticizes attempts to open silk-processing facilities in Tbilisi, where people "avoid even the lightest work," and suggests that Transcaucasia will gain more as a supplier of raw materials.[155] Silk production had been an important part of the Georgian economy since ancient times, when the necessary technology travelled from China through the Great Silk Road. As happened in other colonized regions, such as India, the local crafts were forgotten after colonization in favour of producing raw materials to be exported to the colonizing country. As a part of the Russian Empire, Georgia became a producer of raw silk for the factories located in Russia until the 1920s. In the Soviet period, silk began to be processed in Georgia using new technologies, with the secrets of the ancient craft lost forever.[156]

Instead of silk-processing factories, Abovian suggested building a glass factory to produce bottles that would allow for the preservation and exportation of Trancaucasian wines.[157] He was proud of the fruit the region was producing and exporting: "our lemons, figs, olives, wonderful peaches, apricots, plums, grapes, of such a diverse variety of breeds that can be found nowhere else, our pomegranates, pears, quince, and many and many other fruits." Aligned with the tendency of his time, he suggested that the local population use their own fruits instead of exporting exotic produce from abroad.[158] Abovian seemed to share Zhukovsky's organicist view on economic development, and was against drastic changes and accelerated industrialization of the region. However, he did not share Zhukovsky's concern over the exploitative nature of developing a monoculture, and supported the idea of Transcaucasia as a producer of raw cotton for Russian factories.[159]

Like Griboedov and Zaveleisky, Abovian hoped that the production and export of plant-based dyes would continue to grow.[160] As a supporter of organicist development, he underscored the importance of researching the local soils and of figuring out what new plants could be introduced to the region without destroying its ecosystem,[161] stating that he would be happy to organize and conduct such research if he had the necessary funds. Research and education of local professionals was Abovian's biggest hope for modernizing Transcaucasia. He agreed with Griboedov and Zaveleisky that local merchants were not cognizant of the great potential that entrepreneurship in Transcaucasia could unlock. He also gave a similar explanation of such lack of ambition: that the years of war and insecurity prevented entrepreneurs from making long-term plans and envisioning far-reaching projects. This, he believed, would change with Russian rule, providing not only personal safety but also security of property.[162]

To assist in this change, Abovian proposed to open a boarding school in an area with a pleasant climate and scenic view, not far from the city of Yerevan and the road connecting Georgia with Iran and Turkey – in other words, his native village of Kanaker.[163] Armenian teachers would teach regular subjects, but the school would have its own adjacent land and agricultural facilities where Abovian proposed establishing a German colony of farmers and craftsmen. These people – tailors, coopers, masons, shoemakers, weavers, and farmers versed in advanced technologies for agriculture, gardening, animal husbandry, and operating watermills – would teach their skills to the students of the school, who, after graduation, would relocate to locations in Transcaucasia that needed their skills and technological knowledge. The school would also serve as an example of good agricultural and manufacturing practices for the neighbouring villages.[164]

As a true representative of romantic nationalism, Abovian was interested in ethnographic research and in collecting folklore. It was important for him to preserve the lore and to describe the customs of Armenians and other peoples of Transcaucasia. As well, he avidly explored his native land; among other travels, after settling in Armenia he ascended Mount Aragats with a professor from the University of Munich, Moritz Wagner, and also visited a Kurdish Yazidi community with August von Haxthausen, a German economist and agricultural scientist. It may have been because he was a devoted wanderer that his German wife, Emilia Looze, did not report him missing for a long time after he left home one day never to return. His explorations of the land gave birth to a romantic myth that he disappeared trying to climb Mount Ararat for the second time. Abovian's biographers rule out suicide, although *Wounds of Armenia* reveals that he was depressed, and even admitted that the only things tying him to life were his family and his students. It is doubtful that Abovian's projects of economic modernization of Transcaucasia had any practical results, but his literary and pedagogical activities launched a profound cultural change a few decades after his death, including rapid development of literature in vernacular Eastern Armenian and educational reforms in Transcaucasia.

During the nineteenth century, Transcaucasia served mostly as a supplier of raw materials for Russian silk and cotton factories; during the

Soviet period it became one of the most advanced regions of the Union. Abovian's native village of Kanaker, situated on a hill overlooking the city, is surrounded by apricot orchards and houses four Institutes of Biomedical Research, in one of which I used to work. After the collapse of the Soviet Union, both scientific institutions and industrial manufacturers struggled to survive. Today, while Azerbaijan produces and exports oil, Armenia and Georgia survive through agriculture, tourism, and branches of computer programming companies. Until the recent political upheavals, Russia was Armenia's primary economic partner and political and military ally, but currently people push for more balanced political affiliations.

This brief outline of the nineteenth-century discourse on Russia's imperial expansion and colonial management in relation to the intellectual legacy of the Enlightenment lays the ground for understanding the overarching idea of *The Death of Vazir-Mukhtar*. In that novel, Tynianov exposes the imperialist nature of nineteenth-century romantic nationalism and its Orientalist writing as a disloyal heir of the Enlightenment. The moral compass of the eighteenth century becomes the inheritance of the twentieth century in a descent that skips sons and connects grandfathers with grandsons. The Russian revolutionary avant-garde with its aversion to imperialist ideology is, in Tynianov's view, the true heir of the Enlightenment, while the encroaching Stalinism threatens to beget the new generation of disloyal descendants.

Chapter Two

The "Oriental Journeys" in *The Death of Vazir-Mukhtar*

Among Yury Tynianov's literary works, *The Death of Vazir-Mukhtar* (1927–9) stands out not only because of its Oriental subject matter, but more importantly for the author's insight into the cultural phenomenon that later became known as Russian Orientalism. Written in the late 1920s,[1] the novel anticipates many of the ideas that scholars of Russian Orientalism Susan Layton, Monika Greenleaf, and Harsha Ram put forward in extensive studies over the last two decades.[2] Chief among them are the participation of literature and the discipline of Oriental studies in the process of empire-building, the interconnectedness between ideology and the mode of writing, and the intrinsic specificity of Russian Orientalism in spite of its deriving from a European precursor.

Of course, the genre of the novel does not allow Tynianov to develop these ideas by means of strict analytical argumentation. Instead, he expounds them through his intertextual references to Orientalist writing of the nineteenth century, on the one hand, and to the treatment of the same subject by his contemporaries, on the other.

This chapter views Tynianov's novel as a specific form of scholarly fiction, a study of Russian Orientalism, where parody is one of the methods used in its scholarly explorations. Narrowing Tynianov's complex and multidimensional study of Russian Orientalism to one particular topic, his treatment of Oriental travelogues, it contrasts his parody of Alexander Pushkin's nineteenth-century travelogue *Puteshestvie v Arzrum* (*Journey to Arzrum*, 1829–35) with his intertextual references to the "Oriental Journey" of his contemporary and friend Victor Shklovsky, whose autobiographical book *Sentimental'noe puteshestvie* (*Sentimental Journey*, 1923) contains a chapter dedicated to Persia.

The final part of the chapter analyses the work of each of the three authors, Pushkin, Shklovsky, and Tynianov, in relation to the landmark text *Puteshestvie iz Peterburga v Moskvu* (*Journey from Petersburg to Moscow*, 1790) by the eighteenth-century Enlightenment thinker Alexander Radishchev. In that work, Radishchev condemns imperialism, the inadequate international justice system of the time, and, most importantly, serfdom as a form of internal colonization. We shall see that Shklovsky in his *Journey* expresses similar implacable attitudes towards imperialism by using Radishchev's rhetorical devices. Earlier, Pushkin in his unfinished article "Puteshestvie iz Moskvy v Peterburg" ("Journey from Moscow to Petersburg," 1834) criticized Radishchev, thereby drawing readers' attention to Radishchev's ideas.

While Pushkin questions particular methods of Russian colonization of the Caucasus in his *Journey to Arzrum*, he does not join Radishchev in denouncing imperialism in general. His contemporary Alexander Griboedov, the main protagonist of Tynianov's novel, participated in the imperial project directly, even though like Pushkin he was often critical of the colonial policies of his supervisors. Tynianov in his novel contrasts the attitudes of Pushkin and Griboedov, permeated by both Eurocentrism and romantic nationalism, with the all-inclusive humanism of Radishchev and Shklovsky.

Working in the genre of the novel, a form more synthetic than a travelogue, Tynianov structures his book as a *Journey* that encompasses the *Journeys* of his literary predecessors. He does this by following the road maps of the previous *Journeys*; his protagonist Griboedov travels first from Moscow to Petersburg (an allusion to Radishchev's *Journey* and Pushkin's polemical response), then from Petersburg to Tbilisi (as in Pushkin's and Shklovsky's *Journeys*), and from Tbilisi to Tabriz (as in Shklovsky's *Journey*). While combining the road maps of these three *Journeys* written in three consecutive centuries, Tynianov juxtaposes both the literary devices their authors used and the ideas they adhered to, creating a dialogue around the topics of imperialism and Russian Orientalism.

The Scholarly Novel

Scholars have always been tempted to interpret Tynianov's novels as a continuation of his literary theory and criticism. Such an approach is justifiable, especially since Tynianov himself praised his contemporary and fellow formalist Shklovsky for writing "things" "on the border." In Tynianov's view, Shklovsky's book *Zoo pisma ne o liubvi ili tret'ia Eloiza* (*Zoo, Letters Not about Love, or the Third Heloise*, 1923) fuses together a novel, a satirical article, and a scholarly study, interweaving literature and literary theory in an unusual way.[3]

One early attempt to analyse Tynianov's novels as a specific form of scholarly research appears in Boris Eichenbaum's article "Tvorchestvo Iu.

Tynianova" ("Yu. Tynianov's Works," 1944).[4] Eichenbaum underscores two aspects of Tynianov's scholarly approach in his novels. On the one hand, he sees these novels as contributions to the history of literature, by which Eichenbaum is referring to Tynianov's study of the literary works and biographies of his protagonists: Wilhelm Küchelbecker, Griboedov, and Pushkin. On the other hand, he analyses them as works of literary theory, a way for Tynianov to pose questions of style and of aesthetic methods that he had not yet developed in his scholarly work, and to solve them through experimentation.[5] Eichenbaum rephrases Tynianov's argument about the necessity of scholarly (*nauchnaia*) work in creating new art by stating the opposite: "we need artistic vision, we need work that is artistic in its methodology, in order that new phenomena would appear in science or scholarship."[6]

Tynianov's development of the theme of Russian Orientalism in his novel is an example of such a work, "artistic in its methodology." The "Oriental" subject matter created the necessity to work with Orientalist texts, and the practical task of representing the "Orient" in the novel. Tynianov's evaluation of Velimir Khlebnikov's treatment of the theme of the "Orient" suggests that Tynianov was looking for a new approach: "To zhe i s Vostokom: v 'Trube Gul'-Mully' net evropeiskogo vostoka: ni sniskhoditel'nogo interesa, ni izlishnego uvazheniia. Vroven' – tak izmeniaiutsia izmereniia tem, proizvoditsia pereotsenka ikh." (The same with the Orient: in "Gul'-Mulla" there is no European Orient: neither condescending interest, nor superfluous respect. Equal – thus the measurements of the themes change, they are being re-evaluated.)[7] To find this new way of writing, Tynianov the novelist parodies the texts of his Orientalist predecessors, revealing their underlying ideas and stylistic devices.

The formalists and Tynianov always stressed the orientation of new literary works towards pre-existing texts. Thus, in Shklovsky's words, "Not only parody, but any work of art is created as a parallel and a contrast for some model."[8] Tynianov's view of parody and its creative role in the process of literary evolution anticipates that of Mikhail Bakhtin in his theory of the novel, although Bakhtin's theory contains certain insights missing in Tynianov's theoretical writing that are useful in discussing *The Death of Vazir-Mukhtar*.

Especially useful is Bakhtin's examination of the novel as a dialogic genre, which incorporates in it other non-novelistic genres, such as diaries, biographies, confessions, or travelogues,[9] and combines *belles lettres* with "rhetorical genres" such as moral philosophy.[10] When juxtaposed within a novel, the pieces of writing in different genres enter into a dialogue with each other. This account is especially applicable to

The Death of Vazir-Mukhtar. The genres of the Orientalist writings that the novel alludes to are very diverse and include Pushkin's narrative poem "Bakhchisaraiskii fontan" ("The Fountain of Bakhchisaray," 1824), Griboedov's project on economic development of the Transcaucasia (1928), formal documents, and informal correspondence. This diversity shows the all-embracing way in which the imperial project permeated many aspects of life in all layers of society. Additionally, it allows the author to juxtapose different opinions and attitudes in a comprehensive dialogue about the Russian Empire and its relation to the Orient.

Tynianov's novel also provides an example of what Bakhtin describes as the dialogic resistance of the discourse being parodied. When the subject of the parody is not recognizable, the parodied discourse loses its "objectness [*ob"ektnost'*]" in a process that Bakhtin calls "reaccentuation [*pereaktsentuatsiia*]."[11] Tynianov's writing, if not recognized as a parody of some pre-existing Orientalist texts but taken as a "representation of reality," becomes an Orientalist piece by itself, another sample of the styles and ideas it was trying to parody.

By reading Tynianov's novel as a study in Russian Orientalism and by applying the Bakhtinian notion of dialogism to it, I challenge the view that Tynianov and the formalists saw literature as evolving autonomously and disregarded its connection to history or to life. For example, according to Hans Jauss Tynianov's theory of literary evolution historicizes literature by stressing inner conflict and change over the idea of timeless beauty and tradition. It also reduces this change to "the succession of aesthetic-formal systems," without revealing its "relationship to the general process of history."[12] This relationship, Jauss argues, is not limited to the influence of the socio-economic formation of literature, which was the focus of the Marxist literary theory of Tynianov's time. Literature in its turn influences history through its "formative" social function.[13]

Although the formative function of literature is not at the centre of Tynianov's literary theory, in his article "O literaturnoi evolutsii" ("On Literary Evolution," 1924) he does speak about "a reverse expansion of literature into life."[14] The formative function of literature is more prominent in Tynianov's novel *The Death of Vazir-Mukhtar*, which explores a special case of such expansion, the role of Orientalist texts in the formation of Russian imperial policies. The novel directly suggests the involvement of literary Orientalism in policy planning in an episode where the characters discuss the future of Georgia, and "politics was as if from Pushkin's poem."[15]

Tynianov's "extraliterary interests," according to Steven Lovell, developed "in the second half of the 1920s" and "were largely determined by his interest in historical questions." Lovell argues, "It is via history that Tynianov heads away from 'pure' Formalism" in his theoretical writings.[16] Eichenbaum also stresses the historicity of Tynianov's fiction: "here history owns everything, because each thing exists not on its own, but in correlation with the world."[17] Unfortunately, Eichenbaum and other scholars who analysed historical aspects of *The Death of Vazir-Mukhtar* concentrated on the treatment of Decembrism and autocracy, without noticing imperialism and Orientalism as the underlying themes that pervade the novel.

Eichenbaum, in developing his idea of Tynianov's novel as a scholarly study, argues that while many historical novels are allegories referring to their authors' own times, Tynianov's novel seeks a new understanding of the past. Although this is largely true, Tynianov was certainly aware of the historical parallels between the conquest and annexation of Transcaucasia, which the novel describes, and its re-annexation by Bolshevik Russia shortly before the novel was written. Lenin sanctioned re-annexation of Georgia in 1921 and its forced merging within the Transcaucasian Republic in 1922, despite his previously declared intentions to grant the right of self-determination to all the nations of the empire after the 1917 Russian Revolution. Stalin and his assistant Ordjonikidze suppressed the ensuing discontent and struggle for autonomy in Georgia. This prompted Lenin to advocate for more autonomy in Georgia, and the "Georgian question" became his "last struggle."[18]

Although *The Death of Vazir-Mukhtar* is what Bakhtin describes as a dialogic novel, where different ideas and opinions are represented without favouring one over the other, the author's overall negative attitude towards imperialism and Orientalism often becomes apparent. This overall attitude coincides with the official ideology of the early 1920s, which was based on Lenin's definition of imperialism as the highest form of capitalist exploitation, and which in the 1930s changed to promote a more expansionist and Russocentric worldview. At the same time, as was mentioned above, his negative view of imperialism and Orientalism suggests Tynianov's familiarity with the ideas of the scholars of Rozen's school in Oriental studies, which influenced the Russian intelligentsia of the late nineteenth century and the beginning of the Soviet period. As we shall see, Tynianov states his position indirectly through literary devices, such as parody, allusion, and irony.

Pushkin's Formula

Tynianov's engagement with Pushkin's *Journey to Arzrum* embraces both the artistic experimentation in *The Death of Vazir-Mukhtar* and scholarly analyses, which he presented in his article "O 'Puteshestvii v Arzrum'" ("On the 'Journey to Arzrum,'" 1936). The former seems to precede the latter chronologically: Tynianov's article is based on a presentation he gave in 1927, whereas his archival work on Pushkin's text started only in 1929. Regardless of chronological order, the two methods of Tynianov's research complement each other: in the novel Tynianov reveals Pushkin's manner of writing through parody, while in the article he analyses it in scholarly terms.

Analysing Pushkin's methods of writing his "travelogue," in his article Tynianov notes how the narrator assumes the posture of an uncomprehending civilian, whose "neutral" account of events reveals their absurdity, or how, in using documents, he slightly changes them to give them a new meaning.[19] By suggesting the rationale for using certain literary methods, Tynianov explains Pushkin's ethical position. Thus, discussing the poem "Delibash" (1929), written by Pushkin soon after his return from his journey, Tynianov suggests that Pushkin uses the method of "satirical 'indifference'" to make a "call" "towards peace:"

> Vmesto obychnykh voinstvennykh obrashchenii, svoistvennykh etomu rodu proizvedenii, oba stikhotvoreniia soderzhat prizyvy protivopolozhnogo svoistva, – k miru … vmesto ody byla dana zhanrovaia batal'naia stsenka, v kotoroi lapidarnaia poeticheskaia tochnost' i neposredstvennost' k kontsu perekhodiat v ironiiu:
>
> Mchatsia, sshiblis' v obshchem krike …
> Posmotrite! kakovy? …
> Delibash uzhe na pike,
> A kazak bez golovy.
> Zdes' neitralitet poeticheskogo nabliudatelia iavno perekhodit v satiricheskoe "ravnodushie" poeta.[20]
>
> (Instead of the usual belligerent appeals, characteristic for this sort of work, both poems contain calls of an opposite kind, – towards peace … instead of an ode, there was the genre of the battle skit, in which at the end lapidary poetic precision and immediacy turn into irony:
>
> They rush, they collide in a common shout …
> Would you look at them? …
> Delibash is already on a lance,
> And the Cossack is without a head.
> Here, clearly, the neutrality of a poet observer turns into the satirical "indifference" of the poet.)

This ironic neutrality that at times turns into "satirical 'indifference'" is a characteristic feature of Tynianov's own writing in *The Death of Vazir-Mukhtar*. The following sentences from the novel, describing the fate of Griboedov's remains after the members of the Russian mission in Teheran were killed by an angry mob, read as an exaggerated imitation, or a parody, of Pushkin's style: "Kebabchi votknul golovu na shest, ona byla mnogo legche ego korziny s pirozhkami, i on trias drevkom. Kiafir byl vinovat v voinakh, golode, pritesneniiakh starshin, neurozhae." (Kebabchi stuck the head on a pole, it was much lighter than his basket with patties, and he was shaking the staff. Kiafir was guilty in wars, in famine, in the oppression of the foremen, in the poor harvest.)[21] As in Pushkin's poem, the "satirical indifference" in a representation of violence appears in the context of condemnation of war. Tynianov both emulates the formal aesthetic aspect of Pushkin's writing and recreates its ideological, ethical context.

The entire section describing the fate of Griboedov's remains is built around the following phrase from Pushkin's travelogue: "Obezobrazhennyi trup ego, byvshii tri dnia igralishchem tegeranskoi cherni, uznan byl tol'ko po ruke, nekogda prostrelennoi pistoletnoiu puleiu." (His disfigured body, which was for three days a plaything of Tehran's rabble, was recognized only by his hand, at one time shot through with a pistol bullet.)[22] This statement does not correspond to the documented facts, and has a literary origin – Adam Mickiewicz's improvisation on the death of the patriarch of Constantinople.[23] Note that Tynianov's writing here is particularly susceptible to Bakhtinian "re-accentuation." Reading Tynianov's passage as a "representation of reality" rather than as a parody on Pushkin's texts would turn it into an Orientalist text, a description of "Oriental brutality."

In his article on the *Journey*, Tynianov points out that Pushkin had referred to extensive documents and literary texts in his travelogue: "'Journey to Arzrum' was written in 1835 on the basis of notes of 1829. In the process a big scholarly and literary apparatus was used."[24] Tynianov emphasizes that the *Journey* is not simply Pushkin's travel notes, but a semi-fictional recreation of his travels six years later: "The very method of working on the 'Journey to Arzrum,' the text of which was formed on the basis of notes and books six years after the journey, was not a method of registering the immediate impressions."[25]

Emphasizing the element of parody in the *Journey*, Tynianov juxtaposes paragraph by paragraph the original texts used by Pushkin with Pushkin's rendition of the same texts. The latter appear to be very close to the originals, yet their meaning is manipulated through subtle changes: "Leaving the exposition of the factual side of the event without a change, Pushkin considerably simplifies the pompous style, and with it the pompous meaning of the relation. 'The deputies,' who ask to fire against the 'mutineers,' turn into 'dignitaries,' who are afraid of the fire of their own cannons."[26] Tynianov's own treatment of the original texts in *The Death of Vazir-Mukhtar* is very similar. Thus, in the original text of K.A. Borozdin, which Tynianov used, Alexander Chavchavadze, Griboedov's father-in law, appears as a person of "an ancient family of Georgian princes," who "advanced during the reign of the Georgian tsars Irakli II and Georgi II," was "loved both by Russians and natives," and brought them closer together.[27] In Tynianov's rendering, "the prince" (Chavchavadze) was a man of an excellent "native" "family," and "advanced" "during the reign" of Alexander, by suppressing his own compatriots.[28]

Tynianov follows Pushkin's text closely, and at the same time defamiliarizes the original words by recontextualizing them. One sees this in the following passage where Pushkin develops what Tynianov calls the formula of "the samovar and Christianity":

> Cherkesy nas nenavidiat. My vytesnili ikh iz privol'nykh pastbishch; auly ikh razoreny, tselye plemena unichtozheny … Plennikov oni sokhraniaiut v nadezhde na vykup, no obkhodiatsia s nimi s uzhasnym beschelovechiem, zastavliaiut rabotat' sverkh sil, kormiat syrym testom, b'iut, kogda vzdumaetsia, i pristavliaiut k nim dlia strazhi svoikh mal'chishek, kotorye za odno slovo vprave ikh izrubit' svoimi detskimi shashkami … Vliianie roskoshi mozhet blagopriiatstvovat' ikh ukroshcheniiu: samovar byl by vazhnym novovvedeniem. Est' sredstvo bolee sil'noe, bolee nravstvennoe, bolee soobraznoe s prosveshcheniem nashego veka: propovedanie Evangeliia.[29]

> (Circassians hate us. We forced them out of the spacious pastures; their *auly* [villages] are ravaged, entire tribes are annihilated … They keep the prisoners with the hope of ransom, but treat them with terrible inhumanity, force them to work beyond their ability, feed them with raw dough, beat them, whenever they want to, and assign guarding to their boys, who for a single word have the right to slash them with their child's sabres … The impact of luxury may be favourable for taming them: the samovar would be an important innovation. There is a means more powerful, more moral, more in conformance with the enlightenment of our age: preaching of the Gospel.)

In this passage, Pushkin obviously retells some written or oral source. His missionary "formula" is justified as a more "civilized" alternative to the violence of military subjugation, and as a necessary response to the alleged brutality of the enemy. Tynianov takes Pushkin's formula as well as the idea of a "child's sabre" out of context and combines them with the following passage, where Pushkin describes his encounter during his journey with a family who provided him with food:

> Neskol'ko zhenshchin v pestrykh lokhmot'iakh sideli na ploskoi krovle podzemnoi sakli. Ia iz"iasnilsia koe-kak. Odna iz nikh soshla v sakliu i vynesla mne syru i moloka. Otdokhnuv neskol'ko minut, ia pustilsia dalee.[30]
>
> (Several women in multicoloured, tattered clothing were sitting on the flat roof of an underground *saklia* [house]. I expressed myself somehow. One of them went down to the *saklia* and brought out some cheese and milk for me. After several minutes of rest, I set out further.)

By combining these two passages into one, Tynianov makes the "child's sabre" appear to be a toy rather than a weapon, and Pushkin's desire to "tame" the poor family loses its contextual justification. In the new context, it sounds like a prejudice against their "otherness":

> Zhenshchiny v pestrykh lokhmot'iakh sideli na kamne – ploskoi krovle podzemnoi sakli. Mal'chishka s detskoi shashkoi v ruke pliasal na dozhde.
> – Chaiu, – skazal Pushkin, speshilsia i ukrylsia pod kamennyi naves.
> Emu vynesli syru i moloka.
> Pushkin brosil den'gi. Dozhd' vnezapno, kak nachalsia, tak i konchilsia.
> On poekhal dal'she i oglianulsia.
> Mal'chishka toptalsia v luzhe; zhenshchiny smotreli emu vsled ...
> "Vliianie roskoshi i khristianstva moglo by ikh ukrotit', – podumal on, – samovar i Evangelie byli by vazhnymi sredstvami."[31]
>
> (Women in multicoloured tatters were sitting on a stone – a flat roof of an underground *saklia*. A boy with a child's sabre was dancing in the rain.
> – Some tea, – said Pushkin, he dismounted, and took shelter under the stone awning.
> They brought out some cheese and milk.

Pushkin threw them money. The rain stopped as suddenly as it had started. He set out farther, and looked back.
The boy walked about in a puddle; the women were following him with their eyes …
"The influence of luxury and Christianity could tame them, – he thought – the samovar and the Gospel would be important means.")

The subjectivity of Pushkin's point of view in describing the "other" is underscored by mentioning the gazes of the women, who, on their part, were observing Pushkin. The difficulty in communicating with the women in Pushkin's original text is, in Tynianov's parody, rendered as clear miscommunication: Pushkin asks for tea, and the women bring him cheese and milk. By emphasizing miscommunication between Pushkin and the people he meets in his *Journey*, Tynianov's parody reveals one of the important underlying themes of Pushkin's travelogue, namely, as Monika Greenleaf has put it, the "impossibility of crossing over into another culture."[32] The understanding of this impossibility does not preclude the feeling of cultural superiority over the "Orientals," which Tynianov underscores by having Pushkin throw them money.

It is worth noting also how Tynianov rearranges the two parallel sentences in Pushkin's original, one suggesting the importance of luxury in general and the samovar in particular in "taming" the locals, and the other proclaiming the preaching of the Gospel as an enlightened means of their subjugation. He combines the two sentences into one in such a way that "the samovar" and "the Gospel" become two equally important strategies in dealing with the Caucasus. This combined sentence is rearranged further into the famous formula of "the samovar and Christianity," which Tynianov uses in his article on the *Journey*, completely replacing Pushkin's own words: "Farther Pushkin develops his idea of missionary work in the Caucasus. 'The samovar and Christianity' – such is the formula of colonial politics, he suggests."[33]

In this complete replacement of the original, Tynianov again uses Pushkin's device that he analyses elsewhere in his article. "The tissue of the 'Journey' is so concealed and ironic," explains Tynianov, that Pushkin's intentional misquotation of a certain article "up to now passes" for its "factual exposition."[34] Tynianov's formula once more underscores Pushkin's ironic "neutrality," which at times took the form of "abstaining from judging about the hierarchy of things and events being described, about what is important and what is not important."[35]

Tynianov's interpretation of the passage on the samovar and the Gospel coincides with that of Greenleaf, who reads it as an "ironic glance over his shoulder at other missionary travelogues."[36] In this case, Tynianov's parody aims to reveal and to amplify Pushkin's original, rather than underscore its weaknesses.

The formula of "the samovar and Christianity" sounds like Tynianov's pun on *Pushkin i Khristianstvo* (*Pushkin and Christianity*), the title of a chapbook published in 1915 by the symbolist Vladimir Gippius, who was looking for religious and philosophical meaning in Pushkin's works.[37] Tynianov's formula hints at the manner in which literary and ideological movements of different periods used Pushkin's name to promote their own ideas and worldview. The Silver Age myth, according to Evgeny Dobrenko, perceived Pushkin's value "in the themes of the poetic vocation and freedom of creativity," as opposed to the "messianic nationalist myth" of the nineteenth century that was revived by the "Russocentric populism" of the mid-1930s. The formalists, Dobrenko argues, destroyed both myths by analysing "Pushkin's writing merely as a set of literary devices."[38]

While it is true that Tynianov does not recreate the myths surrounding Pushkin as a literary and historical figure, he does underscore the cultural and historical importance of his *Journey to Arzrum* by placing the parody of it in the epilogue to *The Death of Vazir-Mukhtar*. Tynianov closes his novel with words borrowed from Pushkin and rendered in a parody that can be defined in Linda Hutcheon's terms as "a method of inscribing continuity while permitting critical distance."[39] In his article on Pushkin's *Journey*, beyond the apparent goal of analysing Pushkin's literary devices, Tynianov aims to exonerate Pushkin by showing that his Orientalism was ironic. This irony, in Tynianov's view, was a way to ponder "the questions of Russian colonial politics" that the journey to the Russian Orient "posed to Pushkin."

In the last paragraphs of the article, Tynianov departs from his literary analyses to evaluate Pushkin's *Journey* in terms of the author's moral stance. He gives a complete citation of a passage in which Pushkin describes the miserable condition of the *amanats*, children from the neighbouring mountaineers' tribes, who were kept by the tsarist army as hostages, commenting, "a real collision with the practices of the colonizers forced Pushkin to notice their dark features and to describe them with all the harshness." Tynianov's engagement with Pushkin's *Journey to Arzrum*, both in his novel and in his scholarly work, clearly reveals the ethical principles that guided him as an author and a scholar.

Moral Sentiments

Working on *Vazir-Mukhtar*, Tynianov in turn confronted the same "questions of Russian colonial politics." On the one hand, these questions emerged from the historical material he was using as an author; on the other hand, they were still vital in Tynianov's own time. In his novel, he refers to the "Oriental" encounter of his contemporary and fellow formalist Shklovsky side by side with that of Pushkin, the contemporary of his protagonist Griboedov. Tynianov's novelistic treatment of Shklovsky's *Sentimental Journey*, as well as his evaluation of Shklovsky's other works in his articles, shed light on the ethical nature of Tynianov's engagement with this topic.

The title of Shklovsky's book refers back to *A Sentimental Journey through France and Italy* (1768) by Laurence Sterne, who adhered to the idea of an ethics based on feelings rather than on rationality. Adam Smith gives the philosophical explanation for this idea in his *Theory of Moral Sentiments* (1759), where he argues that the basis of human morality is compassion or sympathy, which, as a necessary precondition of our existence, is one of the "principles" of our nature.[40] In his *Sentimental Journey*, Shklovsky not only imitates Sterne's "literary devices" but also uses the "sentimental point of view" to reveal his attitude towards the First World War, then in progress, and to the Russian presence in Iran.

In this respect, Shklovsky's *Sentimental Journey* does not conform to his statement about art being "pitiless [*bezzhalostno*]" or "outside pity [*vnezhalostno*]" that he makes in his article "*Tristram Shandy* and the Theory of the Novel," which interestingly analyses another work by Sterne:

> Sentimental'nost' ne mozhet byt' soderzhaniem iskusstva, khotia by potomu uzhe, chto v iskusstve net soderzhaniia. Izobrazhenie veshchi s "sentimental'noi tochki zreniia" est' osobyi metod izobrazheniia, takoi zhe, naprimer, kak izobrazhenie ikh s tochki zreniia loshadi (Tolstoi, "Kholstomer") ili velikana (Svift).[41]

> (Sentimentality cannot be the content of art, if only for the reason that there is no content in art. Representing things from the "sentimental point of view" is a special method of representation, similar, for example, to representing them from the point of view of a horse [Tolstoy – Kholstomer] or a giant [Swift].)

Statements like this allowed scholars to view Russian Formalism as a literary theory that does not concern itself with the ethical aspect of the text. Recently, the scholars Ilya Kalinin, Douglas Robinson, and Michael Denner have re-examined this assumption. Thus, according to Douglas Robinson, Shklovsky's statement on sentimentality does not represent the "true core" of his theory of Formalism in general.[42] At the core of Shklovsky's theory, Robinson sees what he calls "somatic mimeticism" or "embodied empathy."[43] Far from establishing the autonomy of art, Shklovsky's idea of estrangement (*ostranenie*) as it appears already in his 1917 article "Iskusstvo kak priem" ("Art as Device") treats art as an essential component of life.[44] In the course of our everyday experience, our sensations or feelings (*oshchushcheniia*) wear away. In losing our sensation of life, we make wrong choices and our life deteriorates. By restoring our sensation of life, art helps us to make it better.

Among the sensations Shklovsky talks about is the sensation of pain, the loss of which brings the world to suicide: "Morskie svinki s pererezannymi nozhnymi nervami otgryzaiut sebe pal'tsy. Mir, poteriavshii vmeste s iskusstvom oshchushchenie zhizni, sovershaet seichas nad soboiu chudovishchnoe samoubiistvo. Voina v nashe vremia mertvogo iskusstva prokhodit mimo soznaniia, i etim ob"iasniaetsia ee zhestokost'" (Guinea pigs with cut leg nerves gnaw off their own toes. The world that together with art lost the sensation of life is now committing a monstrous suicide. The war in our time of dead art passes by consciousness, and that explains its cruelty).[45]

Art, in Shklovsky's understanding, not only restores the worn-out sensual perceptions of the world but also, by restoring the sensation of pain, gives us back the ability to feel empathy, or "sympathy," the "fellow feeling" so important for Smith and the sentimentalists.[46] One of the principal literary devices Shklovsky uses for such restoration is estrangement – by making things, characters, and events strange, art prompts us to see them as if for the first time. In the *Sentimental Journey*, estrangement restores the reader's sensitivity to the horrors and abomination of the imperialistic war, and in this sense Shklovsky follows the tradition of Leo Tolstoy. The abundance of citations of Tolstoy's works included in Shklovsky's article "Art as Device," where he defines and develops the notion of estrangement, is not accidental. According to Denner, Shklovsky's idea of estrangement itself bears the influence of Tolstoy's writing, and his "renovation of perception has an inevitable social result."[47] In the following passage from the *Journey*, Shklovsky uses estrangement to show the unnaturalness of war:

> Posle vzryva soldaty, okruzhennye vragami, zhdushchie podvizhnogo sostava, zanialis' tem, chto sobirali i sostavliali iz kuskov razorvannye tela tovarishchei.

Sobirali dolgo.

Konechno, chasti tela u mnogikh peremeshali. Odin ofitser podoshel k dlinnomu riadu polozhennykh trupov.

Krainii pokoinik byl sobran iz ostavshikhsia chastei.

Eto bylo tulovishche krupnogo cheloveka. K nemu byla pristavlena maken'kaia golova, i na grudi lezhali malen'kie, nerovnye ruki, obe levye. Ofitser smotrel dovol'no dolgo, potom sel na zemliu i stal khokhotat' … khokhotat' … khokhotat' … [48]

(After the explosion the soldiers, who were surrounded by the enemy, waited for the rolling stock and occupied themselves with collecting and putting together the torn bodies of their friends.

They were collecting for a long time.

Of course, they mixed up the body parts of many. One officer walked up to a long row of corpses.

The last deceased was put together from constituent parts.

It was a trunk of a large man. Placed against it was a small head, and on the chest there were small, uneven hands, both of them left.

The office kept looking for a rather long time, then he sat on the ground and started to laugh … laugh … laugh.)

The dehumanizing effect of the war makes it possible to put a person together as a puzzle. Tynianov parodies this passage in his novel, relating the story of putting together the bodies of Griboedov and other members of the Russian mission. Again, rather than entering into a polemic with the parodied text, Tynianov's parody magnifies the effect of Shklovsky's original and spells out his idea of war and violence, turning people into identical, anonymous, inanimate objects:

Vskore obnaruzhilis' chernye, polusgnivshie tela i chasti tel. Ikh vybrasyvali na poverkhnost' rva, i oni lezhali riadom, pokhozhie drug na druga, kak budto pod odnim numerom izgotovila ikh odna fabrika. Tol'ko u odnikh ne khvtalo ruk, u drugikh nog, a byli i vovse bezymennye, ne imevshie nazvaniia predmenty.[49]

(Soon black, half-rotten bodies and body parts were found. They threw them on the surface of the ditch, and they lay side by side, looking alike, as if the same factory manufactured them under the same number. Only some were missing arms, others legs, and there were also completely anonymous objects, having no names.)

In Pushkin's *Journey*, the mutilated body of Griboedov was recognized by his arm and hand with a ring. Tynianov combines Pushkin's version with Shklovsky's description of the soldier with somebody else's arms placed against his body: in his novel Griboedov's hand with the ring is applied to the best-preserved body. According to Ilya Kalinin, the mutilated bodies in both Shklovsky's and Tynianov's episodes allude to fragmentariness in their authors' writing, which in its turn reflects the feeling of fragmentation that the turbulent historical time brings into their lives. Kalinin establishes connections between the formalists' personal experiences of living through the historical times of revolutions, the First World War and the Russian Civil War, and the ideas of estrangement and fragmentation as they appear in their theoretical and fictional writing. The formalists' ideas, according to Kalinin, are a direct response to the traumatic experience of the crucial historical shift, a way to deal with the trauma.[50]

It should be stressed that Tynianov's episode is clearly a parody on Shklovsky's *Journey* and on Pushkin's *Journey*. By juxtaposing the two originals in one parody, Tynianov placed them in dialogue with each other. Pushkin and Shklovsky differed both in their attitude to the Orient and in their evaluation of imperialism, as Tynianov shows in his novel. In the following passage from the *Journey to Arzrum*, replacing the stereotype of "Asiatic luxury" with that of "Asiatic poverty" is a cliché in itself and a parody of preceding travelogues, which does not mean that Pushkin does not subscribe to their ideas:

> Ne znaiu vyrazheniia, kotoroe bylo be bessmyslennee slov: aziatskaia roskosh'. Eta pogovorka, veroiatno, rodilas' vo vremia krestovykh pokhodov, kogda bednye rytsari, ostavia golye steny i dubovye stul'ia svoikh zamkov, uvideli v pervyi raz, krasnye divany, pestrye kovry I kinzhaly s tsvetnymi kamushkami na rukoiati. Nyne mozhno skazat': aziatskaia bednost', aziatskoe svinstvo i prokh., no roskosh' est', konechno, prinadlezhnost' Evropy. V Arzrume ni za kakie den'gi nel'zia kupit' togo, chto vy naidete v melochnoi lavke pervogo uezdnogo gorodka Pskovskoi gubernii.[51]

> (I do not know an expression that would be more meaningless than the words: Asiatic luxury. This saying was probably born during the Crusades, when the poor knights, leaving behind the bare walls and oak chairs of their castles, for the first time saw red sofas, motley carpets, and daggers with multicoloured gems on their handles. Now one could say: Asiatic poverty, Asiatic squalour, etc., but luxury is, of course, the attribute of

Europe. In Arzrum, no amount of money will buy you the things that you will find at a convenience store in the little town of Pskov province.)

In the *Sentimental Journey*, Shklovsky recreates the same situation – a person who arrives in Persia in anticipation of an exotic Orient is bewildered to see only poverty and destruction: "He came to the East and expected it to be multicoloured like a peacock's tail. What he saw was an East made of clay, straw, and an entirely bare war."[52] Poverty here is not a natural state of the Orient, the result of its inner sluggishness or cultural backwardness, but rather the consequence of the "predatory" imperialistic war. Shklovsky blames the Russian and British presence in Persia for its ruined economy: "We came to somebody else's country, occupied it, added to its darkness and violence our own violence, we constrained its trade, we did not let it open factories, we supported the shah."[53] At the same time, he undermines another Orientalist cliché, the notion of inherent "Oriental despotism," by suggesting that the Iranians' initiative to democratize the country failed because the imperialist countries considered it more advantageous to preserve the old regime.

Tynianov uses Shklovsky's motif of Russia's guilt for the 1917–19 famine in Persia,[54] but puts it in the context of events that happened almost a century earlier, in 1829. Trying to analyse the causes of the famine, Shklovsky points to Russian meddling in the distribution of irrigation water and the requisitioning of barley by the troops, which coincided with a poor harvest year.[55] This is a correct assessment – the Russian army was a major contributor to the famine in western Iran, while the British, who caused the famine in the Fars region, also blamed that on the Russians as well as the Iranian democrats.[56]

In Tynianov's novel similar circumstances – war, famine, and the poor harvest – appear to trigger the violent reprisal against the members of the Russian mission: "Kiafir was guilty in wars, in famine, in the oppression of the foremen, in the poor harvest."[57] In spite of the absurdity of blaming the poor harvest on Griboedov, Tynianov's parody introduces into the novel Shklovsky's view of imperialism, and creates the notion of continuity between the events of the nineteenth and the twentieth centuries. It posits the strain of a lost war and economic hardship as the underlying cause of the violence against the Russian mission, rather than inherent cultural and religious differences.

Although both Pushkin's and Shklovsky's *Journeys* combine elements of war memoir and autobiography, they differ in their narrators' involvement in events. Pushkin presents himself as an independent gentleman and an "uncomprehending observer" of the war, whereas

Shklovsky not only participates in events but also is endowed with power and burdened with responsibility. He is an insider, both a military and an ideological leader, and a technician, who knows how to fix and operate military machines. For all that, he often admits his own confusion and lack of understanding: "The cases crept along, swelled through all the committees and investigatory commissions climbing up to me. I understood little in them."[58] Yet Shklovsky's lack of understanding is different from that of an "uncomprehending observer," the narrator of Pushkin's *Journey*. War does not make any sense for Shklovsky exactly because he knows it too well:

> V grazhdanskoi voine nastupaiut drug na druga dve pustoty.
> Net belykh i krasnykh armii.
> Eto – ne shutka. Ya vidal voinu.[59]
>
> (In a civil war, two emptinesses advance on each other.
> There are no white or red armies.
> It is not a joke. I have seen war.)

If Pushkin does not find it possible to "cross over" to the "other,"[60] Shklovsky questions the very division between the "self" and the "other." He shows, if not a complete understanding of other cultures, then a deep care for their representatives. He considers his main mission in Persia to be the withdrawal of Russian troops with the fewest casualities for both Iranian civilians and Russian soldiers. He is especially concerned with the fate of the Aisors, the local people, who put themselves in danger by becoming allies of the Russians. Instead of adhering to a political ideology, he tries to uphold the idea of humanism:

> My naprasno tak umny i tak dal'novidny v politike. Esli by my vmesto togo, chtoby pytat'sia delat' istoriiu, pytalis' prosto schitat' sebia otvetstvennymi za otdel'nye sobytiia, sostavliaiushchie etu istoriiu, to, mozhet byt', eto vyshlo by i ne smeshno.
>
> Ne istoriiu nuzhno starat'sia delat', a biografiiu.[61]
>
> (We should not be so smart and so far-sighted in politics. If instead of trying to make history, we would simply try to consider ourselves responsible for individual events, amounting to this history, then maybe the outcome would not be ridiculous. It is not history one should make, but a biography.)

Here "biography" stands for one's personal moral responsibility, and history for the victory of one's ideological beliefs. As a writer, Tynianov seems to follow Shklovsky's advice literally – all three of his historical novels are biographies. They explore the personal lives of Küchelbecker, Griboedov, and Pushkin, figures that each to a certain degree influenced literary and social history. In *The Death of Vazir-Mukhtar*, Tynianov's protagonist Griboedov, unlike his Decembrists friends who had attempted to make history, felt responsible for the individual events and for the people entrusted to him. Like Shklovsky in the *Sentimental Journey*, Griboedov is an insider endowed with knowledge and power, who at times feels helpless and confused by the complexity of the historical events in which he is participating. His responsibility is to transport safely to Russia its former citizens – mostly Christians from the South Caucasus who lived in the territory contested by the war, which now belongs to Russia, and who find themselves in Persia against their will. This situation is a parallel to Shklovsky's responsibility for the group of Christian Aisors and his attempt to save them from persecution.

Griboedov's refusal to give up just one person – the eunuch of the shah's harem, who asked for asylum – cost him his life. Tynianov, however, complicates the interpretation of Griboedov's motive as humanistic sympathy for the eunuch's fate. He suggests instead that his main motivation was patriotism and his resoluteness in "comply[ing] honestly with the treaty" of Turkmenchay that he himself negotiated with the Iranian government.[62] Tynianov's interpretation of Griboedov's character is similar to that of his contemporary Olga Ivanovna Popova, whose book on Griboedov's diplomatic career was published in 1929, in the same year as Tynianov's novel, as part of a hundredth-anniversary commemoration of Griboedov's death. Popova describes the events of 1819 when, like Shklovsky, Griboedov led the withdrawal of Russian soldiers from Iran: "Despite Griboedov's own humane attitude towards the soldiers … his main concern was not so much his care for the soldiers, but care for Russia's prestige."[63]

Unlike Tynianov's Griboedov, Shklovsky in the *Sentimental Journey* declares that love of humanity (*chelovekoliubie*) was his primary motivation, citing his telegram to his commissary in Iran, "In the name of revolution and love of humanity I demand the withdrawal of the troops," and adding with irony that the commissary "did not like that telegram very much; after all, it is naive and funny to demand the withdrawal of the troops in the name of humaneness. But I was right."[64] That same love of humanity appears as the motivation for Tynianov's writing according to Eichenbaum, who believes that Tynianov's works "are born from worry about man – pity of him, anxiety about him, interest in him."[65]

Tynianov and Shklovsky's all-inclusive humanism and their disregard for national or imperial ideas reflect the frame of mind of the 1920s, with its concern for the well-being of all peoples and anticipation of world revolution.[66] At the same time, their beliefs can be traced back to the anti-imperialist convictions of a number of Enlightenment thinkers in the late eighteenth century,[67] among them the Russian Enlightener Radishchev. Aware of this affinity, both Tynianov and Shklovsky allude in their writing to Radishchev's *Journey from Petersburg to Moscow.*

The Passionate Word

The Death of Vazir-Mukhtar starts as a journey that travels in the opposite direction to the journey described in Radishchev's book: Griboedov travels from Moscow to Petersburg, as the last stage of his mission to deliver the Turkmenchay peace treaty to the emperor's court. This beginning alludes to Pushkin's "Journey from Moscow to Petersburg," his unfinished polemic against Radishchev. According to some scholars, Pushkin's text had a hidden agenda of attracting attention to Radishchev's ideas by lulling the vigilance of the censorship. By imitating the style of both authors in his novel, Tynianov reintroduces the dialogue between Pushkin and Radishchev, transferring its focus from the problem of serfdom to that of imperialism. Just as Pushkin's polemical parody, in deliberately distorting Radishchev's work, at the same time provides an impetus for the reader to check the original, Tynianov's novel "sends" his reader to a number of texts that touch upon the political and cultural life of the empire, leaving "clues"[68] that help to identify the original sources.

As in Shklovsky's *Journey*, Tynianov's novel imitates Radishchev in alternating irony with emotionally loaded passages. These alternations should not be understood in the way Eichenbaum interpreted the intonations of Gogol's narrator in his early article "Kak sdelana 'Shinel'' Gogolia" ("How Gogol's 'Overcoat' Is Made," 1919), as "grotesque, in which the expression of laughter interchanges with the expression of grief – both one and the other appear as a game, with conventional alternations of gesture and intonations."[69] Tynianov's evaluation of Shklovsky's novel *Zoo* argues against such an interpretation: "This novel is emotional, it is not afraid of sentimentality."[70] In his introduction to that work, Shklovsky writes that it is easy to show the world as ridiculous, and asks the reader's permission to be sentimental.[71] He views irony as, on the one hand, a lack of the courage to reveal one's real feelings and, on the other, a device that helps the author to overcome the difficulty of representation.[72] Embarking on their *Journeys*, both Radishchev and

Shklovsky have in mind the *Sentimental Journey* of Sterne, shaped by the philosophy of Smith's *Theory of Moral Sentiments*. Hence, in their writing, irony creates a kind of outward detachment that increases the readers' emotional response in a similar way as "lowering" the "pitch" of one's emotions increases the sympathy of others in Smith's theory.[73]

Shklovsky and Tynianov imitate what Bakhtin calls the "passionate word [*pateticheskoe slovo*]"[74] of the Russian Enlightenment to resume the dialogue around the ethical and political issues associated with it. Radishchev's "passionate word," according to Andreas Shönle, "is replete with exclamations, vocatives and imperatives, rhetorical questions, and other devices mimicking oral speech in its conative function, the function language adopts when it is set toward an addressee."[75] Both Shklovsky and Tynianov use these devices to create an emotional appeal by the narrator to readers, enriched with allusions to the eighteenth-century Enlightenment. An entire section of Tynianov's novel, where he retells the history of the military conquest of the Caucasus through the poetry of Russian classicism and romanticism, and by doing so provides the first "study" in Russian literary Orientalism, is framed with questions: "What is the Caucasus? Who lived in the Caucasus? Who dwelt there? But what is the Caucasus?"[76]

This question-and-answer pattern alludes to the chapter "Novgorod" of Radishchev's *Journey*. While the main theme of his *Journey* is the problem of serfdom, in "Novgorod" Radishchev reflects on imperial domination and the right of nations to self-determination. He begins the chapter by describing the bygone glory of the self-ruling Novgorod and denouncing its appropriation in the fifteenth century by the grand duke of Moscow: "But what right did he have to go on a rampage against them, what right did he have to appropriate Novgorod?"[77] From here, he proceeds to a more general question: "What is the peoples' right?"[78] Using the form of questions and answers Radishchev argues that, as long as the relations between nations are similar to those between individuals in their "natural state," stronger nations will always dominate weaker ones. He therefore questions the state of international relations of his own times, when "peoples' rights" are based on "natural right," implying that nations as individuals should enter into some state of "social contract" preventing domination of one nation over another.[79] To date, Radishchev writes, the only judge between the nations has been the sword, the judgment of which is impossible to appeal.

His discontent with the existing order reflects the vital discussion of his time on the need for some form of international organization to regulate conflict between nations and secure peace in the world. Several Enlightenment thinkers of the eighteenth century had proposed an international federation that would govern relations between nations;[80] their ideas found realization in the twentieth century when, in the aftermath of the First World War, the League of Nations was created.

Alluding to Radishchev's chapter "Novgorod" while writing about the military conquest of the Caucasus as it was reflected in Russian poetry, Tynianov contrasts the romantic Orientalism of the nineteenth century with the anti-imperialist convictions of the late Enlightenment, which disapproved of the very idea of imperial domination. Self-governing Novgorod's loss of freedom parallelled not only the conquest of the Caucasus but also its later reannexation by the Bolsheviks, which became a topic of discussion at, among other forums, the League of Nations.[81]

The late Enlightenment's moral stance against imperialism is rooted in its view of a human being "as an end" and not "as a means."[82] In his *Journey*, Radishchev advances an argument against considering the well-being of any individual as inconsequential in comparison to the history of the society: "no arguments about the insignificance of a particular case can persuade a person, if he himself is that particular case."[83] Shklovsky shares this view. For him the Bolsheviks' readiness to sacrifice the present for the future and their desire to shape human beings according to an idea are moral defects: "The Bolsheviks believed that the material is not important, the design is, they wanted to lose the present day, to lose the biography and to win a stake in history."[84] The material here stands for a life (*zhizn'*) that does not always fit the formula.[85] The negative connotations of the words "design" (*oformlenie*) and "formula" may be a hint at Shklovsky's re-evaluation of his formalist ideas.

Just as no individual should be considered insignificant, no national culture should be labelled as inferior according to Shklovsky. He expresses this point of view in his article "Ob istoricheskom romane i o Iurii Tynianove" ("On the Historical Novel and on Yury Tynianov," 1933), providing another twist in the intertextual dialogue between the two friends. Shklovsky criticizes Tynianov's novel for presenting Nina Chavchavadze, Griboedov's Georgian wife, as a provincial woman, and Georgia as Griboedov's suburban estate in the vicinity of Moscow. These shortcomings are the result of writing "the history" from the centre of the empire, "from Moscow."[86] Georgian and Russian cultures, Shklovsky continues, are different, but one is not inferior to the other; "Georgian princes made good translations of French poetry, and they were people of a culture different from Griboedov's, but not a lower one." (Note that Shklovsky himself cannot avoid a Eurocentric point of view, by appraising Georgians for their cultural connections to France, unmediated by Russia.)

By criticizing Tynianov, Shklovsky disavows his own description, in his *Journey*, of Georgia's capital Tbilisi as a city in the style of Moscow (*pod Moskvu*), a pun on "*pod Moskvoi*" (in the suburbs of Moscow), and of Georgian futurists like the Chekhovian three sisters, dreaming about Moscow.[87] Shklovsky's argument in this article about the futility of comparing the cultures of colonizer and colonized goes back to the ideas of the anti-imperialist Enlighteners, who insisted on the incommensurability of different cultures, undermining the imperialist rhetoric of a "civilizing mission." They saw an inextricable connection between personal and cultural freedom.[88]

For both Radishchev and Shklovsky, cultural and social diversity does not preclude the existence of "a generic point of view, one that would be the expression of humanity itself."[89] Like Radishchev, Shklovsky writes his *Journey* "to compel the readers to experience the otherness by stepping out of themselves."[90] In Tynianov's novel, the allusions to the *Journeys* of his contemporary and friend and of the eighteenth-century Enlightener stand in contrast to his parody of Pushkin's nineteenth-century *Journey*. While disapproving of "Russian colonial politics" in the "Orient," Pushkin questions neither the legitimacy of the colonization in principle nor the stereotype of superiority towards "Orientals," with his main concern being "the aesthetic freedom of Russia's artists" rather than "the political liberty of the Caucasian peoples."[91]

Both Tynianov and Shklovsky are far from being interested only in the formal, aesthetic aspect of literature. Tynianov reveals in his novel the interconnectedness between literary Orientalism and the imperial project, while Shklovsky openly denounces imperialism in his *Journey*. Their moral involvement in the problem shows their affinity with the late eighteenth-century Enlightenment to which, in Tynianov's own words, they "offer their hands over the head of the XIX century."[92]

Chapter Three

A Novelistic Outline of Orientalism

Kavkaz ochen' nas zanimaet. On stol'ko uzhe poezii nashei dal, chto nevol'no zhdesh' ot etogo kraia zolotogo vse bol'she, bol'she.[1]

– Yury Tynianov

(The Caucasus preoccupies us a lot. It already gave so much to our poetry that one unwittingly expects from this golden land more, more.)

The central theme of Tynianov's novel, as I've said above, is not simply Russia's relation to its Orient, but more precisely the question of how Russian writing on the Orient reflects and shapes that relation. Tynianov's significant scholarly insight in his "dissertation-novel" reveals the interconnection between textual Orientalism and the politics of the empire. While in some instances a literary text appears as a prompt response to a political change, in others it functions as an Orientalist discourse that prepares the changes. This chapter considers the literary devices that Tynianov employed in the novel to convey his interpretation of Griboedov's character and his historical time.

Poetic Orientalism and Military Conquest

Different modes of writing in Tynianov's novel are connected with different methods of building the empire. Two consecutive sections, 11 and 12, of chapter 4 each in a different way answer the same question: "What is the Caucasus?" In section 11, the history of the military conquest of the Caucasus reveals itself through poetry, the odes of Mikhail Lomonosov and Gavrila Derzhavin and the poems of Vasily Zhukovsky[2] and Platon Obodovsky.[3] Section 12 describes the Caucasus as a potential site of profitable colonial development, and refers to the texts of Griboedov and Peter Zaveleisky's proposal for establishing the Russian Transcaucasian Company, and the response to the proposal by General Mikhail Zhukovsky.[4] The two sections have parallel development. At the outset, both refer to the Caucasus as a land to be conquered (section 11) or exploited economically (section 12) without mentioning its inhabitants. Only in the second half of both sections are we are reminded that there are people living in that land.

Thus, in the poetic section, Tynianov demonstrates that Derzhavin is substituting the Alps for the Caucasus: "Immediately, Derzhavin gave in the description [*v opisanii*] of the Caucasus a fairly faithful depiction [*izobrazhenie*] of the alpine land," "and especially successful was the icy old man's [*l'dianoi starets*] picture [*kartina*] of the alpine ice."[5] Piling up such words as "description," "depiction," and "picture," Tynianov suggests that Derzhavin's "Ode to Count Zubov" is a conventional artistic representation that obscures rather than reveals the reality.

Inserted in the story of the military conquest, these lines of poetry and Tynianov's remarks on them read as a novelistic hint of an idea later proposed by one of the first insightful scholars of Russian Orientalism, Susan Layton. According to Layton, the images of the "alpine wilderness … averted the eye from military conquest" by concentrating on the "depoliticized experience" of a "communion with nature."[6] Substituting the literary Alps for the Caucasus also severed the connection between the landscape and the people, suggesting the idea of "no one's" land awaiting exploration.[7] Tynianov confirms this reading of the poem, plainly stating that those who were invested in the project of imperial expansion considered the land to be no one's if it was not possessed by another Empire: "And then there were suspicious sultanates and khanates either Persian, or Turkish, or no one's."[8] The notion of "no one's land," as a justification of colonial appropriation of "wasted" land with the goal of "improving" it, was an important part of the Enlightenment's debate on the legitimacy of colonial appropriations.

If in the first half of Tynianov's section 11 the Caucasus appears as a vacant land to be occupied, in the second half Tynianov suddenly "remembers" its inhabitants:

> Kto tam zhil na Kavkaze? Kto obital?
> Zhukovskii poproboval bylo nabrosat' kratkii spisok i utverzhdal, chto tam
>
> Gnezdiatsia i balkar, i bakh,
> I abazekh, i kamukinets,
> I karbulak, i abazinets,
> I chechereets, i shapsug,
> chto oni, kak serny, skachut po skalam, a doma kuriat trubki.

Inozemnaia, barabannaia muzyka imen byla prevoskhodna i slishkom shchedra, potomu chto kamukintsev i chechereitsev – takikh plemen na Kavkaze ne bylo. Byli eshche kumikintsy, a chechereitsev i vovse ne byvalo. Gnezdit'sia oni, stalo byt', ne mogli.[9]

(Who lived there, in the Caucasus? Who were the inhabitants?

Zhukovsky attempted once to sketch a brief list, and he asserted that

The Balkar and the Bakh nested there,
The Abazekh and the Kamoukin,
The Karboulak and the Abazin,
The Checherean and the Shapsoug.
that they jumped about those mountains like chamois, and smoked pipes.

The foreign drum music of the names was excellent and too generous, because, as for Kamuokins (*kamukintsev*) and Chechereans (*chechereitsev*), there were no such tribes in the Caucasus. There were some Koumikins (*kumikintsy*), but no Chechereans ever. So they could not have nested there.)

This passage refers to the idea of knowledge as power, and the lack thereof as a cause of inefficiency. This idea is also raised in another chapter of the novel, in which Tynianov's protagonist Griboedov has to sit through an exam "v Shkole vostochnykh iazykov" (in the School of Oriental Languages),[10] and which demonstrates Russia's attempt to catch up with the European powers both in its imperial enterprise and in the development of the field of knowledge called Oriental studies. Tynianov's depiction of the amateurish level of Oriental studies in Russia coincides with Vera Tolz's opinion that the achievements of the few isolated Russian Orientalists of Griboedov's times were modest. The situation, according to Tolz, started to change only in the 1840s, after Griboedov's death, and by 1890 an original and internationally recognized school of Orientalist studies had developed in Petersburg.[11] The ideas on the connections between the field of Oriental studies and imperialism proposed by the scholars of this school, as well as their critique of the Eurocentric attitudes of contemporary Western scholarship, well known among Russian intelligentsia of the late imperial and early Soviet period, certainly influenced Tynianov's own views either directly or indirectly.

The passage that enumerates the Caucasian tribes stands in contrast to the first half of the section by suddenly suggesting that there are people living in the Caucasus. Tynianov plays with the state of existence and non-existence of the tribes mentioned by the poet Zhukovsky. At the end of the section, the non-existent tribes resist the conquest: "The war in the Caucasus was going on all the time, either with Kamoukins or with Chechereans. And if not Kotliarevsky, then somebody else 'was ruining, destroying the tribes,' according to the rapturous expression of Pushkin."[12] Tynianov refers to Alexander Pushkin's lines from the epilogue to "Kavkazskii plennik" ("The Prisoner of the Caucasus") in which the poet extolls the brutal conquerors of the Caucasus, generals Ermolov, Tsitsianov, and Kotliarevsky.[13] At the same time, the phrase "rapturous expression [*vostorzhennoe vyrazhenie*]" alludes to the following unwavering criticism of Pushkin's narrative poem from Peter Viazemsky's letter to A.I. Turgenev: "Poeziia ne soiuznitsa palachei … gimny poeta ne dolzhny byt' nikogda slavosloviem rezni. Mne dosadno na Pushkina: takoi vostorg – nastoiashchii anakhronizm." (Poetry is not an ally of executioners … poet's hymns should never be a glorification of a massacre. I am vexed with Pushkin: such rapture – is a real anachronism).[14]

As Harsha Ram discusses in *The Imperial Sublime*, Pushkin starts the epilogue "by invoking the elegiac muse" and then abruptly shifts to "a confident prediction of Russia's final conquest of the Caucasus," which is "purely odic" in its tone and rhetoric.[15] Ram reveals that Soviet-era critics, such as Tomashevsky, Blagoi, and Gurevich, use this shift in genre to justify Pushkin's epilogue as overcoming a romantic "idealization of primitive society" and "suggesting the 'historical necessity' of the triumph of civilization," which they associate with "the expansion of the Russian state."[16] Tynianov does not subscribe to this approach, which took shape as a result of the Stalin-era ideology of Russian imperial expansion as a "lesser-of-all-evils civilising project."[17] Thus in his article "On the 'Journey to Arzrum,'" he specifically praises Pushkin because his poems inspired by the trip are "infinitely far from military odes [beskonechno daleki ot voennykh od]."[18]

Because in "The Prisoner of the Caucasus" Pushkin cites the same poem of Zhukovsky with the list of names of the tribes,[19] by alluding to it Tynianov underscores the chain of successive poetic representations of the Caucasian theme in the context of imperial history. The Caucasus as a literary reality is expanding and reasserting itself together with the empire that expands and secures its new borders.

Tynianov juxtaposes Pushkin's support for military suppression of the resistance in his early poem with his missionary formula of "khristianstvo i samovar" (Christianity and samovar) in *Journey to Arzrum*. According to Yakov Gordin, Pushkin's formula is a parody of the

Russian government's plans to move from the stage of conquest of the Caucasus to the stage of peaceful "civilizing" development. In one such project, Admiral Nikolai Mordvinov proposes to "soften" the "mountaineers" by introducing them to "our luxury," and to "bring them closer to us in their ideas, tastes, needs and their demands of household utensils from us."[20] Whether Tynianov had this in mind or not, it is clear that Pushkin's formula in his novel parallels Griboedov's own "civilizing" project.

The opposition between poetry and prose in the novel correlates with that between relying on literary sources and personally witnessing events. Putting Pushkin's phrase "was ruining, destroying the tribes" next to the names of the non-existent tribes, Tynianov underscores the abstract, distant notion of the literary enemy. The following repetition of the names of "Kamukins" and "Chechereans" creates the notion of a shift from enthusiasm and confidence to exhaustion at the core of the empire, and the persistence of resistance at the periphery:

> Kazhdyi raz po doneseniiam iavstvovalo: imeem uspekh i privodim k pokornosti takie-to plemena, ne to kamukintsev, ne to opiat' zhe chechereitsev.
>
> A voina tianulas', i opiat' voevali – mozhet byt', dazhe te zhe chechereitsy. Nessel'rod zhe vse voobshche plemena na Kavkaze nazyval: les cachetiens, tak kak pomnil kislovatyi vkus kakhetinskogo.[21]

> (Every time it was clear from the reports: we have a success, and we bring to submission such and such tribes, either Kamoukins, or, again, Chechereans.
>
> And the war was dragging on, and they were fighting again – maybe even the same Chechereans. As for Nesselrode, he called all the tribes in the Caucasus *les cachétiens*, since he remembered the slightly sour taste of the *kakhetian* [wine].)

Note how "we have success [*имеем успех*]" turns into "the war was dragging on [*война тянулась*]," and "we bring to submission [*приводим к покорности*]" into "they were fighting again [*опять воевали*]." The last sentence introduces the Caucasus from a new perspective as producer of Kakhetian wine, and prepares the shift of focus from the military conquest in the section 11 to the economic exploration or exploitation of the Caucasus in section 12. Tynianov argues that nobody knew "what to do if the Caucasus is suddenly conquered."[22] He ends chapter 11 with the same question that he posed at its beginning: "But what is the Caucasus?"[23] The next section answers this question in a new way.

A Period of Paper Planning

Section 12 opens with Griboedov and Zaveleisky sitting in a hot room in Tiflis, brainstorming their proposal for the Russian Transcaucasian Company. They answer the question "What is the Caucasus?" in terms of the potential profits it promises. Zaveleisky is "chanting [*zaklinaet*]" the names of the minerals, agricultural produce, and manufactured goods Transcaucasia can yield: "Kakhetian indigo … Erivan cochineal of the wild strain."[24] His direct speech is a combination of excerpts from the texts of the proposal. If in the previous section the Caucasus appears as a land to be conquered, now it is described as a land able to yield enormous profits. Again, the inhabitants of the land are not mentioned in the beginning of the chapter. When the natives suddenly appear, they are referred to indirectly, through the parallel Tynianov draws between the Caucasus and Mexico:

> No esli by etot postoronnii byl … syn "velikogo admirala" Don-Diego ili ego general Fernando Kortets, glaza by u nikh zagorelis' tochno tak zhe, kak i u cheloveka v ochkakh. I general, naslushavshis', poslal by odnu armiiu tuda i druguiu siuda, i serebro i zoloto pritekli by k nemu.
>
> A koshenil' on by vybrosil.
>
> Potomu chto on byl syn velikogo admirala, plaval s nim po neizvestnym moriam, travil sobakami tuzemtsev i liubil zoloto, ego ves i zvon.[25]

> (But if that outsider was … the son of "the great admiral" Don Diego or his general Fernando Cortéz, their eyes would light up the same as the eyes of the man in glasses. And the general, having heard a lot, would send one army here and the other one there, and silver and gold would flow to him.
>
> As for cochineal, he would throw it away.
>
> Because he was the son of the great admiral, with whom he sailed unknown seas, sicced dogs on the natives and loved gold, its weight and tinkling.)

Fernando Cortéz now personifies military conquest, while the authors of the Russian Transcaucasian proposal are on the side of "peaceful" colonization through economic exploitation. Comparisons between the military actions of the Russian troops and those of Spanish conquistadors were widespread in the nineteenth century.[26] Decembrist Andrey Rozen, for example, while discussing the most effective ways of colonizing the Caucasus, warned against emulating the "former ancient course of action" of Pizarro and Cortéz, and bringing "weapons and fear" to the Caucasus. Instead of thus making the mountaineers even more "savage and belligerent," one should entice them to the valleys with "different benefits, prospering settlements."[27]

The British way of colonization, according to Rozen, is more worthy of emulation. It is true that they too "shoot the Indians with cannon balls and bullets," but they also introduce them to new tools, trade, education, and religion, and give them hope for "future prosperity."[28] The same idea of luring the belligerent mountaineers into the valleys with the prospect of material well-being, and the desire to emulate the British ways of colonization, is also present in Griboedov and Zaveleisky's proposal for the establishment of their company. Tynianov alludes to this similarity between their plans and the suggestions of the Decembrist Rozen in the following lines:

> I tol'ko staryi anglichanin, odin iz osnovatelei gosudarstva Ost-Indiiskogo ... pykhnul by sigarnym dymom i povtoril by nasmeshlivo i ponimaia vse i dazhe bol'she:
>
> – V Rossii streliat' umeiut, ne umeiut tol'ko otlivat' pul'.[29]
>
> (And only the old Englishman, one of the founders of the East Indian state ... would puff out cigar smoke and he would repeat sarcastically and, understanding everything, and even more:
>
> – They know how to shoot in Russia, only they don't know how to cast bullets.)

Tynianov reveals an important aspect of Russian Orientalism, which Harsha Ram calls "an anxiety to belong."[30] In the novel, Griboedov's persuasions make Russian foreign minister Karl Nesselrode imagine Russia achieving the status of England: "Russia was gaining the importance of, damn it, England! And he will tell Duke Wellington: the peaceful development of our colonies ... God! How come it did not strike him before: Transcaucasia, you know, is a colony!"[31] This passage is true to the fact that throughout the nineteenth century both the Russian government and intellectuals considered the overseas empires, such as the British Empire, to be a more suitable model to emulate than the land-based Austro-Hungarian or Ottoman empires.[32] While the military conquest of the Caucasus is parallel to the conquest of Mexico, the projects of capitalistic exploitation of the region are reminiscent of the colonization of India. The opposition between the two modes of colonization in the novel corresponds to Griboedov's desire for a shift in empire-building policy from further acquisitions of territories to making use of the territories that already belong to the empire: "The thunder of weapons does not bring well-being to the land."[33]

The conquistador discarding the cochineal while keeping silver and gold illustrates another opposition of ideas that Tynianov recreates in his novel. The opposition between cochineal vs. silver and gold refers to the difference between an understanding of the economy in terms of Adam Smith vs. the theory of mercantilism, which suggested that economic success depends on the reserves of bullion.[34] Tynianov makes an obvious literary reference to Pushkin's Eugene Onegin, who was "a profound economist" and had his opinion on "how a state becomes wealthy," and "what it lives on," and "why it does not need gold, when it has a simple product."[35] Griboedov, while not adhering to bullionism, a primitive form of mercantilism, was planning to create a company based on mercantilist principles, such as privileges, monopolies, and protectionism. At the same time, just like Eugene Onegin, he prided himself on understanding economics, and in his travel notes mocked the Iranian Sardar, Hussein Khan, for not being acquainted with Smith's theory and for suppressing internal and external trade in the province of Erivan that he supervised.

Although opposition between freedom of trade and enterprise and monopolization was the most prominent part of the debate between Griboedov and Zaveleisky and their critics, Tynianov either plays it down or thoroughly hides it in his novel. One particular detail of the argument levelled by the proposal's main critic, General Zhukovsky, appears in the novel in a veiled form: "The grey square strikes the eye [*pestrela*] as a frying pan, with fish, tomatoes, capers baking on it."[36] Scholars Dimitri and Zinaida Breschinsky, in their insightful article on Tynianov's cinematic technique in the novel, view the capers as an exotic addition to the plainer ingredients: "The grey square is likened to a frying pan with a fish, tomatoes, and capers in it, the capers for an exotic flavor."[37] However, even seemingly insignificant details in Tynianov's novel usually originate in previous texts. The mention of capers comes from Zhukovsky's argument against granting Griboedov and Zaveleisky's company exclusive rights to cultivate the plants that grew in the region only in the wild, such as wild flax and capers.[38] Throughout the novel, Tynianov uses this method of leaving "clues" for his readers by referring them to pre-existing texts with one memorable or unusual word.[39]

The opposition between military conquest and economic colonization is represented in Tynianov's novel by "fathers [*ottsy*]" vs. "children [*deti*]." Eugene Onegin's father, an old-fashioned landowner, was not able to understand the new economic ideas that his son learned from

Smith; Griboedov's deceased father does not understand his son's preoccupation with entrepreneurial designs:

> I vot esli chelovek drugogo, bolee starogo veka, naprimer papen'ka Griboedova, Sergei Ivanovich, voshel by v etu komnatu, on podumal by: dvoe mal'chishek, odin v ochkakh, a drugoi usatyi, igraiut v strannuiu i dazhe skuchnuiu igru, kotoraia, sdaetsia, nazyvaetsia geo-gra-fiia, togda kak devy, devchonki i dazhe devki zhdut ikh ob"iatii, a koni – shpor.
>
> Prislushavshis', on, pozhalui, briaknul by:
>
> – Mamen'kiny shtuchki. Zhadnosti. Torgashom, chto li, Aleksasha stal?[40]

> (Now suppose if a man of another, older epoch, for example Griboedov's daddy, Sergei Ivanovich, would enter this room, he would think: two boys, one in glasses, and the other with a mustache, are playing a strange and even boring game, which I guess is called ge-ogra-phy, while maidens, girls, and even wenches are waiting for their embraces, and horses – for their spurs.
>
> After listening more carefully, he would probably blurt out:
>
> – His mommy's tricks. Greediness. Did Aleksasha become a tradesman?)

This lack of understanding between father and son is part of the theme of two different generations that plays an essential role in Tynianov's novel. Griboedov and Zaveleisky, bewitched by the names of the exotic colonial products that can be grown or mined in Transcaucasia, chant them, producing "a strange declamation, incomprehensible for anyone besides geographers and children."[41] The word "children," which connotes a love of adventure inherent in childhood, stands in for the new generation's openness to the ideas of daring enterprise. The father expresses contempt for enterprise together with a belief that military service is the most suitable occupation for a nobleman. The position of the father in this chapter aligns with that of Don Diego and Fernando Cortéz, while only the Englishman, one of the founders of the British East India Company, understands the son.

Griboedov and Zaveleisky display childish enthusiasm for abandoning their former aristocratic way of life and embarking on the new adventure of a capitalist enterprise. Their eagerness to enter the "Great Game" of imperial competition against the British reminds of Raynal's admiration of Britain's commercial and industrial success and his desire that his own country emulate it. While Tynianov's novel does not elaborate on the similarities between the ideas expressed by Griboedov and Zaveleisky and those found in Raynal's *History*, it does mention Raynal as a probable inspiration for the former. Colonel Burtsov, a former

Decembrist, to whom in Tynianov's time Zhukovsky's critical comments were mistakenly attributed, during his discussion of the proposal confesses: "I was reading it the whole night long, burnt two candles. I was reading it like at one time I was reading Raynal, and I will probably never read anything more enticing about this matter."[42] He compares Griboedov's proposal to a poem, cancelling the opposition between, on the one hand, poetry and the military conquest of the Caucasus and, on the other, its "prosaic" economic colonization: "The idea of the trading company is a wonderful poem ... Excellent and enticing."[43]

Aleksandr Lebedev views Griboedov's proposal as an alternative to "romantic subjectivism" and the "social utopias" of the Decembrists.[44] Tynianov, by contrast, represents both the proposal and the Decembrists' ideas of social reform as "romantic social utopias." While Burtsov is calling his proposal "a wonderful poem," Griboedov is wondering if he used the same words in his conversations with Pavel Pestel about the latter's proposal for political and social changes after the uprising.[45] Soon Burtsov himself starts talking like Pestel, accusing Griboedov of attempting to create through his project "an aristocracy of wealth" that would lead to "new enslavements."[46] In *Russkaia pravda*, Pestel describes his epoch as one of struggle against the old feudal aristocracy, within which a new and much more harmful "aristocracy of wealth" is starting to develop. The latter, using its money, "gold and silver," brings the entire nation into absolute dependence. Therefore, any prudent government should prevent uneven distribution of wealth that would create such an aristocracy.[47] Pestel's views bear the influence of Jean-Charles-Léonard Simonde de Sismondi, who argued that Smith's system of free trade and free enterprise, if left unchecked, is fraught with crises and will result in the accumulation of wealth in the hands of a few. Sismondi thought that even though economic legislation did not completely reflect Smith's ideas, in many developed countries his "fundamental thesis of free and universal competition has made very great advances." The result was both "prodigious development of the powers of industry" and "frightful suffering for many classes of the population."[48] According to Sismondi, it was the function of the government to soften the divide between different social classes and to alleviate the suffering of the poor:

> We see the government above all as the protector of the weak against the strong, the defender of him who cannot defend himself, and the representative of the long-term, if quiet, interest of all, against the temporary, if vociferous, interest of each.[49]

The ideas of Sismondi appear both in Griboedov and Zaveleisky's proposal and in General Zhukovsky's critical comments. The former agree with Sismondi in expressing their negative view of competition, while Zhukovsky is apprehensive about the future company's contribution to further economic stratification in the society. By putting the Decembrist Pestel's negative evaluation of the "aristocracy of wealth" into the mouth of Burtsov, the supposed author of Zhukovsky's comments, Tynianov unwittingly underscores similarities between the concerns of the Decembrists and those of certain governmental officials. When Burtsov accuses Griboedov of intending to use Russian peasants as forced labour, Griboedov counter-attacks by claiming that if the Decembrist uprising was successful, they would end up employing forced labour to further their own economic self-interest and political goals:

> Vy by kak muzhika osvobodili? Vy by khlopotali, a den'gi by plyli. Den'gi by plyli ... I skazali by vy bednomu muzhiku rossiiskomu: mladshie brat'ia ... vremenno, tol'ko vremenno ne ugodno li vam na barshchine porabotat'? I Kondratii Fedorovich eto nazval by ne krepostnym uzhe sostoianiem, no dobrovol'noiu obiazannost'iu krest'ianskogo sosloviia. I, verno, gimn by napisal.[50]

> (How would you liberate the peasant [*muzhika*]? You would bustle about and the money would float up [to you]. The money would float up ... And you would say to the poor Russian peasant: little brothers ... temporarily, only temporarily, would you mind performing the work for free? And Kondraty Fedorovich [Ryleev] would call it not serfdom anymore, but a voluntary duty of the peasant class. He would probably write a hymn for it.)

Natan Eidelman suggested that in this passage Tynianov refers not only to Griboedov's but also to his own times, the late 1920s,[51] alluding to the new campaign of collectivization. This suggestion is not too far-fetched. While the harshest period of collectivization was still ahead when Tynianov started publishing his novel serially in the journal *Zvezda* in 1927–8, his historical foresight allowed him to recognize that the abuses would only increase in the years to come. The view of collectivization as a return of the old system of serfdom was a widespread one, and the peasants themselves called the requirement to work for the *kolkhoz* a corvée obligation (*barshchina*), complaining that it took away time from working on their own plots of land.[52] The novel creates historic parallels that underscore the role of forced labour in the process of industrialization of Russia. The epoch of Nicholas I, an oppressive autocracy, is also a time of capitalist development and imperialist enterprise. It was the time when the generation of the "children," whom Tynianov's protagonist Griboedov joins in the novel, are eager to launch the industrialization of the Russian Empire without hesitating to use forced labour to achieve their goals:

> Rukami rabov i zavoevannykh plennykh, suetias' ... oni zavintili pustoi Benkendorfov mekhanizm i pustili vint fabrikoi i zavodom.
>
> V tridtsatykh godakh zapakhlo Amerikoi, ost-indskim dymom.[53]

> (With the hands of slaves and conquered captives, bustling about ... they tightened the screws of the empty Benckendorff's mechanism and propelled the spiral motion of factories and plants.
>
> In the thirties, it started to smell like America, like East Indian smoke.)

The final line alludes to the desire to catch up with the West, and at the same time reminds the reader that Western industrialization also to a significant degree relied on the labour of slaves and colonial subjects. It reveals coloniality as "the darker side of modernity," as its "constitutive" without which modernity as we know it would not exist.[54] In his novel, Tynianov creates a parallel between industrialization during the time of Nicholas I and Peter the Great's Westernization, which also heavily relied on forced labour. At the same time, it foreshadows Stalin's industrialization, which used prison labour. Just as Peter's Westernization of Russia was part of his building and strengthening it as an empire, Stalin's industrialization occurred simultaneously with assumption of control over the subjects of pre-revolutionary Russia and colonization of the remote and unpopulated regions of the country, in which the forced labour of the prisoners played a significant part. The political prisoners who were Griboedov's contemporaries, the former Decembrists, served their time in the Caucasian troops and participated in the conquest and colonization of the Caucasus. In the novel, they themselves resemble a foreign colonized nation: "They were in dusty boots. With faces of an earthy colour, so unlike the face of the general, as if they and the general belonged to different nations."[55]

Even though Griboedov's proposal is based on old mercantilist principles and does not advocate new economic policies, he appears in the novel as a person who with childish zeal casts away his old identity as a representative of a feudal aristocracy and tries on the new role of a capitalist entrepreneur. This embracing of the identity of a bourgeois in the cultural atmosphere of *neburzhuaznost'* is, according to Eidelman, the main merit of Griboedov's project, the economic progressiveness of which is questionable.[56] It is not clear, however, if Griboedov himself would agree with Tynianov's representation of the Russian Transcaucasian proposal as the most important creation of his life. In his personal correspondence, the would-be colonial entrepreneur usually complains that his career and everyday activities take time away from his true "goal in life," which is poetry.[57]

The characters of Pushkin and Griboedov personify the opposition between literature and life that Tynianov creates and negates throughout his novel. Scholars have already mentioned that in the novel the relation of Griboedov, the author of one unpublished comedy, to Pushkin, the unquestionable genius, was that of Salieri to Mozart from Pushkin's "Little Tragedy."[58] However, this relation has its reverse side. Pushkin too is envious of Griboedov's achievements, his involvement in real historical events, and his opportunity to travel: "I envy you. You gallop around Persia, and we gallop around journals … Out of my envy towards you, I am starting to write the history of the Caucasian wars."[59] Creating this contrast between the two characters, Tynianov reintroduces in his novel the argument that Dmitry Pisarev puts forward in his article "Pushkin and Belinsky" (1865):

> If the figures of science and life do not write poems or dramas, this of course, happens not because they are not smart enough, and not because their love of the idea is weak, but, on the contrary, because the scale of their mind and the power of their love do not allow them to be satisfied with creating beautiful works of fiction. These people are poets too, but their poems are their great deeds, which, of course, are not only more useful, but also more grandiose than all sorts of *Iliads* and all kinds of Shakespearean dramas.[60]

In a literary work, Pisarev values not its aesthetic form but its content, its relevance, and its usefulness in posing and solving social and political problems. While Pushkin in this article represents pure aesthetics, Griboedov's *Woe from Wit* appears as the only useful literary work of the time. Similar polemics surrounded the name "Pushkin" in Tynianov's own time: some literary movements presented him as a proponent of "pure art" while others underscored the "idea" in his work. He could represent both "progress" and traditional values.

Establishing in his novel the opposition between "literary" and "real-life" creativity, Tynianov eventually negates it. First, he shows how the words of the "Transcaucasian project," Griboedov's "real" historical creativity materialize, turn into products. Then, the "real" things turn into words again, proving their materialization illusory:

> Chto takoe Kavkaz?
> Shafran, koshenil', marena byli slova. No slova okhlop'iami uzhe lezhali v pustoi komnate, lezhali tiukami, i nogi viazli v kakikh-to oshmetkakh: mareny? shelkovichnykh chervei?
> Tak legko zabyt' smysl koshenili.
> Sovershaetsia obratnoe prevrashchenie koshenili v slovo.[61]

> (What is the Caucasus?
> Saffron, cochineal, madder were words. But the words already piled up in the empty room, they were lying in bales, and feet got stuck in lumps of something: of madder? of silkworms?
> Thus, it was easy to forget the meaning of cochineal.
> A reverse metamorphosis of cochineal into a word was happening.)

Interestingly, by 1828 the British East India Company had "entered an age of social and economic planning" of its involvement in India, described as "a period mainly of paper planning."[62] In Tynianov's interpretation, the Russian Transcaucasian proposal was an example of "paper planning" that never found realization and was as utopian as the projects of the Decembrists.

Chapter Four

"The Fountain of Bakhchisaray": The Harem of the Russian Empire

Exploring the relationship between the literary Orient and imperial politics in his novel, Tynianov endows Alexander Pushkin's early "Southern" poem "The Fountain of Bakhchisaray" with special importance. In the following passage, he explicitly suggests that literary Orientalism was involved in political planning, an idea that seems to flow out of Pushkin's "Fountain":

> Oni govorili o Gruzii.
>
> Luna stoiala, i politika kak budto byla iz poemy Pushkina – ne iz unylogo "Plennika," a iz "Fontana"; ona zhurchala, kak zvon podpolkovnich'ikh shpor.
>
> Oni ostanovilis'.
>
> ... I, mozhet byt', esli budet neudacha, – tikho zhurchal podpolkovnik, – my pridem k vam v gosti, v vashu Gruziiu chudesnuiu, i poidem na Khivu, na Turkestan. I budet novaia Sech', v kotoroi zhit' budem.[1]
>
> (They were talking about Georgia.
>
> The moon was standing, and the politics was as if from Pushkin's poem – not the cheerless "Prisoner," but from the "Fountain": it was gurgling like the jingle of the lieutenant-colonel's spurs.
>
> They stopped.
>
> ... and, maybe, if we fail – the lieutenant-colonel was softly murmuring – we will visit you in your wonderful Georgia, and we will march on Khiva, on Turkestan. And there will be a new Sech, in which we will live.)

This well-known poem reflects one of the legends surrounding the so-called Fountain of Tears, in the former palace of the Crimean khans.[2] According to the legend, the fearless and ruthless warrior Khan Giray falls in love with a Christian girl captured for his harem. When she fades and dies in captivity, the grief-stricken khan orders a fountain to be built in her memory. In different versions of the legend, the Christian girl is Greek, Georgian, or Polish. Pushkin chooses to make his heroine, Maria, Polish. He adds to the story a Georgian, Zarema, the khan's beloved wife before Maria made her appearance in the harem. Tormented with jealousy, Zarema murders Maria, and in retaliation is executed by order of the khan. In the character of Zarema Pushkin, according to Susan Layton, Orientalizes the Georgian woman, portraying her as one consumed with violent passions, antipodal to the chaste and spiritual Maria.[3]

Pushkin accompanies his poem with an excerpt from the travel notes of I.M. Murav'ev-Apostol, who, assuming that the girl was Georgian, argues that the locals really wanted to see her as Polish and even gave him her name, Maria Pototskaya. Murav'ev-Apostol attempted to persuade them of the historical implausibility of Tatars kidnapping Poles in the second half of the eighteenth century, but they insisted on their version of the story.[4] The story is a legend, which would seem less historically implausible if we assumed that it originated in the previous century and involved another khan of the Giray dynasty who reigned in the Khanate of Crimea from its inception in the eighteenth century to its annexation by Russia in 1873. The presence of Polish captives in the Khanate of Crimea in the seventeenth century is well documented, and a Polish hetman by the name of Potocki was among the prisoners of the mountainous fortress in the vicinity of Bakhchisaray in 1648.[5] The legend, however, is connected with architectural structures – a fountain and a mausoleum – built during the reign of Kyrym-Giray at the end of the eighteenth century.

Furthermore, the captive girl in Murav'ev-Apostol's account has the same last name as Sofia Pototskaya, the woman who told Pushkin the story about the Fountain of Tears, inspiring him to write his famous poem. Pushkin was fond of inserting in his texts inside jokes or allusions for a close circle of friends and acquaintances. The nationality of his heroine and the appearance of Pototskaya's name in the note could be his way of thanking her for the captivating story she told him.[6]

By attaching Murav'ev-Apostol's matter-of-fact description, as well as a passage from his own letter where he writes that he was not much impressed by his visit to the Bakhchisaray palace, Pushkin underscores the romantic, unrealistic nature of his poetic creation. Yet for the readers of the time the romantic poem replaced the reality by imprinting in their imagination the Orientalist version of the legend. This same version survives to our time, acquiring ever-new Orientalist embellishments, and flourishing now on internet travellers' blogs. Scholars doubt that the fountain was built in memory of khan's wife. The most credible explanation is that it was "constructed as an object of hieratic-sacral sensations" and was connected to Sufi mysticism.[7] The inscription on the fountain invites visitors to drink the pure healing water, and reminds them that in paradise the righteous will drink from the spring Salsabil. Moreover, it became the "Fountain of Tears" only after it was moved in anticipation of a visit by Catherine the Great and the spring of water was reduced to a trickle, creating the illusion of a crying rock.

The cemetery, where the fountain most probably stood before being moved, does have a mausoleum dedicated to a woman named Dilara Bikech. That same name is also mentioned in the inscription on the Green Mosque of Bakhchisaray, which indicates her high status in the court hierarchy. She could not possibly have been a foreign captive, who faded away at a young age.[8] The legends about Khan Giray's tragic love for his captive are an example of self-Orientalization, in this case the adoption of a popular Orientalist story as one's own by the local people partly in an attempt to impress tourists.

In his novel, Tynianov creates a complex system of allusions to Pushkin's poem in which a Georgian and a Polish woman languish in the harem of a Crimean khan. He constantly stresses the parallel between Georgia and Poland, two subjugated provinces of the Russian Empire. The Empire replaces the Crimean khan in the role of the owner of the harem, and the provinces become its unwilling wives and concubines. It is possible that Tynianov's parody reveals the political implication that was already there in Pushkin's original. The Polish captive stubbornly refusing to accept the love of her captor, her privileges in having a room and bath, the privacy that he does not dare to violate, could have been a hint at the nominal sovereignty of Congress Poland with its liberal constitution.

One of the parallels between the Caucasus and Poland, in the context of imperialistic expansionism and management of the colonies, comes up during Griboedov's discussion of the future Russian Transcaucasian Company with co-author Peter Zaveleisky.[9] Griboedov does not want the Caucasus to become a mere supplier of raw materials to Russia and suggests that the company build local processing factories. Twisting "his Polish mustache," Zaveleisky asks whether allowing the factories they are going to build in the Caucasus to "prosper too much" would weaken the "link" between this region and Russia." The question leaves Griboedov wondering: "Exactly what sort of 'weakening of the link' was he concerned about? The Caucasus or Poland?"[10] Griboedov does not doubt the loyalty of the Caucasus to the empire, in the same way that the khan from Pushkin's poem is assured of his Georgian wife's devotion. The nineteenth-century theorists of Russian imperialism were preparing different fates for these countries. As was mentioned before, even the "progressive" Decembrist Pavel Pestel argued that a post-insurrectionary government should permit self-determination for Poles as a fraternal Slavic nation. At the same time, "all peoples and all lands lying to the north of the border extending between Russia and Persia, and also Turkey" were to undergo "decisive subjugation."[11]

Tynianov extensively uses the metaphor of marriage as imperial domination in his scholarly parody. Griboedov's own marriage to a Georgian princess, Nina Chavchavadze, was viewed by their contemporaries in the context of establishing strong bonds between Russia and its recently acquired and expanded province. Nineteenth-century Russian Orientalism developed the metaphor of "voluntary and mutually benefiting ... happy marital union" between Russia and Georgia, and the marriage between Griboedov and Nina Chavchavadze becomes its real-life reference.[12] From the very beginning of the novel, Griboedov thinks of Nina Chavchavadze in terms of marriage. Tynianov stresses that their marriage is Griboedov's initiative; Nina is too young to know what she really wants. Griboedov's thoughts about Nina are the continuation of his plans for establishing the Russian Transcaucasian Company and an attempt to make his life meaningful: "It would be his country, a second fatherland; he would work hard. So much in his young days destroyed, wasted; he was getting on – time to save his soul."[13]

However, Tynianov underscores a problem in seeing the marriage between Griboedov and Nina as a metaphor for the "voluntary and mutually benefiting" union between Russia and Georgia. The dominant position of the Russian side of the marital union is evident from the passage in which Griboedov feels himself to be "a little Asiatic tsar," the likeness of Pushkin's Crimean khan. This scene depicts Griboedov at a dinner table; he will shortly propose to Nina, but at the moment he is still deliberating and comparing her to her friend, Dashinka, sitting by her side. Tynianov parodies the colonialist equivalence of a woman and a land by saying that Griboedov "was looking at Dashinka as at an awakened province."[14]

To understand Tynianov's position, it is important to take into account not only what he included in his novel, but also what he omitted from the memoirs about Griboedov. Almost all memoirs follow a certain formula in describing the marriage between Nina and Griboedov, a canon revived in later Soviet myth-making as an illustration of the fraternal friendship of the peoples of Russia and Georgia. Tynianov does not include in his book the requisite comments on Nina's beauty, intelligence, and education or detailed descriptions of the wedding and the ball. Most significantly, he does not end the story at Griboedov's grave on the mountain in the monastery of Saint David. The memoirs mention the inscription on the grave – "Your mind and deeds are immortal in Russian memory, but what for did my love survive you?" – and admire Nina's fidelity to her late husband and her refusal to remarry.[15] In Tynianov's novel, by constrast, the story of Nina and Griboedov ends with the sentence "In Tiflis she was delivered of a stillborn baby."[16] While this is a callous way of treating the personal tragedy of a loving family, it is effective in undermining the metaphor of marriage as a representation of imperial domination. According to Tynianov, Georgia's marriage to Russia brings her only pain.

Besides being the metaphor for colonialism, the theme of Griboedov's marriage serves Tynianov's exploration of the change in gender relations during the era of romantic nationalism. Romanticism re-evaluated the Enlightenment ideals of gender equality. As Yury Lotman put it: "The Enlightener asserted equality of a woman and a man. He saw a person in a woman and aspired to equalize her rights with those of her father and husband. Romanticism restored the idea of gender inequality, which was constructed according to the models of chivalrous medieval literature."[17] The reverse side of elevating a woman for her finesse and sublimity was demonizing her for a slight deviation from this ideal. Pushkin's "The Fountain of Bakhchisaray" is an apparent opposition to an angelic and a demonic female character.

Romanticism's backlash against attempts to encourage gender equality coincided with its turning away from the Enlightenment ideals of moral universalism and cultural incommensurability and its embrace of Orientalism. In his novelistic exploration, Tynianov implies interconnectedness between these two tendencies. One particularly telling scene is a dinner party at which both Griboedov and Pushkin are present. The scene is a parodic amalgamation of several memoirs of Griboedov's friends and acquaintances, as well as lines from Griboedov's letters and Pushkin's notes, which Tynianov turns into an oral exchange of ideas. At the dinner table two Alexander Sergeevichs, Pushkin, and Griboedov comically join efforts in bashing women. Pushkin argues that women distort poems when they recite them because they only pretend to understand them, while Griboedov suggests that the "Asiatics" have it right: a woman should bear children. Nikolai Grech, also present at the party, comes up with a pun, calling Griboedov "trop perçant," too keen, which sounds like "trop persan," too Persian.[18]

Pushkin and Griboedov's presence at such a dinner party and Grech's pun are attested in the memoir of K.A. Polevoi, but the pun is not prompted by their conversation about women:[19] Pushkin's remark comes from one of his several notes in which he doubts women's intellectual abilities.[20] Tynianov also seems to allude to a stanza from *Eugene Onegin* that was not included in the final version of that work, in which Pushkin's protagonist Onegin jocularly reproaches Russian ladies for not leaving their homes on a "wonderful day" of "frost and sunlight" for a stroll along the Neva river and makes a suggestion similar to Griboedov's, that "the Oriental system is clever, and the custom of old men is right, [women] were born for a harem or captivity."[21] The literary critic Vissarion Belinsky cites this stanza in his essay on *Eugene Onegin*, in which he departs from analysing Pushkin's work to discuss the problem of gender inequality in Russian society.[22]

Griboedov's remarks at the party come from the memoir of A.A. Bestuzhev, who describes at length how the author of *Woe from Wit* did not like women, or at least pretended not to like them. Bestuzhev cites a list of positive qualities that, according to Griboedov, in women are accompanied by negative qualities: their education and enlightenment come with pedantry, sensitivity with affectation, prudence with "ignominious calculation," and moral purity with intolerance and sanctimony. Their feelings are strong but superficial, judgments witty but unfounded, and "quickly grasping the details," they are unable "to comprehend the whole." Just like Pushkin in his notes, Griboedov, in Bestuzhev's account, admits that exceptions exist, but claims that they are rare.[23]

The same account relates that women, in Griboedov's opinion, were responsible for such an odious social ill as nepotism. When the movement of women's fans propels "the mill of public affairs," governing positions are distributed "according to familial ties or whims of benefactors who wear bonnets." For that reason, enclosing women "in the most narrow circle" of the domestic sphere will not only strengthen families but also improve society. Bestuzhev explains Griboedov's inclination to "sentence women for Asiatic or, at the least, Athenian imprisonment" by his life spent "in the Caucasian bivouacs and Asiatic cities of Georgia and Persia." His argument, however, differs from the traditional Orientalist assumption that a person spending time in the "Orient" acquires "Oriental mores." According to Bestuzhev, Griboedov's life, saturated with his travelling and diplomatic work, is entertaining enough for him not to crave the company of women, and having no need of them, condemn them to domestic isolation.

Griboedov himself refers to the authority of George Byron when voicing his opinion on women, thus grounding it in the tradition of romanticism. Women, whom one can make "completely content" by giving them "a cake and a mirror," are infantile "men-children."[24] Tynianov mocks the notion of a woman as a child throughout his novel, and draws parallels with the ideas of a colonized native as a child and a colonized land as a country still in its infancy. Combining these ideas with the metaphor of "imperial power as male dominance over the feminized colonial realm,"[25] Tynianov exposes colonization as a perversion.

While Nina's contemporaries always praised her for beauty and intelligence, in the novel, she is awkward and always changing because she is still a child. She is described as a "cross-eyed" or an "oxen-eyed" girl, "a Caucasian girl with heavy eyes," "still a girl," "a child [*ditiatia*]" who is "tormented with pregnancy."[26] "Going native" and marrying her, Tynianov's protagonist Griboedov is trying to return to his own "primary childhood [*pervonachal'noe detstvo*]," the ideal primitive state of a noble savage. It seems to him that this childhood at an "old age" will absolve him of the sins of his youth, when "a lot was destroyed, a lot pillaged," and reconcile him with the colonized land: "the land will remain with which he will make peace."[27]

Here again, Tynianov is alluding to the relentless criticism of romanticism from Belinsky and his essay on *Eugene Onegin*. Tatiana, the female protagonist of Pushkin's novel, reproaches Onegin for becoming infatuated with her when she had become a prominent figure in high society after rejecting her "love of a submissive girl" when they first met and she was "younger" and "better." Belinsky criticizes her assumption that "younger" is always "better," saying that she "borrowed" it "from bad sentimental novels." He argues that a "society woman tested by life and suffering, who has found words to express her feelings and thoughts" fares better than a "moral embryo," a "mute country girl with childish dreams."[28]

It should be mentioned that marriage between a teenage girl and a man in his thirties was widespread practice in the nineteenth century in both Russia and Europe, which does not mean that it was universally accepted. In 1830, Pushkin became engaged to Natalia Goncharova (1812–1863), who was sixteen at the time, and married her the following year. Soon after his engagement, Pushkin sketched an unfinished fragment "Uchast' moia reshena. Ia zhenius' ..." ("My fate is decided. I am getting married ..."), in which he expressed mixed feelings of happiness and anxiety about his upcoming marriage. He imagines with unease Russian society women who praise his choice to his face but in his absence pity his poor fiancée, who is "so young, so innocent."[29] Tynianov, no doubt, alludes to this fragment in his many-layered parody.

The attribute of childhood makes Griboedov's wife Nina similar to another character in Tynianov's novel: a little girl, Dil Firuz, from the Iranian shah's harem and the captive companion of one of the shah's eunuchs. The story of Dil Firuz, unlike that of most other characters, has a happy ending – she goes back to her family in accordance with the stipulations of the Turkmenchay peace treaty.[30] Her name alludes to Diliara Bikech, possibly the origin of the mythical prototype of Maria, the captive of the "The Fountain of Bakhchisaray." Pushkin's Maria, as a woman-child of the romantic era, also dreams of returning to her father's home, a dream that does not come true. At home, she was the pride and joy of her "grey-haired father," who wanted to give her a life bright as "a spring day," and who fulfilled her every "childood [*mladenchenskaia*] wish," hoping that in her married life she would remember her youthful days fondly.[31] This story of a European captive who longs to return to her father's house also becomes the target of Tynianov's parody. There is a character in the novel that subverts the motif of a paternal idyll and longing for home in captivity – a German woman, Susanna, who decides to stay with her Iranian husband and children instead of taking advantage of the opportunity to reunite with her father provided by the Turkmenchay treaty.[32]

In his signature style, Tynianov creates a parody that refers to sources from both the nineteenth century and his own time. Susanna's character polemically contrasts with that of Maria from "The Fountain of Bakhchisaray" while resembling that of Basia from Isaak Babel's short story "Father."[33] Tynianov stages the episode of Susanna's meeting with her father in the presence of Griboedov and other members of the Russian mission as "the third act of a comedy about the prodigal daughter."[34] While Maria is quiet, graceful, and has "lackadaisical-blue"[35] eyes, Susanna, is "big like an idol, dignified," and speaks in a chest-voice "thick as cream."[36] This imposing appearance is not the only trait modelled after Babel's character. Most importantly, both women know what they want and do not hesitate to assert their right to happiness.

Susanna seems to be quite independent in her marriage to an Iranian seid, who cowers at hearing her voice. Her father is also wary of her assertiveness and addresses her "sweetly, as one speaks to a fat cat, from whom one expects trouble."[37] He tries to create the impression that he was an indulgent father of the kind Pushkin describes in his poem by telling Griboedov and his associates that his daughter lived in his house "as a doll [*wie'n Puppchen*]."[38] She undermines his statement by enumerating the heavy chores she had to perform at home, calling him a "cruel and unscrupulous man," and promising to strangle him on the way if he decides to take her home. Both Susanna's and her father's speeches allude to Babel's character's rapturous description of the young man she took notice of: "Poppa … look at that little gentleman, his little feet are like those of a little doll, I would strangle such feet."[39] This exclamation in turn alludes to Pushkin's stanza from *Eugene Onegin* dedicated to women's little feet.[40]

Although anachronistic, Tynianov's reference to Babel's *Odessa Tales* alongside Pushkin's "The Fountain of Bakhchisaray" can be understood in terms of his desire to inscribe the Orientalization of the Jews in the broader context of colonialism and nationalism. The strong-willed women and daring gangsters of Babel's stories defy the antisemitic stereotypes of Russian literature:[41] they make their own decisions and shape their own destiny, resisting inner colonization.

Tynianov facetiously represents "The Fountain of Bakhchisaray" as the script for imperial expansion, revealing the connection between the literary Orientalism of the Russian romantic nationalism and the politics of colonization in the first half of the nineteenth century. Through parody, he exposes and subverts the metaphor of "imperial power as male dominance over the feminized colonial realm,"[42] as well as romanticism's backlash against the ideas of gender equality.

Alexander Chavchavadze: Russian Empire as the Lesser Evil

Paradoxically, Tynianov's parodic interpretation of Griboedov's marriage as an embodiment of imperial domination that tinkers with the motif of a triangle between a woman, her husband, and her father essentially leaves out the figure of Griboedov's father-in-law. Alexander Chavchavadze, a Georgian political and military figure, poet, and entrepreneur, was a native of the land contested by the Russian and Persian empires. While Chavchavadze's family was "among the Georgian aristocrats who most actively facilitated the colonization of the Caucasus," his "divided loyalties" made him reluctant to accept Russian rule.[43] It is important to consider his views on imperial domination and the future he envisioned for his people and country, in particular because Tynianov's novel distorts Chavchavadze's historical character. In his attempt to subvert the Orientalist trope of a happy marital union between Russia and Georgia, Tynianov perpetuates the equally damaging myth of the "lazy native," portraying Chavchavadze as an absent and disengaged husband and father and an inconsistent politician.

In their project, Griboedov and Zaveleisky highlighted the bountiful nature of the Transcaucasian land and downplayed the amount of labour that the local population invested in it. To justify the colonization of Transcaucasia and persuade the government to support their proposal for establishing an agricultural, manufacturing, and trading company in the region, they argued that the local population was not able to take advantage of its natural resources, portraying the local entrepreneurs as greedy, shortsighted, and corrupt and the producers as lacking skills and efficiency. Such portrayals served to justify their proposed stewardship of the region based on "improvement" of the land.

Besides preventing the "waste" of the natural resources, Griboedov and Zaveleisky's company aspired to soften the cultural divide between the empire and its new colony. Transcaucasian participants in the company, who according to the authors would constitute the majority of the stockholders, would have common economic interest with their Russian partners, which would encourage the two to socialize outside of work and establish strong bonds of friendship.

Nina's father Alexander Chavchavadze was exactly the kind of successful, innovative, and daring private entrepreneur and landowner that Griboedov and Zaveleisky's proposal claimed did not exist in Georgia. He improved the quality of traditional Georgian wines through new European technologies, as well as developing new technologies for producing sparkling wines. Unfortunately, Chavchavadze's archive was severely damaged in 1854 during a fire in his Tsinandali estate, caused by a raid of Imam Shamil's troops. There are no documents revealing his business ethics or his thoughts on the economic development of Transcaucasia.

Therefore, we cannot know the answers to questions such as: Was Chavchavadze a proponent of free trade and free enterprise? Did he support his son-in-law's belief in the usefulness of monopolies and privileges for speeding up the development of certain regions? He was known as one of the "Enlighteners" of Georgia – how did he interpret the ideas of the thinkers of the European Enlightenment, such as Smith and Diderot? What distinguished his perspective on modernizing Georgia from those of his Russian counterparts?

Unlike Chavchavadze's thoughts on the economic development of Transcaucasia, his cultural activities and political views reached us through his own writing and the memoirs of his contemporaries. Chavchavadze played the role of cultural mediator between Georgian, Russian, Polish, and French societies, hosting at his estate artists, literary figures, and businessmen from Georgia, Russia, and Europe and taking upon himself the task of softening the divide between the empire and its colony that, according to Griboedov and Zaveleisky, only their proposed company could accomplish.

Chavchavadze's literary interests and knowledge of languages facilitated his role of cultural mediator. Besides Georgian and Russian, he knew French, German, Persian, and Turkish. His literary translations included the works of Russian, French, German, and Persian authors. His own poems, written in Georgian, gained popular recognition, and his patriotic songs spread widely among people in just a day.[44] Chavchavadze's literary style advanced cultural synthesis, "introducing Russian and European themes and forms into Georgian literature, without severing ties with the Persian tradition that had nourished Georgian verse in the past."[45] It also helped Georgian literature enter modernity through his use of vernacular Georgian.

As a political figure, Chavchavadze was conflicted about the presence of Russian imperial power in Georgia. At different times in his life, he led both rebellions against Russian rule and pacifying operations against such rebellions. The son of Garsevan Chavchavadze, Georgian ambassador in Russia until his country's annexation, he was born in Petersburg. His biographers especially liked to mention that Catherine the Great was his godmother. Returning to Georgia with his family after its annexation by Russia, Chavchavadze joined his first society of rebels at the age of fifteen; the society supported the restoration of Georgia's statehood under the rule of Prince Parnaoz.[46]

When the conspiracy was exposed, the connections of his father helped him to avoid punishment. Instead, the Russian government ordered him to return to Petersburg and continue his education. Becoming a military officer, Chavchavadze participated in the Napoleonic Wars, the Russo-Persian War of 1826–8, and the Russo-Turkish War of 1828–9; he received the rank of major-general and served as military governor of the Armenian province. In 1832, another anti-Russian conspiracy brewed in Georgia. Chavchavadze fell under suspicion and was initially exiled to Tambov but then recalled and forgiven, because the government needed his military leadership in its prolonged war against the North Caucasian mountaineers. Chavchavadze participated in punitive expeditions and received the rank of lieutenant-general.[47]

The trichotomy between Georgia, Imperial Russia, and the North Caucasian mountaineers in the first half of the nineteenth century informed Chavchavadze's political mindset and his artistic endeavours.[48] In his "Kratkii istoricheskii ocherk Gruzii i ee polozheniia s 1801 po 1831" ("Brief Historical Essay on Georgia and Its Condition from 1801 to 1831"), Chavchavadze identified the personal safety and security of Georgians as the main benefit of joining the Russian Empire. The Georgian ploughman, according to Chavchavadze, "tilled the earth armed" and reaped the harvest "under bullets." Georgians, he argued, were safe "neither in cities, nor in villages"; nevertheless they were able to preserve their Christian faith, resisting conversion by either the Persian or the Ottomans, as well as their "martial spirit and love for motherland."[49]

Chavchavadze's animosity towards the mountaineers, like that of another Georgian romantic poet, Nikoloz Baratashvili, was part of "the discourse of retribution," according to which "the participation of Georgians in Russia's North Caucasian wars was just revenge for the raids which the tribes of Dagestan had conducted to devastating effect in eastern Georgia during the eighteenth century."[50] Raiding Transcaucasia, the mountaineers provided slaves for the Persian and Ottoman markets, and in the Georgians' view were on the side of their oppressors.[51] In counter-retribution against Alexander Chavchavadze's and his son David's involvement in the "pacification" of the mountaineers, in 1854 Imam Shamil's troops raided their estate in Tsinandali. They took David's family hostage, to be exchanged for Shamil's son, Jamal al-Din, who from a young age was raised in Petersburg as an "*amanat*," meant to guarantee Shamil's loyalty to the Russian emperor.[52]

Chavchavadze's poetry and political thought were infused with romantic nationalism; however, it is obvious that at his mature age he subscribed to the idea of Russian rule over Georgia as a "lesser evil" compared to the more "Asiatic" rule of Iran. By siding with Russia, Georgia in his view was opening up to enlightened modernity. In his "Brief Historical Essay," Chavchavadze cautiously specified that anti-government uprisings in Georgia were not political in nature and were not anti-Russian. They stemmed from the frustration of the impoverished Georgian population over a particular policy of expropriation of provisions for the Russian army.[53] Legal proceedings of the imperial administration in Georgia were another target of Chavchavadze's criticism. The translations from Georgian to Russian and from Russian to Georgian were "words scattered on paper without any meaning," preventing judges from fully understanding the circumstances of their cases and petitioners from understanding their decisions. To these "unintentional disorders," Chavchavadze added the intentional malpractice of civil servants, who were hired indiscriminately.[54]

Chavchavadze combined criticism of the Russian imperial administration with reluctant admission of the necessity of Russian political presence, and genuine openness towards Russian cultural achievements. The scholars of Chavchavadze's poetic output, Harsha Ram and Zaza Shatirishvili, underscored his complex engagement with the "imperial modernity, which in Georgia as elsewhere meant more than just the bureaucratic or military apparatus of the Russian state."[55]

Both Chavchavadze's and Baratashvili's works "display a profound engagement with the rich and contradictory legacy of Russian (and in one case even Polish) romantic poetry."[56] This assessment meshes with the representation of Chavchavadze's relationship with Russian imperial modernity in Soviet scholarship. Soviet scholars Vano Shaduri and Igor Bogomolov argued that for Chavchavadze the Russia of Pushkin was different from the Russia of Nicholas I, the latter associated with the "chauvinistic policies" of the imperial administration and the former standing for the progressive liberal-minded literary culture.[57]

In reality, as Tynianov shows in his novel, the representatives of "the new progressive romantic trend"[58] in Russian literature were not averse to Orientalism and imperialist ambitions fueled by national pride. Chavchavadze himself displayed a colonialist attitude towards the North Caucasian mountaineers. This trichotomy between Russia, Georgia, and the North Caucasus does not surface in Tynianov's novel, and Chavchavadze appears as a contradictory person, who at times rebels against the Russian Empire and at times helps it "pacify" his own compatriots.

With all that said, Chavchavadze did accomplish a great deal as a cultural mediator, who turned Tbilisi into a culturally vibrant hub where, to the sound of "Oriental" and European music, Georgian and Russian cultures came together and new literary works appeared.[59] Surprisingly, Tynianov does not acknowledge Chavchavadze's role as a cultural mediator, portraying him, if not quite as a "lazy native," then as a husband who escapes his boring family life and aging wife by participating in military campaigns, and as a disengaged father who sends his children to be raised by his neighbour Praskovia Akhverdova.[60] In the novel social mingling between representatives of different cultures takes place at the house of Governor-General Sipiagin:

> No kotil'on skryval po vremenam Mushtaida, kotil'on, v kotorom pleskalis' vmeste s russkimi devami i gruzinki v natsional'nykh kostiumakh. Vot proplyla Nina. Gruznaia cheta gruzinskikh kniazei igrala v mushku, v otdalennom uglu, i – riadom zagliadyval v karty staryi russkii polkovnik s kal'ianom v rukakh.[61]

> (But the cotillion at times hid the Mushtahid, the cotillion in which, together with Russian maidens, Georgian ones in national costumes splashed. There Nina sailed by. A heavyset Georgian princely couple was playing [the card game] loo, in a remote corner, and next to them an old Russian colonel with a hookah in his hands peeked into their cards.)

This description is a parody of the social diplomacy that Griboedov advocated in his proposal and that Chavchavadze implemented, with a wink at similar practices in the Soviet Union. The novelistic governor-general explains its principles to his guest Zaveleisky in a crude and simplistic manner. In his opinion, food and entertainment would appease anyone who is unhappy with the imperial policies, whether they are Persian khans, Georgian aristocrats offended by the Russian officials' condescending attitude, or the prisoners of the Russo-Turkish War of 1828–9. If they cannot dance at a party, they can come for a smoke, to satisfy their "needs of the soul," which according to Sipiagin are central in politics.[62]

If Alexander Chavchavadze in the novel is an active if somewhat inconsistent and uncaring man, his wife Salome's portrayal truly fits the stereotype of a "lazy native." While her husband is distracting himself with military campaigns, Princess Salome is "fading and yawning, like all middle-aged Georgian women, who cannot love their husbands anymore and are unable to occupy themselves with anything else."[63] She is so apathetic and unattractive that her neighbour, Praskovia Akhverdova, who according to Tynianov's invention is raising Chavchavadze's children and cares about Nina more than her mother does, does not want her to be present at the dinner with Griboedov. Akhverdova is anxious that Griboedov could change his mind about proposing to Nina after seeing her mother.[64] It seems that Tynianov wants to subvert the Orientalist trope of a lazy native man in charge of an attractive and passionate native woman in need of being rescued by the Western hero. By doing, however, so he tarnishes the reputation of a real and prominent Georgian family, creating new cultural stereotypes while trying to dispel the old ones.

Chapter Five

Infant Asia and Stenka Razin: Persia in the Works of the Soviet Avant-Garde

Adding to the divergent allusions of "The Fountain of Bakhchisaray" in connection to the ideas of imperialism as male dominance over a feminized colonial land, Yury Tynianov created a scene in which Alexander Griboedov "abducts" a woman, eloping from a ballet performance with the wife of his friend, Faddey Bulgarin, on the pretence that she has a headache. Taking her home, he makes love with her, fantasizing that he is plowing, "entering the rich soil" with a "blunt iron," or conquering a land, "cutting though the Caucasus, Transcaucasia, wedging into Persia." At that moment it seems to him that a "higher power and a higher order" rule the world and that "the power belonged to him." Then "such a time arrived that nothing could stop him anymore." He imagines himself as Stenka Razin, the rebellious Cossack leader whose men once pillaged Persia: "there were raids on a land, the last plunders," "what malice was handling the world." Finally, a "complete equilibrium set in – the infant Asia was breathing beside him ... Faddey's green curtains were lovely."[1]

In this scene, there is an underlying parallel between Griboedov's future Georgian wife, Princess Nina Chavchavadze, and his friend Faddey Bulgarin's German wife, Lenochka, a parallel that appears elsewhere in the novel.[2] The biographical justification of such parallelism is Griboedov's letter to Bulgarin in which he describes how he proposed to Nina and calls her the "second volume of Lenochka."[3] Griboedov also used to call Nina "Madonna Murillo," the name that in Tynianov's novel is given to Lenochka. This confusion is another wink at the author of "The Fountain of Bakhchisaray," whose choice Tynianov analyses in his article "Pushkin."[4] Just as Alexander Pushkin substitutes a Polish woman for a Georgian one in his poem, Tynianov makes a German woman represent the "infant Asia" whom Griboedov is trying to colonize. Playing with the motif of an "Oriental" woman and her European double, Tynianov gives two different nationalities, Armenian and German, to the Christian wives of a Persian khan, the women who decided to seek protection in the Russian mission in Teheran shortly before its destruction.[5] However, if Pushkin in accordance with the Orientalist discourse of the time imagines culturally different women,[6] in Tynianov's novel the wives of the khan are identical. This further underscores the conventionality of Pushkin's characters within romantic literary Orientalism.

Mentioning "Faddey's green curtains" in his passage on the "infant Asia," Tynianov implies that Griboedov has invaded somebody else's territory and interfered with their lives. The complete balance attained when the "malice" is over refers to the idea of a conquest as a "civilizing mission," the illusion that balance and harmony can be attained through force and dominance. Griboedov is impatient to move the empire's relations with its colonies from the stage of the "thunder of weapons" to that of "well-being, and prosperity," from conquering more land to successfully managing what is already there. "Balance" also has a more specific historical connotation: it is an allusion to the balance of power in Europe. Tynianov mocks the European balance in another chapter, where one of the Russian emperors and the European powers appear as tightrope walkers and jugglers in a circus. General Ermolov, the most brutal of the conquerors of the Caucasus, is a horseman riding into the circus arena at the wrong time.[7] The motif of balance is repeated in Tynianov's descriptions of actual street magicians and balance acts both in Russia and in Persia.[8] The references to the circus and to street performance bring into the novel a whiff of Tynianov's own time, when avant-garde theatres, popular performances, and mass spectacles were used for political agitation. It also alludes more specifically to Vasily Kamensky's futurist poem "Juggler," published in the first issue of the Soviet literary journal *LEF*, which compared the craft of a poet to that of a juggler, as bewitching the crowd with his words.[9]

Kamensky, however, becomes the target of Tynianov's parody, not so much for his fascination with the magical power of words over the minds of people in his poem "Juggler" as for his obsession with the figure of the seventeenth-century Cossack rebel Stepan Razin, who came to represent the violent revolutionary transformation of Russian society and culture. Of course, Tynianov's complex net of allusion to Razin's figure in his novel refers not only to Kamensky's works but also to numerous nineteenth- and twentieth-century texts that portray the Cossack rebel as a violent but noble robber and a defender of the oppressed. In addition to folklore accounts, among those who wrote about Razin were Griboedov and Pushkin; the poets of the "*narodnichestvo*" (populism) era of the 1860s through the 1880s, whose poems became popular songs; and especially the writers of the Russian modernism and avant-garde, Tynianov's contemporaries, for whom Razin represented the popular revolution. A violent episode from Razin's legendary rebellious life, his alleged drowning of a captive Persian princess, became the theme of the first complete Russian narrative film, directed by Vladimir Romashkov in 1908.[10] Aleksey Chapygin's historical novel *Razin Stepan* (1925–7) was published at the time when Tynianov was working on *The Death of Vazir-Mukhtar*.[11]

Razin's character is particularly interesting for Tynianov, as a writer undertaking a portrayal of Russia's relations with Iran, because of the Cossack leader's raids of Persian and Caucasian coastal cities on the Caspian Sea in which he was engaged for two years prior to his Volga uprisings.[12] In the above-mentioned passage on "infant Asia," Tynianov compares Griboedov during his "abduction" of his friend's wife to Stenka Razin. This comparison reverses the motif of an abducted captive of an "Oriental" harem, alluding to the story of a Persian princess abducted by Razin and sacrificed to the Volga River. The story of the sacrifice is attested in two memoir accounts, both made by Dutchmen. One was a sailmaker who was in Astrakhan in 1669 at the time of Razin's return from his Caspian Sea adventure; the other was an officer in Russian service, who was captured by Razin's men in Astrakhan in 1670 and escaped to Iran before returning to Russia, retiring from military service, and later continuing his career as a Swedish diplomat.[13] Although it is well attested that during their raids Cossacks captured women, children, and occasionally men for servitude and forced marriage, this particular story seems to be a creation of popular imagination, overheard by the Dutch memoirists.[14]

Tynianov alludes to the story as it appears in one of Dmitry Sadovnikov's "Poems to Stenka Razin" that became a popular song at the end of the nineteenth century.[15] The song depicts Razin celebrating his marriage to the Persian princess in a boat. Razin's crew starts to murmur that he abandoned them for a woman, becoming a woman himself. The princess, sitting next to Razin, is "neither alive not dead," that is, scared to death. Razin shows his loyalty to his men by throwing the princess overboard as a gift to the Russian river Volga, his "dear mother." His fellows seem shocked and repentant, while Razin is trying to cheer them and himself up, ordering: "Hey, you, Filka, devil, dance," and encouraging them to start a swashbuckling (*udalaia*) song "in remembrance of her soul."

In Tynianov's novel, when Griboedov orders his servant Sashka to pack for a journey to the Caucasus and Persia, he adds excitedly:

"Sashka, sing: Down the Mother Volga-river! Sing, Sashka, dance! ... Sashka, devil, dandy-dog, dance!"[16] With his inclination for confusion and mystification, Tynianov gives the name of a different folk song dedicated to Razin. He also makes Griboedov call his servant "Stenka" by mistake: "Stenka sing! I meant Sashka, – Griboedov suddenly says wonderstruck, – Sashka, sing!"[17] While Sashka is singing, his master is imagining the "daring fellows" who, throwing themselves into "light barks" going down Akhtuba river, and eventually venturing into the Caspian Sea, take tribute from the "coastal towns and villages," sparing "neither the grey hair of an old age, nor the swan's down of lovely breasts."[18]

This imagined scene comes from Griboedov's own writings:

> Bylye vremena! kak zhivo voskreshaet vas v moei pamiati eta narodnaia igra: tot vek neobuzdannoi vol'nosti, v kotoryi neskol'ko udal'tsov brosalis' v legkie strugi, spuskalis' vniz po protoku Akhtube, po Buzan-reke, derzali v otkrytoe more, brali dan' s pribrezhnykh gorodov i selenii, ne shchadili ni krasoty devich'ei, ni sediny starcheskoi.[19]
>
> (Bygone days! How vividly this folk game revives you in my memory – that age of unbridled freedom, when a number of daring fellows threw themselves into light boats, went down the channel Akhtuba, the Bouzan-river, dared to go into the open sea, took tribute from the coastal cities and villages, sparing neither the beauty of the maidens, nor the grey hair of the old.)

Griboedov then refers to Jean Chardin, according to whom the daring fellows threatened the very Firuz-Abat and the "brilliant court" of Shah Abbas himself. Griboedov continues his account of the exploits of the daring fellows by describing the loot they brought back from their raids, and the admiration with which they were welcomed back: "Then, getting rich with profits, with countless amounts of patterned fabrics, silver and gold, pearls, they came back home, where love and friendship awaited them; they welcomed them with loud joy, and glorified them in songs."[20] It is evident that Griboedov himself admires these deeds of "bygone days." This admiration is present in Tynianov's novelistic parody, and the parallel with Pushkin's ecstasy about "ruining and destroying the tribes" hardly escapes the readers' attention. Just like Pushkin did, Griboedov allows national pride to take over considerations of humanism. Interestingly, the Cossacks, whose exploits Griboedov admires, were a diverse multi-ethnic group.[21]

Popular imagination and intellectuals celebrated Razin not foremost for his raids, although consistent and resolute disapproval of this aspect of his adventures comes only in the twentieth century, but for his defence of the poor and destitute against the nobility, governmental officials, and wealthy merchants. While the initial goal of Razin's rebellion was to reassert the special freedoms and privileges that Cossacks historically enjoyed, in its later stage it became a truly popular uprising in which different groups, such as the peasants, the soldiers, and the national minorities of the Volga region, joined because of their own grievances against the government.[22] In the novel, Razin's revolt parallels Griboedov's sympathy for the Decembrist uprising, a parallel that parodies the tendency of his contemporaries to represent Razin as a precursor of the revolutionaries, who in Lenin's words "awakened Herzen" and set the path for the subsequent revolutionary movements in Russia. In 1919, Lenin himself gave a speech at the dedication of the monument for Razin on Lobnoe Mesto on Red Square. The monument was short lived – the Persian princess, cast out of cement, and the figures of Razin and his band (*vataga*), carved out of wood, were not weather resistant. In his speech, Lenin called Razin a "freedom fighter" and said that placing his monument at the place of his execution was a reminder of the "many centuries of torment … suffered by the working people under the yoke of the oppressors."[23]

For Tynianov's literary exploration, it was also important that Razin established a short-lived Cossack republic in Astrakhan, and while in Iran attempted to create a semi-autonomous settlement there by persuading the shah to give him land and assuring him of his loyalty.[24] In the novel, he makes his protagonist Griboedov fantasize about creating an autonomous "state" in Transcaucasia that will be ruled by his Russian Transcaucasian Company. Another character of the novel, who strives for autonomy from his motherland and is associated with the figure of Razin, is Griboedov's enemy, renegade Samson Makintsev, also known as Samson Khan. Deserting the Russian imperial army before the first Russo-Persian War of 1804–13, Samson Khan gained the trust of the crown prince Abbas Mirza, and eventually became a general of the Iranian army. Within this army of the new kind, *nezam-e jadid*, which Mirza was building after the model of the Russian army, Samson Khan was the leader of a special Russian unit comprising Russian deserters, prisoners of war, or runaway peasants, whom he persuaded to serve on the Iranian side. The existence of such a unit was an affront to Griboedov's national pride, and one of his missions as a diplomat was to persuade the deserters to return to Russia.

The motifs of treason and betrayal are recurrent in the novel. While Samson Khan commits treason against his state, Griboedov's cooperation with the tsarist government is also a betrayal, an abandonment of the liberationist ideals of his youth. His loyalty to his nation and desire to turn Russia into a competitive state and a powerful empire paradoxically makes him strike deals with his conscience. He has to cooperate with the authoritarian government, and plans to use the labour of former serfs, whom he wants to bind legally to work for his future company. However, Tynianov subsequently dismantles the dichotomy between Griboedov's alleged Decembrist past and his collaborationist present, by showing that the government and the Decembrists agreed in their approval of the imperial expansionism. As for the serf labour, in Tynianov's view the Decembrists would not shun from using it "temporarily."[25] The latter suggestion reads as a covert allusion to Stalinist collectivization.

While Griboedov's character in the novel has obvious parallels to that of the folkloric Razin, he is also in some way similar to the Persian princess. Griboedov feels constrained by his own authoritarian state and his personal life circumstances. He is in Iran against his will, and he feels scared and helpless like the princess, the passive victim of Razin's violence. "Teheran was his final fear" and it "was awaiting him."[26] Razin sacrifices the princess to prove loyalty to his crew; Griboedov sacrifices himself to the patriotic duty of unwavering implementation of the Turkmenchay peace treaty that he helped to negotiate, thus enacting the roles of both the Cossack rebel and his victim. However, there is one passage in the first 1929 edition of Tynianov's novel in which the Iranian government assumes the role of the Persian princess and Griboedov that of the Cossack plunderer. In the passage, Griboedov is described as an undesired bridegroom at the court of Fath Ali Shah, whose ministers "were in white shawls wound around black kajaris, and, despite their red beards, the shawls made them look as if they were brides of masculine gender. They were looking at Vazir-Mukhtar as at a groom who is rich but repellent."[27] Griboedov's exacting demand for timely payment of war reparations from the impoverished Iranian side is, according to Tynianov, similar to Razin's plunder of the same land back in the seventeenth century.

The motif of plundering is another thread in the dialogue between Tynianov's novel and the memoir of his friend and fellow formalist Viktor Shklovsky, *A Sentimental Journey*. As we know, soon after the February Revolution of 1917, Shklovsky found himself in Iran as an assistant commissar of the Persian Expeditionary Corps, where he learned the news of the October Revolution and, ultimately, became responsible for the withdrawal of the Russian troops. Especially distressed by his inability to stop his soldiers from looting, Shklovsky describes in detail an episode where they destroy a Persian bazaar. Some soldiers tried to admonish their fellows and explain to them that looting a bazaar was not the best way of fighting capitalism, which can only be fought in an organized manner. They were not, however, able to dissuade their comrades.

By Shklovsky's estimate, 75 per cent of the soldiers were "passively honest," and yet even "the majority of the passive ones" regarded looting as a "mischievous game." Shklovsky's description of the loot is starkly different from Griboedov's admiration of the "rich profits" of Razin's mates: "It was strange. A man is running with a dagger in his hand and distraught eyes; you catch him, shake him, and he has two gilded frames, two boots for the left foot and a few handfuls of raisins."[28] Rather than judging the soldiers, Shklovsky denounces the war and imperialism that enable such behaviour and turn soldiers against their fellow humans.

Shklovsky called for stopping war and plunder "in the name of revolution and love of humanity."[29] Most of the poets in post-revolutionary Russia saw plunder and violence as an integral part of the elemental force of revolution. The most famous example, of course, is Aleksandr Blok's "Dvenadtsat'" ("The Twelve," 1918), where one of the red guards is similar to Razin in that he is sidetracked by his attraction to a woman, who needs to be sacrificed in order for him to join the revolutionary fight.[30] The fight itself amounts to "having some fun [*pozabavit'sia*]" through revengeful killing and plundering of the bourgeoisie. The motif of revenge for centuries of oppression is central to Maksimilian Voloshin's poem "Stenka's Judgement" ("Sten'kin sud," 1917),[31] in which Razin returns to violently punish the landlords, government officials, clergy, and nobility. In Kamensky's 1912–20 poem about Razin's adventures, the violence of the plunder is also justified as rightful revenge of the poor against the rich.[32] Razin summons his men to "flay" the merchant, taking the "gold-cloth" off him.[33] Even pillaging the "orange gardens" of Persia does not cause remorse, because the victims are the rich inhabitants of the Sultan's palace.[34] Razin's romance with the Persian princess is ridiculously in tune with the Orientalism of the romantic era. The princess is mesmerizing the "oak [*dubovyi*]" and "aspen [*osinovyi*]" ataman[35] with a long ornamental song containing images of carpets, black eyebrows, a fragrant hookah, and leg bracelets, and ending with the lines "My breast is mellow, marvelous. I am all an open window. Ah, my Zarem, my harem, my Persia."[36] He feels guilty about having two lovers, one from home and one from overseas, comparing them to a white and a black swan.[37] Eventually, he sacrifices both women to the cause of rebellion and camaraderie with his crew.[38]

However, Kamensky's interpretation of the episode with the Persian princess changed considerably when he reworked his poem into a novel, and a play, which was timed for the first anniversary of the revolution. The play was successfully staged in Petersburg, Moscow, and Kiev between 1919 and 1924, and was saturated with the atmosphere of circus and folk art, which Tynianov recreated in his novel. Combining narrative in prose with insertions of his own poem, Kamensky creates popular art, in which pillaging of non-Russian peoples becomes problematic. On the one hand, Kamensky feels it necessary to provide in his prose narrative "realistic" psychological motivations for his character's actions that he could omit in a futuristic poem. On the other hand, he seems to be more aware of the importance of demonstrating the spirit of proletarian internationalism when revolution had already won. Thus, he inserts into his play an episode in which Razin's men are robbing a Tatar khan, and the poor Tatars support them by saying in broken Russian that the poor folk, regardless of nationality, have the same heart and the same head (*bashka*). Even the khan feels ashamed and says that "he himself head will hang [*sam bashka poveshu*]," that is, he will kill himself, but is saved by the merciful rebels.[39]

Unlike in the poem, where Razin's men go to Persia after a rich booty, "carpet-gifts [*kovry-dary*]" and "gold-riches [*zoloto-dobro*]," in the prosaic texts Razin comes to the prince Ajar of Resht for peaceful trade. He has his own gold and asks the Persian prince to sell him silk, velvet, and Persian carpets. The prince's daughter, Meiran, and Razin fall in love at first sight and become intimate during the tiger-hunting trip that the prince organizes for Razin. The treacherous prince shoots at Razin instead of the tiger, and Razin shoots back, killing the prince. While the nobility and the rich merchants accuse Razin of murder, "the Persian poor folk, the slaves, the harem of many wives [*mnogozhennyi*], the majority of the palace guard, everyone who suffered long from the prince's cruelty, take Stepan's side."[40]

Thus, the oppressed women of the Orient, according to Kamensky, expressed solidarity with the underclass of their land and with the Russian "freedom fighters." Upon arriving in Russia, the Persian princess also expresses deep care for the cause of the poor there. She approves that Razin distributes his booty to the Russian poor: "I love the poor, I love your people and I love poor Persian people, and I am ashamed, Stepan, my love, that I am a princess, and for that your friends will not like me."[41] The class-conscious and understanding princess absolves Razin from his responsibility by asking him to drown her in the Volga River. She consoles him by suggesting that the river will take her back to Persia. Instead of brutal murder followed by bravado, the story of the princess ends in Kamensky's novel with Razin's lamentation: "The transmarine swan-princess [*lebed'-printsessa*] of Persia is flying away from us ... Volga, Volga, accept her, and keep her, and carry, carry her carefully with love to the Persian shores."[42] Thus, in view of new ideas on gender issues and on international relations, Kamensky feels an obligation to absolve Razin of two grave offences, his mistreatment of a woman and his hostile behaviour towards people of a different nationality.

In Tynianov's parodic paraphrase of Griboedov's "Country Outing," which at the same time alludes to Kamensky's portrayal of Razin, the motif of a swan appears not in a lamentation of a grief-stricken lover, but in a context of pillaging and rape. The "daring fellows" of the "bygone days" venture into the Caspian Sea to raid the coastal cities of Persia, sparing "neither the grey hair of an old age, nor the swan's down of lovely breasts."[43] Among Tynianov's prominent contemporaries, only Marina Tsvetaeva interprets Razin's relationship with the princess as sexual violence. Her princess is not in love with Razin; moreover, she is murdered exactly because she cannot reciprocate his advances. The "mad ataman" throws the princess, with tear-stained eyes and bloody bitten lips, into the water, suggesting that if she does not get along "with our bed [*s nashei postel'iu*]," she has to get along "with our font [*s nashei kupel'iu*]." Instead of international solidarity, Tsvetaeva describes cultural and religious intolerance. Razin's "drunken band [*p'ianaia vataga*]" is angry with him, because he locked himself up with a "basurman dog," that is, with an unchristened foreigner.[44]

Tynianov describes Griboedov himself as a raider, like those "daring fellows" of "bygone days," when he has an affair with his friend Bulgarin's wife: "He burst into the apartment, flew as a bandit over the swan down of lovely breasts – and now the apartment is motionless."[45] Bulgarin's wife, in the novel, is a substitute for Griboedov's future wife Nina and her land, the "Infant-Asia" of his imperialist desire. In folklore and mythology in Russia and Eurasia, hunting for swans appears as a metaphor for conquering enemies, and at the same time for wooing and marrying a woman. Tynianov uses this image to expose through parody the representation of imperialism "as male dominance over the feminized colonial realm."[46]

In other instances, the motif of a swan in the novel appears in passages that paraphrase "The Tale of Igor's Campaign," consolidating Griboedov's identity in the novel as both an imperialist and a literary "archaist-innovator," who wants to move Russian literature forward by revitalizing it through ancient written and oral tradition. In Tynianov's novel, Griboedov's love of poetry is imbued with romantic nationalism.

Alluding to Griboedov's essay "Country Outing," in which the narrator admires the outfits and the singing of Russian peasants, and calls his Westernized compatriots a "damaged class of semi-Europeans,"[47] Tynianov says that Griboedov's life goal was creating a song:

> Pesnia v nem guliala, bolela, nazrevala, brodila i rassypalas' ... Teper', kogda on postarel i molodost' sniali s nego, kak tesnoe plat'e, on eto ponial ... khotel on postroit' prostuiu, priamo russkuiu ... drevniuiu pesniu, polunoshchnoe slovo o novom polku Igoreve.[48]
>
> (The song was wandering in him, aching, brewing, fermenting and scattering ... Now, when he grew old, and they took off the youth from him as a tight dress, he understood that ... he wanted to construct a simple, outright Russian ... ancient song, a midnight tale of a new Igor's campaign.)

During his last days in the Russian mission in Teheran, feeling his captivity, Griboedov imagines his Georgian wife, Nina, in the role of Yaroslavna, the wife of Prince Igor, who mourns her husband's captivity at the hands of the Cumans (*Polovtsy*). Ironically, his "Yaroslavna is weeping in the city of Tabriz on an English bed," in the house of John MacDonald, the envoy to Iran representing Russia's rival, the British Empire,[49] for Griboedov left her behind, believing it was dangerous to take his pregnant wife to Teheran. Unfortunately, unlike Prince Igor, he did not have a chance to escape his captivity and reunite with his wife.

As a poet who wants to modernize Russian literature and society using the archaic lore of texts and songs, Tynianov's protagonist Griboedov is similar to Russian futurists Kamensky and especially Velimir Khlebnikov. In his article on Khlebnikov ("O Khlebnikove"), Tynianov praises the poet's childlike non-discriminatory openness towards different "literary traditions," which "fly open" before his innovative inquiry. Because of this openness, "Igor's Tale" for Khlebnikov "suddenly becomes more contemporary than Brusov."[50] Just like Griboedov, Khlebnikov is both an archaist and an innovator. His poetry, according to Tynianov's cherished idea of literary descent from grandparents to grandchildren, is akin to that of Mikhail Lomonosov and is alien to the literary culture of the nineteenth century.[51] This, Tynianov points out, "is not a return towards the old, but only a struggle with the fathers, in which the grandson turns out to resemble the grandfather."[52]

Just like his eighteenth-century polymath "grandfather," Khlebnikov regards "things as phenomena, with the judgment of a scientist, penetrating into the process and passing."[53] His many-faceted personality propels him to pay attention to "random street conversations," as well as to the "events of world history."[54] This ability, according to Tynianov, gives Khlebnikov an insight into the true life of the "East," which he encountered in 1921 in Iran as a "Kul'tprosvet" ("Cultural Education") lecturer in the headquarters of the Russian Revolutionary Army that was helping the short-lived Republic of Gilan. His poem "Gul-Mulla's Trumpet," based on his Persian impressions is Tynianov's standard for depicting a different culture. In it, the "East" does not appear through the gaze of a European amateur outsider; one can find "neither condescension, nor excessive respect," but rather a "close-up" and "level" point of view.[55]

It seems that Tynianov endows Khlebnikov with his own anticolonialist sentiments and cultural sensitivity, which he traces back to the moral universalism and the ideas of cultural incommensurability of the thinkers of the Enlightenment. Opposing this stance to the romantic nationalism of Griboedov and Pushkin's era, he reiterates his cherished idea of the Russian avant-garde shaking hands with the eighteenth century "over the head of the XIX century."[56] Tynianov and his fellow formalist Shklovsky explicitly express their anticolonialist convictions, and undermine the attitudes that later become known as Orientalism. Khlebnikov's views are harder to pinpoint because he voices them in an obscure and oracular style, but his pacifist, anti-imperialist, and internationalist stance is apparent in his poetry and prose.

Khlebnikov's humanism, akin to that of Shklovsky, manifests in his anti-war poetry. In his poem "Voina v myshelovke" ("War in a Mousetrap"), he promises to create another "Igor's Tale" or "something similar," as a response to the atrocities of the First World War, when the burnt-down globe will ask itself, "Who am I?"[57] For him, this ancient text is a powerful warning against prideful bellicosity, a mystical charm against another disaster, rather than simply an object of national pride as it was for the poets of romanticism. This perception is very different from the belligerent pan-Slavism of Khlebnikov's pre-futurist youth, the time when he gravitated towards the symbolists. Just like Shklovsky, Khlebnikov undoubtedly blames world imperialism in starting and perpetuating the war, and supports revolution. In his "Pis'mo dvum iapontsam" ("Letter to Two Japanese Men"), he calls for the creation of an age- (and gender-) exclusive international of young men (*iunoshi*). Like the narrator of Remarque's famous anti-war novel *All Quiet on the Western Front*,[58] Khlebnikov accuses the older generation of sowing animosity between nations in his "Letter" and in "War in a Mousetrap," where he regrets having to forgo"the sweet commonwealth of twenty-two-year-olds, free from the foolishness of the older ages."[59]

Khlebnikov's poems and letters show his openness towards the culture of Iran. His perception of himself as an unappreciated prophet, a feature more characteristic of romantic poetry than of the works of the Enlightenment, prompts his curiosity about the land of his precursor Zoroaster. He is grateful to Persia for accepting him as its own:

"Nash!" – skazali sviashchenniki gor.
"Nash!" – zapeli tsvety ...
"Nash!" – zapeli dubrovy i roshchi ...[60]

("Ours!" – said the priests of the mountains.
"Ours!" – sang the flowers ...
"Ours!" – sang the oak-woods and groves ...)

Khlebnikov's adventures in Iran resonate in many ways with Pushkin's *Journey to Arzrum*. His description of the little town Anzali on the Iranian coast of the Caspian Sea differs in its tone from Pushkin's description of Erzerum, a town with stone buildings and turf-covered roofs, which looks "extremely strange" from above, and is mired in "Asiatic" poverty and squalor.[61] Unlike Pushkin in Erzerum, Khlebnikov is delighted to spend time in Anzali, and wishes that his family could join him there:

Enzeli sostoit iz mnozhestva cherepichnykh domikov, pokrytykh kovrami zelenogo mokha, milovidnymi krasnymi tsvetochkami. Zolotye narynchi i portakhaly unizyvaiut vetki derev'ev. Dervishi s uzlovatymi posokhami, pokhozhimi na klubiashchikhsia zmei, surovymi litsami prorokov – svoim peniem oglashaiut ulitsy.[62]

(Anzali consists of many little tile houses, covered with carpets of green moss, with pretty red flowers. Golden narynchs [Persian *narenj* – orange] and portaxalars [Persian *porteqal* – orange] bead the branches of the trees. Dervishes with knotty staffs that look like swirling snakes, with austere faces of prophets, fill the streets with their singing.)

In the *Journey*, Pushkin is introduced as a poet to a prisoner-of-war Ottoman official, who pays him a compliment:

"Blagosloven chas, kogda vstrechaem poeta. Poet brat dervishu. On ne imeet ni otechestva, ni blag zenmykh; i mezhdu tem kak my, bednye, zabotimsia o slave, o vlasti, o sokrovishchakh, on stoit naravne s vlastelinami zemli i emu pokloniaiutsia."[63]

("Blessed is the hour, when we meet a poet. A poet is a brother of a dervish. He has neither a fatherland, nor earthly comforts; and while we, the wretched ones, care for fame, power, treasures, he stands on a level with the lords of the Earth and everyone worships them.")

While Pushkin admits with self-irony that he enjoyed the "Oriental greeting" of the official, he pokes fun at his suggested familial ties with dervishes later in the day, when he sees "a young man, half naked, in a sheepskin hat, with a club in his hand, and a sheepskin on his back. He was yelling at the top of his lungs. They told me that it was my brother, a dervish, who came to greet the victors. They were barely able to drive him away."[64] Unlike Pushkin, Khlebnikov took to heart the label of Russian dervish that people gave him in Iran, and cherished his title of Gul-Mulla, the priest of flowers: "Nothing as honorable as being the Gul-Mulla, spring's treasurer of golden ink."[65] Paradoxically, while Khlebnikov was not very useful as a political lecturer in Gilan and spent most of his time in a teahouse smoking opium as his friend, the artist Dobrokovsky, drew caricatures and talked to the locals, his revolutionary comrades in arms viewed this behaviour as a kind of "cultural diplomacy" that promoted their cause:

> Nesmotria na strannost' etikh shtatnykh agitatorov. Revvoensovet armii spravedlivo schital ikh sovershenno neobkhodimymi rabotnikami. V religioznykh i bytovykh usloviiakh togo vremeni, pri nastorozhennom vnimanii k russkim revoliutsioneram, nesushchim na svoikh znamenakh sovershenno neobychainye lozungi, "russkie dervishi" kakim-to trudno ob"iasnimym obrazom usilivali nashi politicheskie pozitsii.[66]

> (Despite the strangeness of these staff agitators, Revvoensovet [revolutionary army council] rightly considered them to be absolutely indispensable workers. Within the religious and living conditions of that time, with wary attention directed to the Russian revolutionaries, who carried on their banners quite extraordinary slogans, these "Russian dervishes," in a way that is hard to explain, strengthened our political positions.)

In his turn, in a letter to his family Khlebnikov describes the multiethnic group of Russian revolutionaries in Persia as "adventurers from the gangs of Amerigo Vespucci and Ferdinand Cortéz [Hernán Cortés]."[67] "Amerigo, Cortés, Columbuses [Columbus and his brothers]" also appear in Khlebnikov's anti-war poem "War in a Mousetrap."[68] While Tynianov uses the names of Cortéz and Columbus in his novel to denounce colonization, Khlebnikov's view of these historical figures is harder to interpret. Although the word "gangs" (*shaiki*) clearly has a negative connotation, adventurers and conquistadors could also represent courage and the ability to see the world afresh, as they do in Nikolay Gumilev's poetry. Gumilev's praise of the "captains" in search of new lands, "all those who dare, who want, who search, who are weary of the countries of the fathers,"[69] seems to have inspired Khlebnikov's poetic prediction that

Ot startsev glupykh veshchie iunoshi uidut
I osnuiut mirovoe gosudarstvo
Grazhdan odnogo vozrasta.[70]

(From foolish elders the prophetic youths will go away
And found a world state
Of citizens of the same age.)

Khlebnikov's adventurers may represent revolutionary zeal rather than colonization. The idea of a new state appears in Tynianov's novelistic parody as the conspiracy of the Decembrists to found a new state in the Caucasus, and Griboedov's dreams of revolutionizing the Transcaucasian economy, making it autonomous from the rest of the empire.

Khlebnikov's creative convergence with acmeism and adamism, a poetic movement that prompts one "to look at things already known with a fresh and enthusiastic gaze, like Adam on the first day of creation,"[71] is apparent in his Persian poems. In "Gul-Mulla's Trumpet," he calls Persia "the country where all people are Adams," a pun, since the word "adam" means "man, human person" in Persian.[72] The "Nowruz of Labour" welcomes the fresh beginning that revolution was meant to bring to Persia:

Snova my pervye dni chelovechestva!
Adam za Adamom
Prokhodiat tolpoi …[73]

(Once more, we are the first days of the humankind!
Adam after Adam,
They pass in a crowd …)

Representing a new beginning and at the same time destruction of the pristine New World, the discoverers and pioneers evoke mixed feelings in Khlebnikov. So does the figure of a Russian adventurer, Stenka Razin, with whom Khlebnikov identifies. Stenka the revolutionary and the daring seafarer arouses Khlebnikov's admiration, but the notorious affair with the Persian princess requires reconsideration, and the poet comes up with the formula in which he is Razin with an opposite sign:

Ia – Razin naprotiv,
Ia – Razin navyvorot …
On grabil i zheg, a ia slova bozhok …
Razin devu
V vode utopil.
Chto sdelaiu ia? Naoborot? Spasu![74]

(I am Razin the opposite,
I am Razin inside out …
He plundered and burned, and I am an idol of the word …
Razin drowned the maiden
In water.
What will I do? Quite the reverse? I will save her!)

Real-life "Oriental" maidens waiting to be saved watch the red banners carried during the New Year revolutionary procession in "Nowruz of Labour:"

Poodal', kak budto u russkoi svobody na paperti,
Revnivoi temnitseiu zaperty,
Strogie grustnye devy islama.
Chernoi chadroiu zakutany,
Osvoboditelia zhdut oni.[75]

(Further off, as beggars on the porch of Russian freedom,
Locked up by a jealous dungeon,
Austere sad maidens of Islam.
Enveloped in a black chador,
They are awaiting a liberator.)

In "Gul-Mulla's Trumpet" women in black chadors and white headscarves appear to the poet as bottles of wine with "little white heads over black glass" that he is planning to uncork "lazily."[76] They have "animalistically scared eyes, stupidly adorable."[77] Khlebnikov's poetic representation conforms to the stereotype of helpless, "infantile," and irrational "Oriental women" awaiting their saviour, which neither his new revolutionary consciousness nor his fresh poetic outlook were able to erase. It is hard to agree with Tynianov's statement that "Gul-Mulla's

Trumpet" is a poem written from a level point of view without a Westerner's condescension or exoticizing reverence.

Local men in Khlebnikov's *Persian Poems* appear as primeval Adams, mighty workers, and savage horsemen "with a bandit charm" of mountaineers.[78] It seems, however, that they too are ready to accept guidance from the Russian revolutionaries. An interesting detail, both in "Gul-Mulla's Trumpet" and in the "Nowruz of Labour," is that Khlebnikov describes men wrapped in shawls:

V shaliakh voiny ... [79]
Ikh smuglye litsa okutany v shali.[80]

(The warriors are in shawls ...
Their swarthy faces are wrapped in shawls.)

In Tynianov's parody, as noted above, the Iranian shah's ministers wrapped in shawls are like brides, looking at Griboedov as at a rich but repulsive groom.[81]

During his employment with the Persian Red Army, Khlebnikov wandered off to a mountain village, where he stayed with the family of a local khan and tutored his son and daughter. While imaginary Persian women-children, whom the poet promises to save, are painted in the impersonal style of post-Impressionist primitivism, the real child of this hospitable country awakens his true empathy:

I vot zelenoe ushchel'e Zorgama.
Khannochka, kak babochka opustilas',
Prisela na tsynovku i vodit ukazkoi po uchebniku.
Ogromnye slezy katiatsia iz skorbnykh bol'shikh glaz.
Eto gore.
Slabaia, skorbnaia ulybka krivit guby.
Pervoe detskoe gore.
Ona spriatala knizhku, chtoby propustit' urok,
No ee bol'shie liudi otyskali i prinesli.[82]

(And here is the green gorge of Zorgam.
Khan's little daughter like a butterfly came down,
Sat on the mat and
Is moving the pointer along the textbook.
Enormous tears are rolling
From sorrowful big eyes.
This is grief.

A weak, sorrowful smile is twisting her lips.
The first childhood grief. She hid
The book, in order to skip the class,
But the big people found it and brought it here.)

According to Ronald Vroon, the girl in Khlebnikov's poetic imagination is combined with the images of a mermaid and the drowned Persian princess, whom he vowed to save. While this is definitely true, Vroon's assumption that Khlebnikov's attitude towards the girl "implies something more than a platonic relationship – in thought, if not in deed" is not plausible. Vroon argues that the sequence describing the girl is followed by a dream, in which "the poet sees a gypsy woman singing and dancing suggestively," and thus "the little princess" transforms "into the provocative gypsy."[83] This interpretation is not convincing. The dance of the "gypsy" in blue and black tatters with a bucket on her head is spirited and self-asserting rather that suggestive. She is not the Persian princess, because she and her camp are moving towards Persia, and the poet is joining them. The multi-ethnic, colourful Persian Red Army, which Khlebnikov joined and which was formed in Baku to aid the revolution in Gilan, is a better biographical prototype for the dancing and singing gypsies. Initially joining the camp, the poet himself would like to become the leader of the revolutionary transformation that is taking place in Persia. He wants to "jump from the mountains and sweep along" with him the "population of these mountains" carried by "the avalanche of wild life and laughter."[84]

A "gypsy" camp as a carrier of progress appears also in Khlebnikov's "Letter to Two Japanese Men." In the letter, among the suggested topics to be discussed at the "Asian Congress" of young men is a proposal to organize inventor camps (*tabory izobretateli*) and to "obligate the neighbouring towns and villages to nourish them and worship them."[85]

In his poem, the futurist Khlebnikov leads his fellow travellers into the "sounds populated by people," the city of "sound logs" and "sound stones," of "sound food" and "sound eaters," in which "logs are made of laughter and streets of singing."[86] From there he takes them to the happy city of the future in which little children, "leaning against the windowsill," could read "glass books," "the city of glass pages."[87] Finally, he invites them to the city made of "austere logs of time." He asks his fellow traveller "carpenters" to "chip centuries into carpenters' boards."[88]

The "carpenters" appear to be ethnically Russian, since Khlebnikov suggests that they tie up their "Slavic curls" with "linden bast" before getting started with their task. He asserts the messianic role of the Russians in bringing revolutionary change to Persia, the country of "swarthy ancestors" and "black browed boys" who "quietly look at the mountains" with "Russian sadness in their eyes." The boys are "savage" and "resemble goats."[89] They call the poet "urus dervish," Russian dervish, "tovarishch," comrade, and "gul'-mulla," the priest of flowers.[90] The pacifist Khlebnikov is hopeful of bringing revolution through poetry, prophecy based on the law of numbers that he discovered in order to be able to predict history and avert future bloodshed.

At the end of the poem, Khlebnikov sees Persia as a "pot of passion" to which he would like to add his "futurist's fire [*budetlianskii ogon'*]." Finally, he looks at it as a scientist, and before his "intelligent eyes of a chemist," this "country with its past millennia is a glass tube ... and his brain depends on the kinks of happiness." Into this mix, he would like to "throw [surfaces and angles], a piece of another world."[91]

Khlebnikov's poetry is abundant in sequences in which the transformation of Persia depends on the help of an outside agent, a scientist, a carpenter, a poet, or a prophet. That being said, "Gul-Mulla's Trumpet" and "You See, Persians, Here I Come" do refer to events in Iranian history, in which men and women of the country have agency in initiating and pushing for social change:

Klianemsia volosami Gurriet el' Ain,
Klianemsia zolotymi ustami Zaratustry –
Persiia budet sovetskoi stranoi.
Tak govorit propok![92]

(We swear by the hair of Gurriet el Ain [Qurrat al-'Ayn],
We swear by the golden mouth of Zarathustra,
Persia will be a soviet counry,
Thus spoke the prophet!)

Here Khlebnikov connects current revolution with the religious teachings of the past, somewhat similarly to Blok, who puts Jesus Christ in charge of the red guards in Petersburg in his poem "The Twelve."[93] The golden mouth (*zolotye usta*) of Zarathustra brings together Zoroastrianism and Christianity, alluding to John Chrysostom (Zlatoust), an early Church Father, who denounced abuse of authority. Qurrat al-'Ayn is a nineteenth-century poet and thinker, whose religious quest resulted in her belief in a continuous spiritual evolution and progress of humankind.[94] Joining the like-minded Babi movement, she became a religious teacher and a charismatic leader "equal to the Bab himself, at times even more determined than him and other leading Babis to register her rejection of the prevailing order."[95]

Qurrat al-'Ayn considered her time to be a transition, during which, in expectation of the new divine emanation, the old religious obligations lost their meaning. She appeared unveiled before the congress of her co-religionists, and received support from Bab, who called her Tahira (pure) to shield her from charges of immorality.[96] Qurrat al-'Ayn's teaching was not feminist, although it attracted a large number of female followers. However, her belief in "human progression," as well as her desire for freedom of inquiry and an opportunity to establish the truth through debate, inevitably resulted in her revolt against the tradition.[97] In 1852, she was tried and executed after a group of Babis unsuccessfully attempted to assassinate the shah.[98]

She was strangled in secret in a garden, and her body was dumped in a well. Different accounts mention that she was strangled with her own handkerchief that she had previously chosen, with a rope, or with her own hair. Khlebnikov in his poems mentions both hair and a rope, and also underscores Qurrat al-'Ayn's volition in choosing the terms of her own execution:

> Gurriet-el'-Ain,
> Takhire, sama
> Zatianula na sebe kontsy verevok,
> Sprosiv palachei, povernuv golovu:
> "Bol'she nichego?"[99]

> (Gurriet-el-Ayn,
> Tahire, herself
> Tightened the ends of the ropes,
> Having asked the executioners, turning her head: "Nothing else?")

Khlebnikov studied Bab's teachings and was eager to see it as an anticipation of the future revolutionary movement. As a "Kul'tprosvet" lecturer, he was preparing a talk that would compare Babism with Christianity:

> Uezzhaia iz Baku, ia zanialsia izucheniem Mirza-Baba, persidskogo propoka, i o nem budu chitat' zdes' dlia persov i russkikh: "Mirza-Bab i Iisus". Persam ia skazal, chto ia russkii propok.[100]

> (Leaving Baku, I started studying Mirza-Bab, a Persian prophet, and I will give a lecture about him here both for the Persians and the Russians: "Mirza-Bab and Jesus." I told the Persians that I am a Russian prophet.)

A more militant Babi movement eventually evolved into Baha'ism, with its emphasis on religious universalism and a pacifist outlook. Khlebnikov, who was against war, adhered to the idea of spiritual revolution that would eliminate violence once and forever. This spirituality is universalist and absorbs all previous religions and liberation movements. In his poem a Persian woman, Qurrat al-'Ayn, has agency in bringing forth the spiritual transformation of her country. However, after her martyrdom she becomes the Persian land itself, a passive victim of oppression in wait for a liberator:

Eto ee mertvoe telo – snezhnye gory.
Temnye nozdri gor
Zhadno vtiagivaiut
Zapakh Razina,
Veter s moria.
Ia edu.[101]

(It is her dead body – the snowy mountains.
The dark nostrils of the mountains
Avidly draw in
The smell of Razin,
The wind from the sea.
I am on my way.)

Qurrat al-'Ayn is at the same time the Persian land and the Persian princess ready to meet her Razin, none other than Khlebnikov himself. While the revolutionary-minded poet inverts the image of Razin and presents himself as anti-Razin, his final message is traditionally Orientalist: the futurist poet and prophet from the West will save the woman of the East together with her country.

In Tynianov's novel, Griboedov-Razin does not save the princess. He feels guilty for ruining the life of his young wife, Princess Chavchavadze, the colonized "infant Asia" of his imagination, asking himself, "Why did you marry the girl, the child, and leave her? She is tormented now with pregnancy waiting for you."[102] Juxtaposing the representation of Stepan Razin in the works of his nineteenth-century protagonist, Alexander Griboedov, and his contemporaries, the futurists, Tynianov reveals both the imperialist agenda of the former and the revolutionary expansionism of the latter as problematic approaches to the relationship between Russia and Iran, or Russia and its "own Orient," Transcaucasia.

Chapter Six

The "Treacherous Eunuch": Search for Authenticity

Starting chapter 6 of his novel *The Death of Vazir-Mukhtar* with a parodic Orientalist reference to the "treacherous" nature of eunuchs, Yury Tynianov proceeds to sketch a number of relatable human characters.[1] The most important among them is the character of Mirza Yakub, the eunuch from Fath Ali Shah's harem and the shah's treasurer. Mirza Yakub's request for asylum in the Russian mission and his declaration of a desire to become a Russian citizen were the main triggers for the 1829 tragedy in Teheran, recorded in both the accounts of his contemporaries and the historical re-evaluations of the events. Siding with a British conspiracy theory as one of the possible causes of the tragedy, Tynianov clears Mirza Yakub of accusations that he was collaborating with the British. Nor does he interpret Mirza Yakub's desire to flee the shah's harem as a pursuit of financial gain, of which the eunuch was also accused. Instead, Mirza Yakub's longing to return to the place of his birth appears in the novel as a quest for authenticity and personal freedom.

The conflict in the novel between individual happiness and confinement in a harem follows the pattern established by Montesquieu in his *Persian Letters*.[2] Like the eighteenth-century Enlightenment thinker, Tynianov uses the image of the harem to allude to the status of personal freedom in his own country, Stalinist Russia. At the same time, Tynianov, scholar of nineteenth-century literature, reveals how the motifs of the harem and "Oriental despotism" changed during the period described in his historical novel. In nineteenth-century Russian Orientalist texts, and most importantly the writings of Alexander Pushkin and Alexander Griboedov, veiled criticism of the Russian Empire as an "Oriental despotism" coexists and at times is outweighed by criticism of the Orient itself and justification of Russian expansionism as a "civilizing mission." Tynianov's novel is a parodic representation of despotism in Iran as viewed by Russian Orientalist writers, who are either promoting colonialism or criticizing the autocracy of Nicholas I. At the same time, their references to "Oriental despotism" serve Tynianov as an Aesopian language to vent his own anxieties about the tightening grip of Stalinism in the late 1920s.

The Mighty Three

To introduce the motif of castration, Tynianov provides a graphic description of the gelding of a horse, which reacts to that treachery with tears falling from his "crazed" eyes into the snow and yet, since horses have short memories, soon becomes an obedient worker and stops neighing for good,[3] an allusion to Tolstoy's novella "Knolstomer."[4] Unlike horses, humans have long memories, and "the hollows in their bodies are dreadful."[5] They retaliate with their own treachery and avenge their humiliation. Tynianov goes on, overwhelming the reader with an enumeration of treacherous, revengeful, and cruel castrates described in the ancient Greek sources.[6] The only truly evil castrate from recent Iranian history, however, is Agha Mohammad Khan, the founder of the Qajar dynasty, who centralized Iran and restored its domination in the South Caucasus. Tynianov describes the brutality with which he sacked and burned down Tbilisi in 1795, killing many people and taking the surviving population back to Iran.[7] Establishing a symbolic and factual connection between enslavement and castration, Tynianov depicts an embittered eunuch who inflicts on other people the same calamity he had suffered.

Creating several parallels between Iranian and Russian rulers, he depicts the cruel autocrat Nicholas I as an "incomplete man." While trying to subvert the Orientalist image of a treacherous eunuch, Tynianov himself falls prey to the gender stereotypes of his time. His Nicholas is an effeminate creature with "perfect thighs" dressed in moose-skin leggings of a "sweet," "almost edible" white colour, who like "a woman has a habit to ponder a lot on what people talk and think about him, and whose treatment of others was not manly."[8] The emperor and Griboedov watch a ballet performance in which the male dancer, looking like "a flying fool," has "silly white thighs" just like Nicholas. The dancer performs the part of Acis, possibly from Handel's pastoral ballet "Acis and Galatea,"[9] whose name sounds similar to "Attis," name of the Greek god who castrated himself in ecstatic dedication to the goddess Cybele. The myth of Attis rendered by the Roman poet Catullus appeared in the 1918 article "Catilina" written by the Russian symbolist poet Alexander Blok in the wake of the October Revolution.[10] Blok equates Attis's ecstasy and self-castration to the transformative power of revolution that he eagerly welcomes.

In his novel, Tynianov counters the idea of revolution as castration. The castrate is the revengeful tyrant, such as Nicholas, who strangles the revolution, represented in the novel by the Decembrist uprising, and turns the survivors into eunuchs – collaborators in his despotic regime. While equating revolutionary zeal with masculinity reveals Tynianov's traditional view of gender roles, the fundamental tragedy of castration is in one's alienation from one's former self and the submission to someone else's will, and affects both male and female characters in the novel. By rebutting Blok's idea of castration as a desirable and sublime state, Tynianov goes against the irrationalism and mysticism of the Silver Age, whose artists were fascinated with the Russian religious sect of Skoptsy and with their practice of self-castration as a means to overcome lust and achieve spiritual purification. Tynianov cites a stanza from a Skoptsy song about bridling a horse as an epigraph for the chapter that tells the story of Mirza Yakub's enslavement and castration.[11] Bridling or shoeing a horse represented castration in Skoptsy's imagery; they also believed that after the final stage of initiation, the consecrated members of the sect would be able to mount the white horse of the Apocalypse and escape from hell. The sect was not averse to accumulating wealth and high social status and believed that Russian tsars were secretly Skoptsy too, a myth that makes Tynianov's representation of Nicholas as a eunuch more grounded in folk imagination. Parodying the mystical millenarianism of the Silver Age, Tynianov falls back on the rationalism and humanism of the Enlightenment thinkers, such as Montesquieu who interprets the characters of the three eunuchs of the shah's harem Tynianov depicts in his novel.

At first Tynianov makes his reader believe that, similar to the cruel former ruler of Iran and his autocratic Russian counterpart, the three eunuchs from Fath Ali Shah's harem who appear in the real time of the novel will conform to the stereotype of an evil overseer. This stereotype is exploited in Russian romantic Orientalist writing, such as Pushkin's early poem "The Fountain of Bakhchisaray."[12] Soon after, however, Tynianov inverts the image of eunuchs as villains, depicting instead traumatized individuals who cope with their past, each in his own way. The "hollows" of their bodies come with spiritual emptiness that each of the three is trying to fill with his own passions and ambitions. The oldest eunuch, Manuchehr Khan, accumulates wealth and expands his power; the youngest, Khosrow Khan, collects and trains horses that outshine those from the shah's stables; while Mirza Yakub, the most important eunuch in the novel, has a passion for knowledge and spends most of his time reading books.[13]

The three eunuchs of Tynianov's novel differ a great deal from Pushkin's lifeless "dummy" whose "soul does not seek love," and who responds to neither the abuses nor the pleadings of the wives he is in charge of.[14] Far from being apathetic, Tynianov's eunuchs experience a wide range of emotions akin to the characters from Montesquieu's *Persian Letters*, who are saddened by and angry at losing their "humanity," and at being separated "forever from their very selves."[15] In both Tynianov and Montesquieu's books, the eunuchs compensate for their loss with an increase in their social status, power, and wealth. Whereas in Montesquieu's depiction of the harem as a model of a stratified society eunuchs exercise their power solely over the wives, Tynianov shows them as important administrative figures of the shah's court.

Representing them as influential administrators, Tynianov facilitates a parallel between the eunuchs and Russian administrative officials, most importantly Griboedov himself. The emphasis on Mirza Yakub's scientific or scholarly aspirations – as the Russian word *nauka* refers to both science and scholarly pursuit – also prompts the reader to compare him to Griboedov, who complained in letters to his friends that his diplomatic work did not leave him time to keep up with the advances of science. At the same time, that emphasis implies the eunuch's similarity with Tynianov, the literary scholar and theorist. The position of the eunuchs within the harem as both victims and benefiting collaborators of despotism reflects what Tynianov perceives as similar arrangements between Griboedov and the autocratic government of Nicholas, and, at the same time, the novelist's own compromise with the Stalinist regime.

This compromise is at least semi-voluntary in Montesquieu's *Persian Letters*, as a boy, before becoming a eunuch, had to agree to castration. Reflecting on that pivotal moment of his life at an older age, one of the eunuchs views it as a practical calculation on his part, an agreement to trade his masculinity for financial security and higher social status, rather than as a decision made simply out of fear of punishment. Senior eunuchs in the harem help the young ones to undergo the same transition, soothing their tears and explaining to them the benefits of their compromise.[16] As Corey Robin points out, Montesquieu's book reveals that fear alone is not enough to support a despotic regime. It is fueled by ambition and the promise of social advancement and cemented by the mentorship of senior members of the society, who advise the young on how to survive and live comfortably in given circumstances.[17]

Tynianov's collaborators, who are being transformed (*prevrashchaemye*), seem to have even less choice than the boys who are coerced to choose the path of eunuchs. His view of history as a blind and brutal force expresses itself in the image of the sack they fling on the horse's head when they geld it. Griboedov's "transformation" takes place after the failed Decembrist uprising, when he is forced to collaborate with the officials, who executed some of his friends and sentenced others to hard labour in Siberia or penal military service in the Caucasus. Tynianov, as noted above, describes the suppression of the Decembrist uprising as a moment in which "time suddenly broke in two,"[18] alluding to Stalin's slogan of the *velikii perelom* (great break), the name he gave to the second cultural revolution of 1927–31.[19] This transformation forces Tynianov to scale down his aspirations to revolutionize literary theory, and to watch the demise of many avant-garde artists and writers. Ironically, the restraints on his freedom as a literary theorist launch his career as a novelist. Both his protagonist, Griboedov, and, implicitly, the novelist himself are alienated from their former identities by relentless and blind despotism.

In Montesquieu's book, it is the most oppressed members of the system, the wives of the harem, who initiate a rebellion against despotism and attempt to reconnect with their lost identity. They do it through asserting their natural right to choose whom they love. The more privileged eunuchs do not rebel because they have more to lose, as they had sacrificed much to acquire their wealth and social status. At the same time, being unable to love and to procreate, they are devoid of both the means and the goals for a rebellion. The lack of ability for physical love, according to Montesquieu, does not eliminate the desire, and so castration is not simply a trauma of the past but a deep loss of which the eunuchs are constantly reminded. Tynianov further develops this motif of impossible love in his novel. While the oldest eunuch, Manuchehr Khan, seems to be content with his power and chests full of money, Mirza Yakub and Khosrow Khan long for something greater than their passion for knowledge or for beautiful horses.

The Story of Dil Firuz

Alluding to Montesquieu, Tynianov wonders about the dark and incomprehensible love of a eunuch, and then proceeds to describe the bond between the youngest eunuch, Khosrow Khan, and a captive little girl, Nazlu. Khosrow Khan gives Nazlu a new name, Dil Firuz, which Tynianov translates as "joy."[20] It alludes to the name of Dilara Bikech, who according to popular imagination was a captive in the Crimean khan's harem and the prototype of Pushkin's Maria from "The Fountain of Bakhchisaray."

Castrated in early childhood, Khosrow Khan barely retains his "masculine memory" and is the most content of the three eunuchs with his present identity of an "amazon"; he is "indecisive as a woman and brave as an equestrian," an effeminate lover of horses, which he collects and trains.[21] He starts to spend less time with his horses, however, when a friend of his gives him a captive girl as a present. The girl is smart, talkative, and likes to giggle, and Khosrow Khan bonds with her by telling her the funniest stories he knows, buying her dresses and jewelry, and indulging her with her favourite dishes. The girl grows to like Khosrow Khan's mascaraed eyes and his "unmanly gaiety" and feels proud and anxious watching him train his horses through a coloured window. Although the girl and Khosrow Khan laugh together and horse around on the carpet (*vozilis'*), their physical contact is devoid of eroticism and their relationship reminds one of that between a girl and her adoptive mother.[22] Yet, while not violently, Khosrow Khan attempts to erase Nazlu's childhood memories and to make her forget her former identity just as he was once forced to do. This erasure of memory is similar to training a horse rather than gelding it, and while not physically brutal, is spiritually devastating.

Unlike Khosrow Khan, Mirza Yakub was enslaved and castrated as a young adult when, carrying only a bag of books on his back, he joined a caravan of Georgian volunteer fighters and Armenian merchants on their way to Tbilisi, intending to study with a famous Armenian scientist who had just moved there. He joined the caravan when it was passing by the monastery of Ejmiatsin, where he, a son of poor Armenian parents, enrolled to perfect his knowledge of the medieval Armenian language. Enroute, an Iranian detachment attacked the caravan, and those who survived were enslaved and sent to Tabriz. There, as Tynianov puts it, "the Persian state castrated him without malice or hatred because it was in need of eunuchs."[23] Being educated, he soon found himself in the shah's harem in charge of his finances. Together with two other eunuchs, he founded a business selling merchandise to the shah's wives and was able to send money back to support his parents.[24]

Unlike Montesquieu, Tynianov does not present the eunuchs as being constantly repressed and humiliated while taking revenge by exercising power over the wives. Guarding the wives does not seem to be the responsibility of the three eunuchs that appear in the novel. They are political advisers and administrative managers of the shah, whose lives are comfortable and respectable. Yet "wealthy, shapely, and educated" Mirza Yakub, who has the luxury of spending most of his time in the library he had collected, cannot sleep at nights: "With dry eyes he stared at the smooth ceiling. Emptiness lay next to him. When it became too large, he fell asleep."[25] He fills this spiritual emptiness with his thoughts of Nazlu, whom he first sees when he visits Khosrow Khan to discuss business. He starts visiting her often, brings her presents, hugs her, and tries to persuade her to come and live with him. The two eunuchs ask Nazlu whom she would prefer to live with, and she chooses to stay with Khosrow Khan.[26]

Soon Nazlu faces another choice: whether to stay with Khosrow Khan, to whom she has become attached, or return to her family. In conformity with the Turkmenchay peace treaty, which Griboedov helped to negotiate and was charged with implementing, the captives, who were born on the territory that was now under Russian government, were given a chance to return to the place of their birth. Nazlu's family delegated her uncle to come to Tehran to take her home. Being used to the luxury that Khosrow Khan had surrounded her with, she is appalled by the treats that her uncle brought: two sweet lemons and cheap candy covered with dirt from his pocket. But when the uncle begins to weep and ask her if she remembers him, the girl squeals like a dog, hides her face in her uncle's hands, and starts licking them instead of kissing.[27]

This behaviour, reminiscent of a dog that lost and then found her owner, is an allusion to Anton Chekhov's popular story "Kashtanka." A seemingly simple story, often included in reading lists for middle-school children, it explores the mysteries of life and death, memory, loyalty, and identity. It describes the adventures of a dog that lost her owners: a carpenter and his young son, a boy who used to play roughly and abuse Kashtanka. A nice circus performer adopts the dog and takes care of her, while training her for one of his shows. During the very first show, the carpenter and his son happen to be in the audience. They recognize the dog and call her name. Kashtanka with a "joyful squeal" runs through the audience towards the top rows, "being transferred from hands to hands, and licking people's hands and faces."[28] Going back home with her former people, the dog thinks that "she has been following them for a long time, happy that her life was never interrupted even for a moment," while her days at the circus performer's place "appeared to her now as a long, deranged, heavy dream."[29]

The allusion to Kashtanka marks Nazlu and Mirza Yakub as the only "transformed" characters in the novel who are determined to return their former identities. The eunuch's vigils are similar to those of the dog in Chekhov's story. While both are content with their daytime routines, at night Mirza Yakub is overcome with gradually growing emptiness,[30] and the dog with sadness that "crept up to her insensibly and overtook her gradually, the way darkness overtakes a room." Before she falls asleep, in her imagination the carpenter and his son come to her as "two indistinct figures, either dogs or people, with physiognomies likable and sweet, but incomprehensible," and she feels that she saw them somewhere and that she used to love them, and they "smell like glue, wood shavings and varnish."[31]

During the emotional scene when Nazlu decides to go home, Khosrow Khan also starts to cry without knowing if he was feeling sorry for the girl, her uncle, or himself. Only Mirza Yakub was standing "lost in thought," pondering the possibility of his own return to his birthplace.[32] Just like Kashtanka, Mirza Yakub imagines the two important people he left at home, his parents. His memories are as sensual as those of the dog. If for Kashtanka memories of the people she loved are inseparable from the smell of glue and wood shavings, Mirza Yakub's mental recreation of his parents lingers on the tangible images of the evening table "at which his father is sitting talking to a neighbour," and "the clean tablecloth" with which his mother is covering the table.[33] And like Kashtanka, who felt continuity between her past at the carpenter's house and her present reunion with him and his son, Mirza Yakub sees the fifteen years in Teheran, his "temporary life of a castrate," as a mere interruption of his real life.[34] After making up his mind to ask for asylum in the Russian mission, "Hodja Mirza Yakub never hesitated anymore. It seemed to him that all his life the only thing he thought about was the Russian embassy."[35]

To contemporaries of the historical Mirza Yakub, his determination appeared to be the inexplicable stubbornness of a person willing to give up a life of wealth, power, and security. Iranian sources, such as Fath Ali Shah's letter to his son and heir Abbas Mirza, argued that Mirza Yakub owed money to the shah's treasury and accused him of insulting the faith of Muslims in the Sharia court, where he was summoned after requesting Russian asylum and a return to the place of his birth. Russian sources also speculated on the reasons for Mirza Yakub's determination, one of them arguing that the eunuch secretly remained a Christian, did not hold the distinctions granted him by the Iranian court in high regard, and always dreamed of returning to his motherland. Mirza Yakub countered the Iranian accusation that he wanted to escape his debt to the shah's treasury by accusing the court of wanting him to stay because it inherited the possessions of eunuchs after their death. Another interpretation of events suggested that British diplomats were the ones who incited Mirza Yakub to leave the palace and instigate the ensuing massacre of the Russian mission, because of their animosity towards Griboedov and the rivalry between the Russian and British empires.

In Tynianov's novel, the angry mob that attacks the Russian mission is galvanized by economic and cultural oppression, by poverty exacerbated by the war and high indemnity, while a British conspiracy only serves as the last impetus to the disorder. As for Mirza Yakub's decision to return to the newly acquired Russian territories, the place of his birth, Tynianov suggests of him the innermost motivations of searching for one's identity, leaving aside other possible reasons such as religious beliefs or national pride. In this quiet but resolved rebellion of personal freedom against domestic and societal tyranny, Tynianov's character follows that of Roxane, the wife of Usbek from *Persian Letters*, who asserts her personal liberty by choosing her love partner in defiance of the rules of the harem.[36] For Mirza Yakub, his path towards liberation lies through restoring his spiritual wholeness. He decides to restart his old life, returning to the place where he lived as a free man as if his captivity never happened.

In Montesquieu's book, only the wives are inclined to rebel, while the eunuchs, unable to see their own existence outside of the harem hierarchy, try hard to suppress that rebellion. In Tynianov's novel, the eunuchs not only collaborate among each other, but also display solidarity with the captive wives who want to take advantage of the right to return home that the Turkmenchay treaty grants them. Mirza Yakub and the eunuch of Alayar Khan, the shah's son-in-law, help two of the latter's wives to seek and receive asylum in the Russian mission, by informing Griboedov about their captivity and desire to return to their motherland. Tynianov uses the revolutionary term "*stachka*" (strike) to describe the collaboration of the two eunuchs, although he claims that the wives bribed the eunuch of Alayar Khan,[37] who was among the most important instigators of the Russo-Persian War of 1826–8, and continued to propagate mistrust of Russia and its representative, Griboedov, after the peace treaty was signed. Tynianov, however, does not implicate Mirza Yakub in a political conspiracy against Iran and in favour of Russia, and interprets his decision to go home, as mentioned above, as exercising personal freedom.

Griboedov as a Eunuch

The parallels between the character of Mirza Yakub and the main protagonist, Griboedov, are many in Tynianov's novel. They are both influential administrators and scholars fluent in a number of languages, and at the same time are both individuals who had been "transformed," "castrated." They are victims of the despotic political systems in which they live, and the blind cruelty of history that does not have regard for individual lives and freedoms.

Another common feature of the two characters is their loyalty to their families. Both endure the unfreedom of their social position in order to help their families by sending money home. Tynianov imagines Mirza Yakub's poor parents exclaiming "Thank God!" whenever they receive his money.[38] While this does seem like a betrayal and exploitation of their son's misfortune, the novelist judges Griboedov's mother even more harshly: Nastasia Fedorovna, as Tynianov portrays her, consciously manipulates her son into accepting the position of the head of the Russian mission in Iran, as the most lucrative of the careers he could choose from after his successful negotiation of the Turkmenchay treaty. Griboedov's mother in the novel is both greedy and prodigal, calculating and impractical, and in constant need of money. Examining her attempts to redecorate the house while he was away, her son views the result as a pathetic transformation of his childhood home into an ornamental, "Asiatic" dwelling to which he feels attached nevertheless:

> Vse bylo neudavshaiasia Aziia, razorenie i obman.
> Ne khvatalo, chtoby steny i potolok byli okleeny raznotsvetnymi zerkal'nymi kusochkami, kak v Persii. Tak bylo by pestree.
> Eto byl ego dom, ego Heim, ego detstvo. I kak on vse eto liubil.[39]
>
> (It all was Asia manqué, devastation and deception.
> They could as well glue varicoloured glassy pieces on the walls and the ceiling, like in Persia. That would be more variegated.
> This was his home, his Heim, his childhood. And how he loved all this.)

Introducing "Asiatic luxury" mixed with "Asiatic impracticality" into her son's childhood home, she inadvertently reminds him about the dreaded diplomatic appointment in Iran, which she wants him to accept. Both Nastasia Fedorovna's insistence that her son become a diplomat in Iran and Griboedov's persistent desire to avoid it are documented in the letters and memoirs of their contemporaries. Describing their family relationship, Tynianov adheres to his usual manner of introducing words and phrases from the original texts while misplacing them or slightly changing their meaning for comical effect. Thus, in a letter to a friend, Stepan Begichev, Griboedov complains that his mother applied a *patka* with cologne to his forehead to cure his headache, instead causing burns on his skin.[40] Tynianov uses the word *patka,* which apparently means a pat or a dab in the original, to describe Nastasia Fedorovna's hair, "not grey but colourless," that she shakes during the conversation with her son about his possible appointment to Persia.[41]

It is not a coincidence that the complaint about the *patka* comes from one of Griboedov's many letters in which he disparages Iran, calling it a "stupid land [*duratskaia zemlia*]" and its inhabitants "savage-looking Asiatics [*dikoobraznye aziatcy*]."[42] Many scholars of Russian Orientalism describe it as different and somehow "milder" than its Western variety, because of Russian intellectuals' recognition of their country's separate path, its role of a middle ground between the East and the West. This does not quite apply to the literary figures of the 1820s, including Pushkin and Griboedov. Instead, as Elena Andreeva points out, anxiety over belonging to the "civilized" nations makes their criticism of the Orient harsher.[43] While in Russia, Griboedov laments the Westernization of the country's elite and longs for the return of the Russian national dress; in the Caucasus and Iran he presents himself as a European, burdened with a "civilizing mission."

Griboedov often reiterates the Orientalist trope of his time about finding depravity and desolation while expecting to see sophistication and luxury. The usual complaint of travellers of his period about the lack of fine European linen in the "Orient" also becomes subject matter for Tynianov's parodies. Thus, for example, the crown prince Abbas Mirza in the novel, deep in thought about the ways he could influence Griboedov to reduce the amount of the war reparations, takes out "a European handkerchief and blows his nose."[44] The eunuch Mirza Yakub's most vivid recollection of life in his childhood home is the moment when his mother covers the table with a clean tablecloth.[45] His forceful captivity keeps him away from this modest but essential luxury, which in his imagination represents his motherland. At the same time, one of the main reasons he tolerates his captivity is the opportunity it affords him to help his parents financially.

Financial help to his mother is also the main reason for Griboedov's voluntary captivity in the "Orient" that he despises, and separation from his motherland. Having a motherland in Tynianov's novel goes hand in hand with having fine linen. Unlike the poor uprooted pianists of his epoch, who wear tailcoats over their naked bodies, "Griboedov had beautiful fine linen, and he had a motherland."[46] The juxtaposition of "linen and motherland" is similar to that of "samovar and Christianity" in Tynianov's parody of Pushkin's formula of colonial policies that would "tame" the "savage" peoples of the Caucasus through sharing with them the material and spiritual wealth of "civilization."[47] This new formula is just as subversive. As we find out from another passage of the novel, Griboedov's "white, fine, nobleman's linen" is "woven by serf women, the very same ones who one fine day roused a riot."[48]

Thus, the motif of fine linen transmutes from a symbol of progress into a reminder of oppression. It alludes to the despotism of Griboedov's mother, who, according to Griboedov's biographer Piksanov, was not only an authoritarian parent but also an oppressive landowner. The linen produced in her factory, using the forced labour of serfs, was of fine quality; Piksanov mentions that during the sixteenth and seventeenth centuries the linen from the same factory was exported to Holland.[49] He accuses Nastasia Fedorovna of violating her serfs' personal and economic freedom in many ways, including demands that they pay her with the fine linen they produced.[50] She was among those landowners who justified oppressing their serfs on the assumption that God gave them a different constitution, able to bear physical labour and corporal punishment. As for Griboedov, who was a co-owner of his mother's estate and enterprises, Piksanov blames him for his non-interference in her oppressive practices. He also accuses Griboedov of spending the money produced by the serfs' hard labour on women, referring to Griboedov's letter to Begichev in which he arranges for the money arriving from the estate to be given to a woman he calls Didona.[51]

Griboedov's main point of discontent with the Orient is not the lack of everyday conveniences, but the feeling that it is oppressive and stifling for an educated and free individual like him, and that the people who surround him are slavish, flattering, and dishonest. Ironically, as Tynianov's novelistic study implies, his very presence there is the result of his enslavement in his own homeland by such forces as financial circumstances, family obligations, societal norms, authoritarian government, and his own notions of national pride. He prides himself on retaining his "Western" independent stance devoid of diplomatic games and "Asiatic" flattery, as opposed to the British, who abide by the rules of Iranian courts and wear red socks when brought into the presence of the shah: the British "took off their boots, put on red stockings, and stood as red-legged birds before the shah."[52] Russians, Tynianov continues, had secured for themselves the right not to follow this etiquette after Ermolov – empowered by his military conquests, during which people on both sides "bowed to the ground to each other, never to get up" – sat in front of the shah on a chair in his soldier boots.[53] This entire passage is a parody of Griboedov's bragging to his friend Begichev about the Russians' privilege to use chairs and to trample "multicoloured" Persian carpets with their "thick soles," while the British were required to sit on the floor without their shoes.[54] Tynianov's Griboedov is determined not to return to the red-sock etiquette.

In one of his last letters, addressed to Varvara Miklashevich, Griboedov argues that he never regretted not making friends in Iran by ingratiating himself with the "future Persian friendship." In the same letter, he welcomes the nickname "Sakhtir" that he received in Iran, and provides a French translation, "coeur dur," hard heart.[55] The superintendent of the Russian secret police, Maxim von Vock, quotes passages from this letter in a report under the subtitle "Different discourses and rumours between close friends of Griboedov." In the report he ennobles Griboedov's nickname by translating it as *tviordoe serdtse* (firm or adamant heart) as well as further deprecating Iranian diplomatic circles by replacing "future Persian friendship [*budushchuiu Persidskuiu druzhbu*]" with "Persian soulless friendship [*Persidskuiu bezdushnuiu druzhbu*],"[56] thus giving indirect approval of Griboedov's diplomatic stance vis-à-vis the Iranian court.

By relentlessly following the stipulations of the Turkmenchay treaty, Griboedov both upholds Russia's prestige and power and demonstrates his adherence to the "European" principle of abiding by the law to the lawless "Orientals," who in his opinion are accustomed to respect only despotic authority. In Tynianov's interpretation, however, Griboedov's rigidity causes the annihilation of the Russian mission in several ways. His rudeness angers the Iranian court and alarms the British, who have a great diplomatic influence in Iran, but most important, his insistence on speedy repayment of reparations drives the already impoverished people of Iran to desperation, and makes them susceptible to indoctrination by the clerics and the elite. In the novel, it is a poor old man from a crowd who nicknames Griboedov "hard-hearted," and not the Persian courtiers or diplomats. Griboedov does not understand the meaning of the name and asks another member of the Russian mission, Doctor Adelung, to translate it for him. The latter looks it up in a pocket dictionary: "Coeur dur, cruel heart – he read, – maybe there is also another meaning, but this edition is already old."[57]

In the novel, Griboedov enjoys his power over the "Orientals" in a scene where he, following the example of his predecessor General Ermolov, sits on a chair in the presence of Fath Ali Shah, who stays standing for the duration of the audience. While he sits in front of the shah, Griboedov remains silent as if deep in thought, prolonging the uneasy and awkward confrontation that must have felt humiliating for the Iranian court. While Griboedov is dressed in high boots and cocked hat, projecting masculinity and power, the shah is wearing a bejewelled dress. Even the gilded statue of Napoleon that stands beside the shah does not endow him with power and only "gloomily observes what is happening."[58] Not only the shah's eunuchs, who are present at the scene, have feminine attributes, but also his ministers, who are wearing white shawls over their dresses.[59] Just like the traumatized and hardhearted eunuchs of Montesquieu's *Persian Letters*, who take revenge for their enslavement by oppressing the wives, Griboedov, unable to strike back at his persecutors at home, vents his bad temper by harassing the Iranian court.

Tynianov omits Griboedov's statement that his diplomatic goal was to make the Iranians "fear Russia and comply with what the sovereign Nikolai Pavlovich orders."[60] Yet Nicholas I is indirectly present in the scene, as the narrator "guesses" that the Russian emperor is whom Griboedov is thinking about during his prolonged silence in the presence of the shah: "Maybe he is comparing the appearance of the Asiatic despot with wings that fly nowhere, in the garment that weighs one and a half poods, with the appearance of the other one, who is fine and round, like a doll, in a blue coat of a heavenly gendarme color."[61]

In Tynianov's interpretation, Griboedov is a true representative of the romantic nationalism of the nineteenth century: he continues the tradition of the Enlightenment by using the example of the imagined "Oriental harem" to criticize despotism in his own country, but he also engages in more direct criticism of "Oriental practices" as a way to nourish his sense of cultural superiority to "Orientals" and serve the political interests of his own country.

Griboedov wanted to escape from his unwished-for diplomatic career by dedicating himself to what he sees as his true calling – poetry. Yet at times even poetry feels like voluntary enslavement: "Dependence from my family, another one from my employment, the third one from the purpose in life that I set for myself, maybe athwart my fate. Poetry!!," he writes in another letter to his loyal friend Begichev.[62] However, he is unable to write after his spiritual castration, which in the novel is the trauma resulting from suppression of the Decembrist uprising, and Griboedov's survival guilt. Just like the eunuchs, who long to love but are unable to, Griboedov is "mute as a coffin." Here, Tynianov uses Griboedov's own words from yet another letter to his friend Begichev.[63]

The leitmotif for both Griboedov's and Mirza Yakub's thoughts of escape is Pushkin's poem "Pora, moi drug, pora! pokoia serdtse prosit …" ("It's time, my friend, it's time! My heart is asking for peace …").[64] Just like the lyrical persona of the poem, Tynianov's protagonists gave up searching for happiness but long for "peace and freedom" in a place that, while not quite their own, would allow them to be themselves. Mirza Yakub dreams about his parental home, and Griboedov, "the tired slave," envisions his "escape into a remote tenement of labours and pure pleasures,"[65] namely his father-in-law's estate in Tsinandali. However, only the literal eunuch had the resolve to put his thoughts of escape into practice.

From the moment of their first meeting, Tynianov describes Mirza Yakub as an equal to Griboedov: "In his stature he was not shorter than Vazir-Mukhtar, his passionless face not less handsome."[66] The literal eunuch from the Orient, according to the novel, was able to preserve more dignity and courage than the one castrated by the authoritarian government and conformist society of the Russian Empire.

Despite giving his book the title *The Death of Vazir-Mukhtar*, Tynianov does not dwell much on the way his main protagonist dies. The memoirs of contemporaries provided him with an array of different descriptions of Griboedov's last moments, from an account of a heroic death to a statement that he hid in an oven and was glimpsed through a chimney pipe, dragged out, and beaten to death. Tynianov chooses to grant his protagonist an easy death: the beams on the ceiling above him break, people fall down, and one of them hits Griboedov in the chest with a sabre.[67] This description only partially conforms with Pushkin's famous romantic affirmation from his *Journey to Arzrum* that Griboedov's death was "instantaneous and beautiful."[68]

Glossing over the death of Vazir-Mukhtar himself, Tynianov depicts in a memorable way the deaths of the Russian mission's doctor and Orientalist scholar, Adelung, and the eunuch Mirza Yakub. Both meet their death with courage, the doctor as a fighter and the eunuch as a martyr. Adelung dies in a sword fight, without giving up even after losing his left arm, which he hastily wraps with a rag to stop the bleeding.[69] Mirza Yakub quietly sits on a carpet waiting for his persecutors, and when he sees them looking in the door, he rises "slowly and solemnly." They step back astonished at his imposing appearance.[70]

With bared teeth, which, according to Tynianov, can be interpreted either as a grin or as jaws clenched to suppress fear, the eunuch steps forward to meet them and challenges them to kill him, stating that he is unarmed. Then follows a prolonged and gruesome depiction of his torturous death at the hands of his attackers, reminiscent of scenes of religious martyrdom.[71] Though he titles his novel *The Death of Vazir-Mukhtar*, Tynianov's description of his protagonist's death is overshadowed by that of the eunuch, whose death is significant because he is a martyr professing his belief in the importance of authenticity. Griboedov, by contrast, in Tynianov's interpretation acts out of duty and national pride rather than true humanism, and is hesitant to assert his own authenticity; therefore his death qualifies neither as heroic struggle nor as courageous martyrdom. This harsh judgment reflects Tynianov's guilt and anxiety over losing his own authenticity in the political atmosphere of the late 1920s.

Chapter Seven

An Iranian Delegation's Visit to Petersburg in 1829 and Its Interpretation in 1929

To this day, when Iranians face an injustice or calamity they exclaim, "Vay vay Turkmenchay," referring to the peace treaty that ended the Russo-Persian War of 1826–8. For Iran, the treaty was a painful and embarrassing defeat marking a time of clear realization that the country needed to modernize. For Russia, it was a moment of triumph, an important step in its empire-building project and competition with the British.

As we have seen, one year after the treaty was signed Alexander Griboedov and the rest of the Russian diplomatic mission in Iran were killed by an angry Teheran mob, and soon thereafter a delegation led by the shah's grandson, Prince Khosrow Mirza, arrived in Petersburg to apologize to Nicholas I for that incident. Below I analyse Yury Tynianov's portrayal of Khosrow Mirza's visit to Petersburg in *The Death of Vazir-Mukhtar*. I compare Tynianov's depiction of Khosrow Mirza's visit to Petersburg with an account of the same event by Mirza Mostafa Afshar, the personal secretary of Mirza Mas`ud, one of the four most important members of the prince's delegation. While in these pages I refer to Mirza Mostafa Afshar as the single author, I should mention that his patron Mirza Mas`ud both edited the diary and added information about events to which his secretary was not invited. As well, in some cases, the author could have written down what he heard from other members of the delegation.[1]

Tynianov was not familiar with Mirza Afshar's diary, which had not been translated into Russian.[2] This circumstance, however, makes it even more important to compare the way he imagined the visit of the Iranian delegation with the first-hand impressions of the visitors themselves. Tynianov's imaginative writing replaced the historical account of the event, influencing even the iconic scene of the meeting between the Persian prince and the Russian emperor in Alexander Sokurov's famous one-take film *Russkii kovcheg* (*Russian Ark*, 2002).[3] The span of time across which Tynianov viewed the encounter imbued his writing with a cynical and pessimistic tone of historical determinism and the inevitability of imperial domination. Living in the moment, the Iranian delegation was hopeful of overcoming the challenges of modernity and open to change.

There are several conflicting or converging explanations of what triggered the tragic events in Teheran. The most frequent are that the shah's government, incited by the British, instigated the murder, or that Griboedov and his employees angered the inhabitants of Teheran with their arrogant behaviour and disrespect for local religious and cultural traditions. While not trying to invalidate these two conjectures, Tynianov proposes as deeper cause of the tragedy: Russia's imperialist designs in Iran and the debilitating indemnity that the impoverished Iranian side was obliged to pay after the Russo-Persian War of 1826–8.

Following in Vazir-Mukhtar's Footsteps: The Audience Ceremonies as Depicted by Tynianov and Mirza Afshar

Tynianov foreshadows the ceremony of the prince's apology and gift giving with a parallel scene of Griboedov's audience with the Russian emperor. The two scenes frame the novel, with Griboedov's audience taking place at the beginning and Khosrow Mirza's at the end. The prince presents the emperor with the shah's letter of apology; Griboedov delivers the treaty of Turkmenchay that he helped to negotiate after Russia's victory over Persia. Both the arrival of the treaty and the arrival of Khosrow Mirza in Petersburg are greeted with discharges from the cannons of Peter and Paul fortress.[4] There is a tragic irony in this parallelism. The treaty obliged the already impoverished Persian side to pay a considerable amount of money, which, according to Tynianov, was crucial in igniting the starving Persian mob's rage against the Russian mission. And Khosrow Mirza's visit to the emperor had as its goal not only to apologize for the Russian mission's deaths, but also to negotiate a reduction of the war reparations.[5]

Griboedov and Khosrow Mirza's audiences with the emperor each appear as both a smoothly operating mechanism and a perfectly choreographed ballet. Tynianov's overarching image of the Russian Empire is that of a rigidly organized, strictly hierarchical militarized mechanical universe, "the kingdom of absolute order, immutable truths," where "the colour of linings and the shape of hairdos were predesignated, and harmony was preinstalled,"[6] at the head of which was the most cunning emperor of emperors, God.[7]

This formidable machine did at times malfunction, as it did during Griboedov's audience with the emperor. After Griboedov handed the Turkmenchay treaty to Nicholas I, the cannon volley in honour of Russia's victory over Persia did not follow immediately. As Tynianov explains: "The mechanism was organized thus: the thread went from a certain well-known person through the Marshall of the House to the Peter and Paul cannons. The person performed a gesture, but the cannon was late – so now he was vexed."[8]

Tynianov compares the militarized machine of the empire to a theatre machine (*teatral'naia mashina*), which is also prone to malfunctioning. In a scene of a ballet performance at which both Griboedov and the emperor were present, the mechanism lowering the dancers to the stage broke down, leaving them in the air. This vexed the emperor, who "was sensitive towards such accidents. He could not stand surprises. Today a theatre machine breaks and the muses got stuck, tomorrow something else gets stuck and breaks hopelessly."[9]

At times, the dance itself appears as a dutifully performed job, a mechanical movement, in which the dancers "with an inexplicable enthusiasm" perform "duty-imposed jumps, flights and beatings of one leg against the other."[10] At other times, the dance resembles a military parade with the dancers "raising their faces somewhat up like horses gnawing on their bits." During one particular dance, the pairs one by one moved away from the core and "ducked to curtsey with unnecessary dancing politeness."[11]

The scene of Griboedov's audience presents a similar ceremonial dance of courtesy and "unnecessary politeness," so superfluous that it felt to Griboedov incomprehensive and scary. While in the ballet performance the participants moved away from the core of dancers, in Griboedov's case they are joining it one by one. As Griboedov and Chancellor Karl Nesselrode walk up the stairs and through the many rooms of the Winter Palace to present the Turkmenchay treaty to Nicholas I, numerous courtiers with different titles and responsibilities join and accompany them. Tynianov names five of them, implying that there were more, and insisting that the official of ceremonial affairs (*chinovnik tseremonial'nykh del*) is not to be confused with the chief master of ceremonies (*Ober-Tseremonimeister*):

> Ikh vstrechali v kazhdoi novoi zale, prisoedinialis' molchalivo i, ne gliadia drug na druga, shagali, kto po bokam, kto vperedi – veroiatno po pravilam.

Tikhaia detskaia igra, v kotoruiu igrali rasshitye zolotom stariki, razrastalas'.

Kak tol'ko prisoedinialsia novyi chin v kazhdom novom zale, Griboedov ispytyval detskii strakh: tak terprelivo oni podzhidali ikh, tak nezametno otdelialis' ot pestroi steny i sosredotochenno sorazmeriali svoi shag s ostal'nymi.[12]

(They met them in every hall, joined them silently, and, not looking at each other, some of them walked by their sides, some in front of them, apparently following some rules.

The quiet children's game that the old men, embroidered in gold, were playing was swelling up.

As soon as a new rank would join them in every new hall, Griboedov felt scared as a child: so patiently they waited for them, so insensibly they separated from the patterned walls and intently synchronized their steps with the others.)

Just like Griboedov before him, Khosrow Mirza is accompanied up the stairs and through the halls of the palace by an ever-increasing number of courtiers and governmental officials.[13] They bring Khosrow Mirza, just as they brought Griboedov, to the waiting room where he is greeted by the chief marshal of the house.

While resembling Griboedov's audience in its perfectly choreographed ceremonial formality, Khosrow Mirza's visit is more festive and pompous. Music plays at the prince's arrival, guardsmen stand "along the walls in every room, as raised ornamentation," and in the waiting room the prince is offered coffee and sherbet specially prepared by "Tatar-Shias," discovered and recruited by Petersburg's police for the sole purpose of performing that task. Most importantly, the prince's apology was a public event at which the nobility, "the most celebrated persons of both sexes," were present, while the merchants had an opportunity to see the prince separately in the Marble Hall after paying for admission tickets.[14]

In his depiction of the two scenes, Tynianov uses a number of devices from the formalist kit, which includes parallelism and gradation within and between the two scenes, the second audience being an amplified version of the first; defamiliarization in presenting them from the point of view of someone who can see the ceremonial movements of their actors but cannot comprehend their meaning; and retardation achieved by many repetitions.[15]

Comparing Tynianov's depiction of the two ceremonies with that of Mirza Afshar's diary, we find what seems to be the same elements of repetition, parallelism, gradation, and retardation. Here, however, they are the result of the author's commitment to recording the prince's visit with as much detail and precision as possible. While Tynianov playfully imitates "literature of fact," Mirza Afshar strives to create a factual account that will speak for itself. In the diary, the "joining game" is a prominent feature of the narrative, simply because the author perceives it as an important part of the historic meeting between Iranian prince and Russian emperor. As in the novel, the "joining game" appears twice in the diary but describes the same audience, first as it was planned and then as it actually happened.

The first description summarizes the official program for the ceremony of Khosrow Mirza's audience that the Iranian delegation received from the Russian government while still in Podolsk.[16] This text creates a gradation of parallel successive ceremonial processions:

1. sailing from Peterhof to Petersburg, where smaller boats join and accompany the prince's boat on his way to his residence in Tauride Palace (Tavricheskii dvorets);
2. arrival at Tauride Palace, where the prince was to be met and accompanied by the governor of Petersburg, guardsmen, and representatives of nobility;
3. the ride from Tauride Palace to the Winter Palace in a long and pompous procession, and finally the arrival at the Winter Palace.[17]

In the Winter Palace, Mirza Afshar describes the meticulously planned journey up the stairs and through the halls and pavilions towards the place of the audience with the emperor in the Hall of Saint George. The Iranian delegation was to be successively joined and accompanied by "the chief usher and two pages (chamber junkers)," chief marshall of the house, chief chamberlain, and the chancellor. In the waiting room, the prince was to be offered coffee and "chilled refreshments."[18]

The audience in the Hall of Saint George itself is outlined as a perfectly choreographed performance, where every actor – the emperor, the members of his family, the chancellor, vice chancellor, members of the council, generals and commanders of special regiments, and army and navy engineers – all have spots specially designated for them. The prince and his delegation were to join in performing their parts with a dutiful precision. The prince was to bow for the first time upon entering the hall; he and his delegation would proceed to the centre of the hall, where he would bow for the second time; his delegation would remain standing in the centre while the prince, separating from them, would continue to move towards the throne and bow for the third time. Then he would stop and give a speech in Persian, which a specially appointed translator would repeat in Russian. The prince would give the shah's letter of apology to the emperor, who, accepting it, would give it to his vice chancellor. The latter would reply to Khosrow Mirza on behalf of the emperor.[19]

The scene was to be repeated with exact precision in the Small Throne Room, where the empress, surrounded by her female companions, would be waiting for the prince after his short private audience with the emperor. Again there were to be three bows, the prince's delegation would pause in the middle of the room, the prince would go forward and give his speech in Persian. It would be translated to Russian, and the vice chancellor would reply to the prince on the behalf of the empress.[20] On the actual day of the ceremony, this program was faithfully enacted as a well-rehearsed dance performance.[21]

The meticulous descriptions of the choreography of the ceremonial audiences have different functions in Mirza Afshar's and Tynianov's writings. Mirza Afshar's writing is a semi-official account of what was not only a diplomatic visit charged with a delicate mission, but the Iranian's personal encounter with the achievements of Russian modernization. It took place at a time of full realization that Iran must enter *asr-e jadid*, a new era that requires knowledge of sciences and technology and a new "ordered" government that would allow the country to modernize, lest it lose its independence to Britain or Russia. Mirza Afshar and other members of the delegation arrived in Russia eager to observe and possibly transplant modes of modernization.[22] For them the very orderliness and meticulous planning of the audience ceremony were indicative of Russia's Westernization and thus worthy of detailed recording.

Tynianov's descriptions, by contrast, are clearly parodic. Any novel has an element of parody in it, and the more so a novel written by the theorist of parody Tynianov. Mocking the official Russian accounts of the ceremonies, he turns their instances of repetition into a literary device of retardation. Tynianov builds up the reader's expectations during the "joining game" of Griboedov's ceremonial ascendance up the stairs and through the palace towards the emperor, only to crown this ascendance with a disappointingly banal encounter – the emperor reminds Griboedov that they met three years before, and Griboedov replies that His Majesty has an excellent memory, wondering to himself if it was worth it to endure the discomfort of a month of travelling to Petersburg in order to make "a platitudinous compliment."[23]

The prince's audience ends more theatrically – when the emperor grants Persia forgiveness for Griboedov's death, the entire scene freezes for eternity:

> I tak kak bylo tikho, kazalos': vremia ostalos' za stenami, zdes' zhe vechno stoit generalitet i znameniteishie osoby oboego pola, raznykh tsvetov, vechno i tonko razduvaiutsia zhenskie nozdri, chtoby vpitat' chastitsy garemnogo vozdukha, navsegda zastriali kuchei posredine zala persiiane, davno ros zdes', kak derevo, stroinyi Khozrev.[24]
>
> (And since it was quiet, it seemed time was left behind the walls, while here eternally stand the generals and the most celebrated persons of both sexes and different colours, eternally and nicely swell the nostrils of women, to soak in the particles of harem air, forever get stuck as a heap in the middle of the room the Persians, forever was growing here, as a tree, the slender Khosrev.)

Making his performers and onlookers freeze, Tynianov creates the impression of the closing scene of an elaborate ballet. The entire empire-building project is compared in the novel to a "serf ballet," which Griboedov mocks in *Woe from Wit*, a symbol of imitating the West in form while changing little in the society's hierarchical and autocratic structure and tolerating bond service.[25] Reappearing juxtapositions of military service and dance also allude to Griboedov's expression "constellation of manoeuvres and mazurka," by which he describes one of the negative characters in his comedy, the obsequious social climber Colonel Skalozub.[26]

Tynianov's recurring motif of performance and theatricality simultaneously alludes to the theatre and mass spectacles regaining their central role during the second cultural revolution of 1927–31 that accompanies the implementation of the first five-year plan.[27] Curtailing the freedom of artistic expression of avant-garde artists and writers, this period paradoxically actualizes their radical vision of creating a new human and a new society. An allusion to the second cultural revolution, which Stalin christened the *velikii perelom* (great break),[28] appears in the very first paragraph of Tynianov's novel: "On a very cold square in the month of December of the year of one thousand eight hundred twenty-five people of the twenties with their leaping walk ceased to exist. Time suddenly broke in two."[29]

This break creates a chasm between the generations of fathers and sons, the Decembrists and those who collaborate with Nicholas's autocratic and imperialist regime, the avant-garde artists of the first cultural revolution of the 1910s and early 1920s and those who joined the second one that emphasized rapid industrialization, collectivization, militarization, and consolidation of imperial power. In this light Khosrow Mirza's cortège and audience appears akin to a mass spectacle of the late 1920s, and freezing the last scene may allude to an attempt to build a "living utopia" in Tynianov's own time, to "efface change, to create conditions so perfect that time would cease to exist."[30]

After playing his part in this ceremonial performance, Khosrow Mirza in the novel is treated to a real ballet performance – Catterino Cavos's "national-pantomimic" ballet "The Prisoner of the Caucasus," choreographed by Charles Didelot. Tynianov defines the genre of this ballet as "pastoral and military."[31] There are no records of Khosrow Mirza ever watching this ballet, neither in the Russian sources nor in the diary of Mirza Afshar, who dutifully recorded the titles of the numerous performances the prince attended. Moreover, choosing a ballet based on the imperial conquest of the Caucasus as entertainment for the delegation from the defeated Persian Empire, which not so long ago lost those territories to Russia, would be insensitive, and the Russian government was committed to reconciliation.

The introduction of this ballet, based on Pushkin's homonymous long poem in which he infamously extolls Russia's conquest of the Caucasus, was another one of Tynianov's many mystifications. "The jumps and the waltzes" of the ballet, he reminds the reader, "were inspired by Pushkin's poetry." "But," argues Tynianov, paraphrasing Pushkin's famous lines from *Eugene Onegin*,[32] "Didelot became boring for Pushkin." Therefore, at the time the prince was watching a ballet based on Pushkin's poem, "Pushkin was not in the audience. He was in the theatre of war."[33] Tynianov here refers to Pushkin's 1829 journey to the South Caucasus, where, after victoriously ending the 1826–8 war with Iran, Russia engaged in the 1828–9 war with the Ottoman Empire. Pushkin's seemingly factual description of this trip in the *Journey to Arzrum* had its own falsifications, such as his encounter with the body of Griboedov being transported from Iran to Georgia, and meeting with Prince Khosrow Mirza's delegation on their way to Petersburg.[34] In the travelogue, Pushkin comes across a manuscript of his early poem "The Prisoner of the Caucasus," and upon rereading it is pleased to find that although the writing is "weak, immature, incomplete ... many things are guessed and expressed correctly."[35]

Pushkin's departure to the "theatre of war" is prefigured in a parallel scene at the beginning of the novel, in which Pushkin meets Griboedov while attending another ballet performance. In this scene, Pushkin expresses his envy of Griboedov's involvement in the East, which puts the latter in the vanguard of the Russian imperial project, while he, Pushkin, appears to be "thrown from the steamboat of modernity," as the futurists would say. Similar interest in the country's periphery reflects the second cultural revolution's centrifugal aspect, Orientalist aesthetics, and imperialist tendencies.[36] Describing Emperor Nicholas I as "cheerful' and "honest," Tynianov's Pushkin cites his own poem "Druz'iam. Net, ia ne l'stets, kogda tsariu ..." ("To my friends. No, I'm not a flatterer when for the king ..."), in which he praises the tsar for "enlivening" Russia through "the war, hopes" and "labour."[37]

While "hopes" and "labour" referred to expectations of easing the fortunes of the sentenced Decembrists and achieving the solution of the problem of serfdom, counting the Russo-Persian War as one of the emperor's merits connects the desire for Russia's modernization with its imperialistic expansion in the East. Expansion of the empire in the Caucasus and efforts to extend influence in Iran appear in the novel as a part of an attempt to catch up with the European empires, in which Griboedov himself plays an important part. Yet an impressive performance in the "theatre of war" does not lead to successful or even profitable management of the conquered territories, because of the government's autocratic conservatism and rigidity.

Projecting Taylorism on Nicholas's Era

The novelistic genre in general tends to connect history to the present,[38] and Tynianov, the scholar of the past and theorist of the present, has a strong propensity for "writing a usable past."[39] In Tynianov's depiction of Griboedov's time, the "serf ballet" symbolizes arts in the service of autocracy, military expansion, and internal and external colonization. In reference to Tynianov's own time, the mechanistic "duty-imposed" dancing steps allude to the productivist fervour of the art and literature of the 1920s, which Tynianov's association with the journal *LEF* (Left front of the arts, 1923–5) helped to uphold. Although the subsequent journal *Novyi LEF* (New left front of the arts, 1927–9) that appeared while Tynianov was working on his novel focused its theoretical quest on "factography" rather than on productivism, the latter had already "expanded" from art to "life,"[40] and was part of the industrialization, collectivization, and militarization plan. Literary and artistic productivism drew its inspiration from Frederick Winslow Taylor's method of scientific management, aimed at increasing the efficiency and productivity of labour. Theatrical producer and director Vsevolod Meyerhold used Taylor's ideas to develop biomechanics, his famous system of training his actors. The physical movements of Meyerhold's biomechanical études came from sources such as the circus, boxing, kabuki, and military discipline, among others.[41] It is possible that Tynianov's description of the dancers "raising their faces somewhat up like horses gnawing on their bits," an allusion to Griboedov's *Woe from Wit*, is simultaneously a parody of one of Meyerhold's études called "The Horse and Rider."[42]

"Duty-imposed" movement performed "with an inexplicable enthusiasm"[43] appears in Dziga Vertov's poetic documentary *Man with a Movie Camera*, stills from which were printed in *Novyi LEF* in 1928, the same year that Tynianov's novel was being published in chapters in *Znamia*. The film alternates footage of a dancer with footage of a textile-spinning machine, both joining the exuberant rhythm of productive and recreational activities in the new Soviet society. This society is advancing towards modernity with an accelerating speed symbolized, among other images, by an ever-quickening pendulum and by scenes of people and vehicles moving at times simultaneously and at times alternating towards and away from the viewer as well as to the left and the right.[44] In Tynianov's novel, Griboedov, who has just returned to Moscow to deliver the Turkmenchay treaty to the tsar, finds himself in a city bustling with activity and "seething with motion," as if it had sprung out of Vertov's film. It seems to him that the same people and vehicles "go forward and then return back," while his heart palpitates as a pendulum, "now it is young, now old." He finds that the movements of the Muscovites had acquired new "ease and slickness," a remark that would remind Tynianov's contemporaries of biomechanics. Even *muzhiks* lost their ursine awkwardness (*medvezhevatost'*). He saw one of them carrying a barrel of herring "swaying his torso and arm with mechanical grace" and "balancing like a ballet dancer."[45]

This new slickness and purposefulness were symptoms of a modernizing Russia, which Nicholas I "enlivened" with new imperialistic wars with Iran and the Ottoman Empire. As confirmation of Russian acquisition of the Erivan province, according to the treaty that he is delivering to the tsar, Griboedov sees two dandies in Erivan hats (*erivankas*) moving in carriages towards each other.[46] Wearing the same hats, they look like a Vertovian superimposition of the same object moving in opposite directions. Modernization itself enters the country as "two winds" blowing in opposite directions, "to the East and to the West."[47] Catching up with the West requires domination over the East. Griboedov, the protagonist, has jumped on the bandwagon of Nicholas's modernization, with youthful enthusiasm rendering his services as a negotiator during the Russo-Persian War and developing an innovative project of colonial management in Transcaucasia. Yet, in an opposite swing of his pendulum-heart, he realizes that this modernization is inseparable from coercion, despotism, and surveillance, and that the same hands of "slaves" and "prisoners" who "screwed together the empty mechanism" of Benckendorff's secret police were "winding up and releasing the screw" of mills and factories. At this realization, his youthful enthusiasm turns into tired disappointment and the chill touches even his cherished project.[48]

The parallels between dancing, marching to music, and the movements of the smoothly running parts of a coercive authoritarian machine appear in Yevgeny Zamyatin's 1921 novel *We*, published in Russian in Prague and smuggled back into the USSR in 1927, at the time that Tynianov was working on *The Death of Vazir-Mukhtar*. The protagonist of the novel is the proud builder of a spacecraft that has a mission to colonize other planets, imposing on them the rational, equalizing, and efficient civilization of the totalitarian One State. Admiring the harmonious work of the machine, in which

> s zakrytymi glazami, samozabvenno, kruzhilis' shary reguliatorov; motyli, sverkaia, sgibalis' vpravo i vlevo; gordo pokachival plechami balansir; v takt neslyshnoi muzyke prisedalo doloto dolbezhnogo stanka. Ia vdrug uvidel vsiu krasotu etogo grandioznogo mashinnogo baleta.[49]

> (with their eyes closed, forgetting themselves, the spherical regulators were twirling; the operating cranks, sparkling, were bending to the right and to the left; the balance-beam was proudly waggling its shoulders; the chisel was curtsying to the beat of an inaudible music. I suddenly saw the whole beauty of this grandiose mechanical ballet.)

Trying to understand what makes dance beautiful, he concludes that it is the "ideal non-freedom" of its movements. Defined by its non-freedom, the dance represents and promotes the strictly regulated totalitarian One State. The technical achievements and the mechanistic cheerful art simultaneously achieve two goals, the internal colonization of the citizens of the One State and the conquering of new frontiers. Poetry glorifying the spectacular achievements of the One State was supposed to be part of the "first cargo" that the spacecraft would carry towards the unknown primitive cultures of the universe.[50]

Zamyatin's dystopia satirizes this zeal for colonization and the method of scientific management used to carry out the "civilizing" and modernizing mission. Unlike Zamyatin, avant-garde poet and member of Proletkul't Aleksey Gastev, Tynianov's contemporary, was an earnest proponent of scientific management, which he put into practice in 1920 by founding the Central Institute of Labour. For Gastev, scientific management was not only a means of optimizing work output, but also a path to cultural self-colonization and to overcoming the weaknesses of character that he associated with Russianness, such as impulsiveness, sloth, or disorganization.[51] Leaving behind the traditional national disposition that impedes progress towards a modernized industrialized society would, according to Gastev, allow Russia to become more like America. He celebrates Russia's entrance into transnational modernity as a merging of the Russian Eastern and American Western frontiers in his favourite poem "Ekspress" ("Express"), dedicated to the completion of the Trans-Siberian Railway in 1916.[52]

Tynianov refers in his novel to Griboedov's time as one when "it started to smell like America," superimposing cultural trends and political realities of the nineteenth and the twentieth centuries. The "smell of America" was quite distinct in twentieth-century Russia, well before the October Revolution. Thus, Alexander Blok in his 1913 poem refers to Russia as the "New America" where "it smells with burning, combustible and free."[53] The post-revolutionary avant-garde embraced this vision of America as Russia's modernized and industrialized future. In the late 1920s, this artistic fascination was replaced with actual emulation and involvement of American firms in the major Soviet industrial projects.[54]

In reference to the nineteenth century, the "smell of America" alludes to the Russian-American Company's advances in colonizing Alaska; Griboedov's friend and Decembrist Kondratiy Ryleev became the manager of the company one year before the uprising. It also refers to Decembrist Dmitry Zavalishin's proposal to colonize northern California. Both Ryleyev's participation in the Russian American Company and the debate surrounding Zavalishin's proposal influenced Griboedov's own ambitious project of colonizing Transcaucasia with the help of the Russian Transcaucasian agricultural, manufacturing, and trading company.[55]

Just as Gastev's scientific management was a path towards self-colonization and cultural modernization, Griboedov's proposal of colonial management aimed not only at the rapid economic and industrial development of Russia and Transcaucasia, but also at the creation of a new type of human, a responsible worker and daring entrepreneur, and a new culture of capitalist enterprise. Applying the Orientalist notion of a "lazy native" to the "timid" Transcaucasian merchants, while at the same time criticizing the apathy of the local Russian officials, Griboedov sought the assistance of the government in his proposal to invigorate these cultural backwaters with modernizing capitalist zeal.

Unlike Gastev's strive towards transnational modernity, Griboedov's proposal revealed national pride and a desire to compete with European empires as an important component of the authors' motivation.

In his capacity as an "archaist-innovator," Tynianov's Griboedov resembles the futurist poets Velimir Khlebnikov and Vladimir Mayakovsky more than Gastev. While working to advance Russia to the vanguard of history, he strives to create its new song from the lore of its archaic written and oral traditions, which Gastev dismissed for their "patriotic sloppiness."[56] Griboedov's fascination with the archaic and his experimentation with the Russian language, as well as his involvement with the Orient, allows Tynianov to draw parallels between his protagonist and Khlebnikov.

Griboedov's linguistic patriotism should have resonated for Tynianov with Mayakovsky's well-known poem "Nashemu iunoshestvu" ("To Our Youth"),[57] written and published in *Novyi LEF* in 1927 while Tynianov was working on *Vazir-Mukhtar*. In the poem, Mayakovsky ridicules the citizens of Tiflis for dressing up in the most fashionable hats and long-nose shoes and imagining themselves to be Parisians, and laments that the academies of Tiflis and Kazan correspond in French rather than in Russian. Similarly in his *Woe from Wit*, Griboedov's protagonist Chatsky resents the attention that Moscow society gives to "the little French from Bordeaux," and wonders if Russians will ever "be resurrected from the foreign domination of fashion" and communicate in Russian so that the common people will not take them for foreigners.[58] In spite of the apparent similarity, there is a difference between the two examples: for Georgians, using French could be an attempt to proclaim their cultural independence from Russia, their own affinity with the West and modernity that does not need Russia as an intermediary. For contemporary readers, Mayakovsky's poem evoked memories of the Georgian uprisings that culminated in the August uprising of 1924 and aimed at restoring the independent Georgian Republic subjugated by Bolsheviks in 1921. Tynianov hinted at the same events in his novel by mentioning several Georgian uprisings of the nineteenth century.[59]

Mayakovsky's rhetoric is in tune with the increasing Russo-centrism of Stalin's rule, although the poet had declared independence from the influence of Paris and the French avant-garde long before, as a beginning futurist. He specifies that his promotion of Russian is not based on outdated notions of nationalism, but on the importance of that language as the bearer of the new socialist mentality. Moscow is not an imperial centre, dragging other lands in a "noose" behind itself, but "the fiery banner" of revolution showing the new path to progress; not a colonizer, but a beacon for those who hope to enter modernity free of the shackles of colonialism. Because it is the language of Lenin, Mayakovsky infamously declares, he would learn it without "despondency and idleness" even if he would be "a negro in declining years." He ends his poem by rearticulating his appreciation of multiculturalism and the need to know one's own roots, claiming that he himself is "a Georgian by birth," being born and raised in Georgia. This in his view gives him the right to satirize the West-emulating philistines, both in Georgia and in Russia.

Griboedov's own criticism of West-emulating Russian elites distancing themselves from the common people, as well as his interest in Russian language, folklore, dress, and traditions and his perception of Peter the Great's reforms as a tragic disjunction of Russian history, anticipate the soon-to-come Slavophilia and the search for Russia's own path.[60] Yet the modernity that he envisioned for Georgia and Transcaucasia was that of Western technological advances, and a Western type of self-disciplined, goal-oriented worker and entrepreneur. He believed that Western capitalist enterprise would propel both Transcaucasia and Russia into a prosperous and more democratic future, while Persia represented the past, to which Griboedov did not want to return.

With all his reservations about the cultural gap between the people of Russia and its Westernized elite created by Peter's reforms, he does not hesitate to express his feelings of superiority over his Persian hosts, whom he compares to amiable pre-Petrine Muscovites, while he imagines himself to be their Western guest the seventeenth-century German scholar and traveller Olearius.[61] The German scholar's prejudiced description of Russian backwardness must have been an affront to Griboedov's national pride, which does not make him less judgmental in his own description of his intercultural encounters in Iran. Based on Griboedov's accounts of his interactions there, Tynianov creates the overarching parodic image of Persia as Russia. If the "smell of America" brings a whiff of the future to Griboedov's Russia, the sights of Persia are reminiscent of her past.

Tynianov uses Griboedov's own references to Persia as pre-Petrine Russia to infuse his protagonist's trip to that country with the sense of a journey down memory lane, a subjectively interpreted historical memory. For his protagonist, Persia becomes the "usable past" he ponders while trying to make sense of the present in his own country. This present has pockets of the past within itself. The similarities between Moscow and Tabriz that Griboedov notices upon his return create a parodic opposition between Petersburg, the capital and city of the future, and Moscow, the abode of the past in which, as *Woe from Wit* tells us, "the houses are new, but the prejudices are old."[62] Interestingly, Mirza Afshar corroborates the parallels between Moscow and his own country, mentioning in his diary that the Kremlin reminded him of Iran.[63]

While *Woe from Wit* was only a satire of mores that did not propose any solution to the problem, Griboedov's proposal for the establishment of the Russian Transcaucasian Company did outline his plan of bringing both Transcaucasia and Russia from past to future. According to this plan, economic and industrial progress would lead the way and cultural change would follow. The company would help to shape "people enterprising in trade and industry, striving through their private gains to further the betterment of the society."[64] One can discern the influence of Adam Smith in this argument. Assigning Persia a place in pre-modern history, Griboedov accuses Erivan governor Sardar Hussein Khan of stifling domestic and foreign trade, because "Adam Smith's system was not written while he was around [*ne pri nem*]."[65]

Ironically, Griboedov himself was contravening Smith's principles of free trade by requesting special privileges and monopolies for his company from the Russian government. His point of persuasion is that while in general monopolies and privileges are detrimental to the economic development of a region, Transcaucasia, ravaged by wars and backward, is a special case where they would be of a great advantage.[66] Critics of the proposal viewed this claim as anachronistic at a time when popular opinion preferred "natural," "bottom-up" development through free trade and free enterprise that would put Russia and its newly acquired territories on track for slower but steadier progress.

Tynianov overlooks this criticism of the proposal in his novel, instead having the cautious officials of Nicholas's "mousy state" reject Griboedov's daring project of modernization out of fear that his company will acquire too much power and escape the tight grip of tsarist despotism.[67] He glosses over the question of free trade, most probably because it would distract from the parallels that he was drawing between his protagonist's and his own times. He does, however, highlight the other profound demerit of Griboedov's proposal, his intention to use forced labour for his grand modernizing project. Keeping the motif of the serf ballet in the spotlight throughout his novel, Tynianov juxtaposes Griboedov's condemnation of serfdom in his play *Woe from Wit* and his readiness to use forced labour in his modernizing economic enterprise. His allusions to Taylorism and biomechanics refers to similar attempts to modernize through coercion in Tynianov's own time. To stress the imperialistic aspects of Nicholas's modernization, Tynianov introduces the ballet "The Prisoner of the Caucasus," which further refers the reader to the *Journey to Arzrum*, in which Pushkin is "pondering" Russian colonial practices. Soviet imperialism appears in Tynianov's allusions to the Georgian affair and the uprising of 1924. Like Yevgeny Zamyatin before him, Tynianov sees modernization in Russia as inseparable from internal and external colonization, while at the same time admiring its daring and innovative aspect. Thus, Tynianov's protagonist Griboedov's spiritual death starts with his final abandonment of his cherished project for modernizing Transcaucasia.

Tynianov's Griboedov is akin to the Soviet literary avant-garde, the "leaping" fathers,[68] in his desire to bring a radical change to Transcaucasia, his belief that changing the periphery will also transform the core of the empire, and his confidence in his ability to lead those who are not mature enough to initiate the change on their own. Griboedov's revolutionary character reveals itself in the following passage comparing "theatre machines" to guillotines:

> On ne byl zdes' dva goda, i vse ismenilos'. Zal byl zanovo vykrashen, plafon byl lazurnogo tsveta, kakaia-to lepka otiagoshchala ego ... On zhe liubil stroguiu pustyniu starogo teatra, gde stsena byla eshafotom, lozhi – sud'iami, parter – tolpoi, teatral'nye mashiny – gil'otinoi.[69]
>
> (He was away for two years and everything has changed. The hall was painted anew, the ceiling was azure, some kind of plasterwork was weighing it down ... As for him, he preferred the severe desert of the old theatre, where the stage was the scaffold, the loges – the judge, parterre – the crowd, theatre machines – the guillotine.)

Applied to Tynianov's own time, this passage reflects the turn towards conventionality and pompous style in literature and arts. The scaffold reminds the reader not only of the French revolutions, but also of the executions of the Decembrists, with whom Griboedov, the protagonist, clearly sympathizes. Yet when the former Decembrist Colonel Burtsov rebukes him about his plan to use forced labour in his future company, Griboedov, as mentioned above, replies that if the Decembrists won they would "temporarily, only temporarily" use corvée labour. Thus, the novel implicates the romantic "leaping fathers" along with the more practical collaborator children. Griboedov abandons his project both because the government does not support it and because he admits to himself that it is morally wrong. It seems that Tynianov feels similar ambivalence towards his own formalist project: vexation about the rejection of his creation and at the same time a realization of its shortcomings.

For Zamyatin, the conflict between the creative thrust of innovation and the stifling rationalization of coercion will be forever resolved and re-established through new revolutionary movements, when the pendulum swings from the entropy of conformism towards the energy of revolution. Tynianov's novel ends with the victory of the mechanical "mousy state" and with the pendulum frozen forever on its way from enthusiasm and support to disappointment and alienation.

Order and System: *Nazm wa tartib*

Tynianov's depiction of the two audiences with the emperor, Griboedov's and Khosrow Mirza's, was clearly a parody. Let us now return to the question: What impelled Mirza Afshar to describe so meticulously every step and gesture of the actors of the grand ceremonial play put together for the prince and his delegation by the Russian court? Were they impressed by the reception, as Tynianov suggests? Mirza Afshar does not use a single evaluative word in the entire description of the ceremonial arrival and the audience. Moreover, he does not give away his disposition by describing how people, places, and things look. What he does describe in detail is movement through space, the names of the buildings, the streets, the bridges, and the parks of the city that the delegation passes on the way to the audience; the rooms of the Winter Palace through which they pass; the precise location of the actors in relation to each other, their movements and gestures. He underscores that each person or group had their own specially designated space in the ceremony, which they did not transgress.

It was this perfect order and military discipline, mocked by Tynianov as an expression of autocracy, that impressed Mirza Afshar the most. Having just lost the rest of the South Caucasus to Russia, economically debilitated and experiencing the diplomatic pressure of the British, the Qajar dynasty of Iran at the time was trying to consolidate its power over a decentralized country ruled by many local governments. The ability to create a strong autocratic state modelled on the experience of Peter the Great and Catherine the Great became, in the eyes of Qajar reformers, the guarantee of Iran's progress and independence.[70]

In order to protect Iran's independence from British and Russian encroachment, it was necessary to modernize its army. Peter the Great's rapid creation of an army and a navy to be reckoned with appealed to the Iranian elite as a model to be emulated. Although modernization meant adoption of European practices,[71] Iranians considered Russian modifications most suitable for their country. While French, British, Italian, and Spanish officers were helping Fath Ali Shah and Abbas Mirza build a regular disciplined army during and between the two Russo-Persian Wars of 1804–13 and 1826–8, the system of indirect conscription that relied on landowners resembled the Russian system introduced by Peter the Great.[72]

Aware of the efforts to create *nezam-e jadid*, new-order regiments,[73] back home, Mirza Afshar scrupulously describes everything related to the Russian army and navy. He seems to share the belief that the most important qualities of modernized military forces were regularity, order, and discipline. In his descriptions of the processions that accompanied the prince's arrival and his audience with the emperor, as well as the many military drills he was invited to observe, Mirza Afshar especially stresses their order. The words *nazm wa tartib*, order and system, appear again and again in the part of his diary dedicated to Petersburg.

Discipline and order take root, as Mirza Afshar suggests, because they are inculcated at an early age. He relates that children of the nobility, in compliance with Nicholas's military aspirations, spend several months of the year in the army or navy. He believes that during this training, the children are treated equally; the sons of generals are not shown any favouritism and comply with the rules as does everyone else.[74] This remark is indicative of the growing desire among the Iranian elite for their country to democratize. Many considered constitutional monarchy an appropriate model of government to emulate. Mirza Afshar admires the sons of the nobility, whose ages range from eight to fourteen years old and who spend one month every year training as sailors, for being able to climb rope ladders to the very top of the mast as fast "as lightening" at the sound of the whistle. He also described the students of the cadet corps, who participate in drills during breaks between their classes, and notices the special little guns manufactured for their training.[75]

Order and system, *nazm wa tartib*, in Mirza Afshar's account are present not only in the Russian military but also in the general organization of public life in Petersburg and Peterhof. He notices the regularity of the buildings, streets, and canals, and pays particular attention to the parks and public gardens. The trees in these parks, although fruitless, are perfectly groomed and trimmed, the paths covered with fine, soft, pounded sand, and fall leaves are promptly removed. In regular intervals from each other stand green benches, on which people can relax during their daily promenades.[76]

The garden of the Tauride palace, according to Mirza Afshar, becomes the centre of the social life of Petersburg for the entire time Khosrow Mirza and his delegation reside there. From the day of the prince's arrival until the day of his departure, the men and women of Petersburg stop visiting any other gardens or places of recreation. Instead, they come to the Tauride garden, where by the emperor's order a music band plays every evening. They stroll along the alleys of the garden or ride the small boats hoping to come across Khosrow Mirza, who, seeing their eagerness to meet him, would go out of the palace to take part in the social gathering.[77] Nicolai Gogol unwittingly "confirms" Mirza Afshar's account by making his character, the Nose, choose Tauride garden over Nevsky prospect as his favourite place of promenade. While according to Mirza Afshar Petersburg society indulges itself in voyeurism, in Gogol's story it is the prince who observers the effect of "the playfulness of nature," the Nose.[78]

Just as in military spheres, in participation in social life orderliness and cooperation are instilled, in Mirza Afshar's view, from an early age in both men and women. He stresses the importance of girls' education by noting that a girls' school the delegation visited, the Smolny Institute for Noble Maidens, was not smaller than other schools and that the rank of the female supervisor was equal to that of a general.[79] The students of the school impressed the visitors by displaying formidable cooperation in playing a musical piece in unison on twenty-four pianos with forty-eight participants.[80] Enumerating the useful subjects that children study in several educational institutions they visited, Mirza Afshar does not fail to notice the incorporation of recreational activities in their schedule. Thus, the cadet corps has a playground equipped with toys, where the boys can escape from boredom.[81]

Organized games in which adults participated alongside their children also attract Mirza Afshar's attention. Count Sukhtelen gives a brief account of two evening parties the empress hosted for the prince and certain members of his delegation in Tsarskoe Selo. He enumerates the salon games that Khosrow Mirza enjoyed participating in alongside children and adults from the royal family.[82] Mirza Afshar finds it important not only to name the games that the prince and his retinue played, such as "Rope" and "Cat and Mouse," and the one they refrained from, "Musical Chairs," but to describe all these games in detail and to explain their rules.[83] In another day's entry, he describes the tableau vivant with which the children of Count Kochubey and Prince Trubetskoy entertained Mirza Mas'ud, Mirza Saleh, and the doctor of the Iranian delegation, Mirza Baba.[84]

Order and system are also prerequisites for learning science and technology, and museums are the best training aids. Mirza Afshar describes in detail the museum of the Mining School, the educational institution, which according to his diary and the notes of Count Sukhtelen impressed the members of the Iranian delegation the most. The collections in the museum contained samples of solids from all over the world displayed in perfect order and system. These collections often served as tools for educating the students in different stages of the mining process, such as recognizing veins of minerals in mountains and deserts, or calculating their profitability. While in most of his descriptions Mirza Afshar gives the Russians credit for successfully emulating European practices, here he claims they outperformed their teachers by creating a museum unequalled in Europe.[85]

Even more detailed is Mirza Anshar's description of the museum of the Imperial Academy of Sciences, the Kunstkammer. Here everything is systematized and preserved in spirits for posterity, or covered with glass to protect it from the dust. An identifying tablet accompanies each museum piece. The preserved animals are classified into subgroups, while historical artifacts, such as a collection of coins that includes middle Persian samples, are organized and catalogued. The museum allows scientists and scholars to conduct their research, while younger students come here to witness and comprehend divine wisdom.[86] This and similar statements reveal that, in Mirza Afshar's view, the modern developments in natural and social sciences did not undermine but confirmed religious postulates and were easily transferable to Iranian society.

Mirza Afshar praises the preservation and display of objects and clothing that belonged to former monarchs as a means to promote the idea of stability and continuity in the dynastic succession and steady development of the country. He sees a great advantage for the development of Russian society in the ability of each successive monarch to build upon the achievements of his or her predecessor rather than begin entirely anew.

The one museum piece that attracted the special attention of the prince and the rest of the delegation was a wax effigy of the founder of the museum, Peter the Great himself. This sculpture by Carlo Bartolomeo Rastrelli became the character of Tynianov's 1931 novella "Voskovaia persona" ("Wax Effigy")[87] that he wrote soon after *The Death of Vazir-Mukhtar*. If Tynianov had had access to Mirza Afshar's description of the Iranian delegation's encounter with the great reformer, it is possible that he would have given the effigy a role to play in his novel too. With his propensity for drawing parallels between countries and epochs, Tynianov could have elaborated on the similarities between Russia's modernizing projects and the advance of the *asr-e jadeed* in Iran.

The prince and his mission took the time to stop in front of Peter's figure and to share their reflections on his role as a reformer who brought Russia prosperity, splendour, and stability, and who encouraged the development of sciences and industries. The prince asked that Mirza

Afshar stand next to the effigy. A man taller than average, he was still a span shorter than the wax figure.[88] Perhaps the prince was wondering if he himself would measure up to the daring and self-disciplined character he ascribed to the great reformer. According to Adolph Berzhe's account of the same visit, when someone remarked on the roughness of Peter's clothes, the prince answered that if the great monarch had not worn those clothes Russia would not have a navy.[89] Regardless of the factual correctness of Berzhe's account, the prince's remark is consistent with the general attitude of the Iranian delegation as expressed in Afshar's diary. It reveals the desire for urgent self-colonization as a means of preventing colonization by others. Back at home, it was Khosrow Mirza's father, the reformer Abbas Mirza, who looked up to Peter as his role model, a "monarch-artisan, innovator and imposer of order," and strove to educate himself before educating his subjects.[90] Mirza Afshar confirms this reputation of Peter the Great as one who mastered foreign knowledge and new technologies, and describes one of the stone-cutting and -dressing machines that the emperor brought from abroad.[91]

Developing industries and technologies, according to Mirza Afshar, is even more important than fundamental sciences. He tries to record in his diary every little detail of the manufacturing technologies he observed, such as, for example, the process of paper production. No less minute is his description of the process of lowering a new ship into the water, as if the author strives to master the know-how in its entirety. The fastest transfer of industrial expertise to Iranian society, he suggested, would be through inviting foreign teachers to Iranian schools. They would teach sciences, industrial technologies, and laws of commerce, while their Iranian colleagues would complement these studies by teaching ethics and religion.

Since these schools would advance public welfare and guarantee political stability, the citizens whose children attend them should pay for most of the expenses, while the government supplemented their payments with additional financial assistance. However, no effort to modernize Iran would work, according to Mirza Afshar, unless there are laws and order regulating private property and preserving social and political stability. An effective army would ensure Iran's modernization on its own terms and not as a receptor of a "civilizing mission" from Europe, while educational reform would be the fastest way to bring about profound cultural change, and create a new citizen ready to enter the new era, *asr-e jadid*. Without doubt, many of the other members of the Iranian delegation shared Mirza Afshar's vision of the new order. One of them, the future prime minister Amir Kabir, put the ideas conceived during his visit into practice, implementing educational reforms in Iran twenty years after the trip.[92]

Imperious Heaven and Hell of Colonization

In his novel, Tynianov creates a parody of Griboedov's comparison between Iran and pre-Petrine Russia. The Persia of 1829, he writes, "resembles Russia of the times of Ivan III or, maybe, Aleksey Mikhailovich. Apparently, there was no Peter there, or they haven't noticed him."[93] This subversive parody recognizes the tendency of romantic nationalism to see Orientals as "people without history."[94] It presents Persia as an old country not aware of its own age "because there were people living there."[95] This phrase draws from from Leon Trotsky's 1923 critique of formalism, which he argues does not take into account the fact that both writer and reader are human beings, "living people," whose psychology is shaped by their social conditions.[96] Here again, Tynianov interweaves his satire of Griboedov's imperialism and Orientalism with criticism of the formal method for not taking into account human psychology and social conditions. He admits his own short-sightedness when he states that his protagonist Griboedov mistook different people moving back and forth on a Moscow street for the same person because "that's what it seemed to him, he was short-sighted."[97] Similarly, drawing "Asiatic comparisons," that is, comparisons between Persia and Russia, stemmed from Griboedov's "laziness of mind."[98]

If Iran is old and tired, Russia is characterized by youthful zeal for reforms that is displayed in an awkward and inefficient way, as for example in General Ermolov's attempt to wrest Tiflis from the clutches of the old Orient and turn it into a European city:

> V slepoi i gruznoi zhazhde preobrazovanii, pokhozhei na liubov' soldata, Ermolov velel lomat' balcony, na kotorykh sokhranilas' staraia Aziia. On khotel sdelat' Tiflis evropeiskim gorodom i rubil ulitsy po voennoi privychke, kak lesnye proseki …
>
> Evropa v Tiflise skoro okazalas' riadom kazarm. Takovy byli glavnye ulitsy.
>
> Kak neudavshaiasia liubov' polkovodtsa, voznik gorodskoi sad s temnoi listvoi, s lampionami, s prosekami dorozhek.[99]

(In a blind and awkward thirst for reforms that resembled a soldier's love, Ermolov gave the order to break the balconies that retained the old Asia.

> He wanted to make Tiflis a European city and hacked the streets through as forest paths following his military habit …
>
> … Europe in Tiflis soon turned out to be a row of barracks. That was what the main streets were like.
>
> As an abortive love of the general, the city garden appeared with dark leaves, lampions, with glades of the paths.)

Describing colonialism as "a soldier's love" alludes to Peter the Great, who started his Westernization project by reforming Russia's army and creating a strong navy, making it ready to compete for imperial dominance. The straight streets and an orderly public garden modelled on the ones Mirza Afshar admired in Petersburg appear as a violation of the city's nature. Tynianov connects the views of Petersburg as an artificial city created by Peter's volition with the idea of employing deforestation in an attempt to subjugate the Caucasus, which appears in the novel as a continuation of Peter's empire-building aspirations. The motif of deforestation alludes to Leo Tolstoy's early story "Rubka lesa" ("Forest Felling," 1853–5)[100] and his late anti-imperialist novella "Haji-Murad" (1896–1904).[101] The straight lines Ermolov is trying to cut through Tiflis also resemble the parallel streets of Andrey Bely's Petersburg, where the lines that Peter once drew "on the swamps were trying to catch the entire world within their rectilinear mesh."[102] Both Tynianov's Tiflis and Bely's Petersburg resist this straightening, the former growing balconies and the latter fences and columns to deviate from the rectilinear order.[103] Against this, the streamlined, transparent, geometrical urban design of Zamyatin's utopia, the opposite of the chaotic, gaudy, and opaque "ancient house," is a testimony to the One State's successful self-colonization and a facilitator of the further spread of its "civilizing mission" in the universe.[104]

In contrast, Ermolov's zeal to "civilize" the Caucasus appears in Tynianov's novel as barbaric hacking rather than a feat of engineering, and its result has the orderliness of military barracks rather than the stately imperial city of the future. Tynianov's Ermolov is an ambiguous figure just like Peter is in his novella "Wax Effigy." The vigour and scope of Peter's transformative reforms in the novel are a thrust towards the future, but the archaic brutality of their methods belongs to the past.[105] As we have already seen, Tynianov's protagonist Griboedov is also a reformer who wants to modernize Transcaucasia with the help of his new and dynamic company while using the forced labour of former serfs.

The myth of Peter's transformative reforms as Petersburg's salvation from stagnation, his self-colonizing "triumph of intention over habit," in which the new enlightened order is equated to heaven and the old obscurantism to hell,[106] becomes the object of Tynianov's parody. In this parody, visiting Petersburg appears as ascension, a movement that is the opposite of descending to Old Persia. The scene of Griboedov's visit to Abbas Mirza's mint is parallel and opposed to the scenes of Griboedov's and Khosrow Mirza's audiences with the Russian emperor, in which, as we have seen, they ascend stairs with new courtiers joining in the ceremony on each landing and then process through the splendor of the rooms and galleries of the Winter Palace.

The vertical hierarchy of Petersburg society ends in heaven with the most cunning emperor of emperors, God, the twist being that God himself reports to the Russian emperor. This twist is an allusion to Leo Tolstoy's novella "Haji-Murad," in which God "salutes and glorifies" Nicholas, who accepts it as his due, believing that the "welfare and happiness of the entire world" depends on him. "Haji-Murad" is a re-evaluation of the mid-nineteenth-century Caucasian wars in light of new anticolonial movements unfolding in the early twentieth century. Tolstoy unambiguously condemns imperialism and joins his voice to the growing support for anticolonial struggle around the world.[107] In "Haji Murad," he draws parallels between Nicholas and the leader of the mountaineers' resistance, Shamil, both blinded by megalomania and thirst for power. Another parallel is drawn between the ordinary mountaineers and simple Russian peasants, both suffering from the senseless war of imperial conquest.[108] The similarity between Nicholas and Shamil in "Haji Murad" does not conceal the overwhelming dominance of the political and military power held by the imperial core. Following Tolstoy, Tynianov creates mirroring images of Russia and Persia, Nicholas and Abbas Mirza, with a stronger emphasis on the idea of economic inequality between colonizer and colonized.

Visiting the Persian mint, just as during his audience with Nicholas, Griboedov walks through numerous rooms and courtyards, while courtiers of Abbas Mirza join in the procession to accompany him. This procession is very different from the well-choreographed ceremony in Petersburg. The guards, who stand on a platform that reminds Griboedov of Moscow's Red Arch, look like gapers, and the courtiers that successively join him are wearing "Oriental caftans." Instead of the magnificence of the Winter Palace, the visitor sees panes with multicoloured glass that remind him of a kaleidoscope, a European toy the Persians are said to be fascinated with.[109]

To enter the small dark room of the mint, Griboedov has to lower his head. The description of the interior with its earthy floor and half-naked people making a fire is infernal. Tynianov's description alludes to Khlebnikov's poem of the revolutionary Gilan cycle, "Kave-Smith:"

Byl sumrak ser i zaspan.
Mekha dyshali naspekh,
Nad grudoi seroi pepla
Khripeli gorlom khriplo.
Kak babki povial'nye
Nad plachushchim mladentsem,
Stoiali kuznetsy u tela polugologo ...[110]

(The dusk was grey and sleepy.
The bellows were breathing hastily,
Over the grey pile of ashes
They were roaring throatily.
Like midwives over a crying newborn,
The smiths were standing
Next to the half-naked body ...)

Here the smiths are midwives that ensure the birth of a new kind of labour, "first labour." They are participating in the "night tempering of freedom," while their tools are singing in praise of the "dawn of labour." Thus, the smiths in Khlebnikov's poem are the agents of modernity who will revolutionize life in the new Soviet Republic of Iran. In Tynianov's novel, the fire of the mint is necessary to melt ancient vessels and chandeliers in order to pay the war reparation to the Russian side. Griboedov is here to ensure the timeliness of this payment. The old has to perish for the new to come forth, yet the new is not benefiting Persia, but leaving the country.

In another allusion to Pushkin's Orientalist tale "The Prisoner of the Caucasus," Tynianov makes Griboedov feel atrociously lonely, as if he had spent all his life in an earthen cellar. Abbas Mirza, who is sitting next to him, becomes alien, as if they are separated by "a thousand of versts and a thousand of years ... more alien than the melted chandeliers." At that moment, "it did not come to his mind that he, Griboedov Alexander Sergeevich, is burying the empire of Qajars. That made him feel neither warm nor cold."[111]

The artificial, oppressive, and inefficient heaven of the imperial centre is in the novel opposed to the hell of the "Oriental" periphery subjected to colonization and driven to poverty. Bely's Petersburg waited with apprehension for the "Asiatic" periphery and the working class to sweep away its rectilinear order. Zamyatin's One State barely survived the rebellion of the people from the wilderness outside its orderly civilization. The onslaught on the Russian Empire takes the form of destroying its mission in Teheran and murdering Griboedov, who, according to Tynianov's interpretation, is held accountable for the poverty caused by heavy reparation payments.

Thus, in Tynianov's interpretation, Russia's relationship with Persia in the aftermath of the war is tainted with Orientalism, and with imperial expansion, in which the legacy of Peter the Great played a pivotal role. Mirza Afshar in his contrasting account concentrates on teasing out the perfect recipe for modernization as concocted by Peter, the great reformer, which in his optimistic prognosis will deliver Iran from Western domination and launch its progress towards a politically stable and prosperous future.

Chapter Eight

The Death of Vazir-Mukhtar as a Parody of a Spy Novel

Within the tapestry of interwoven parodies through which Yury Tynianov explores nineteenth-century political and cultural imperialism, there is a clearly discernible thread of adventure literature and its subgenre, the spy novel. Tynianov's characters Alexander Griboedov and Colonel MacDonald lose themselves in *The Prairie*, the newly published adventure novel by James Fenimore Cooper (1789–1851).[1] According to Angela Brintlinger's insightful article, the historical Griboedov viewed his own life as "The Persian Prairie," in which he, like Cooper's characters, explored the frontier, defined as "a place of cultural mixing and cultural contest."[2] *The Death of Vazir-Mukhtar*, however, is more akin to the spy novel *Kim* by Tynianov's contemporary Rudyard Kipling (1865–1936).[3] In 1907, the author of this famous novel received the Nobel Prize in Literature "in consideration" of his "power of observation, originality of imagination, virility of ideas and remarkable talent for narration."[4] Kipling's interest in the diplomatic intrigue surrounding the British and Russian imperial expansionism stems from his experience as special correspondent for the *Civil and Military Gazette*, based in the city of Lahore, India, then in the British Indian Empire.[5] The first assignment that truly excited Kipling was reporting on the Afghan Boundary Commission dispatched "to demarcate Afghanistan's northern borders."[6]

> The Commission – thirty Raj officials, loaded with gifts, escorted by some 500 troops – traveled into Afghanistan in considerable style, hoping to negotiate locally with Russian commanders who threatened Afghan borders from the north and the west. It was partly a fact-finding trip, partly an amiable gesture, partly a way to send the message that India was serious about protecting Afghanistan's integrity, and partly – that peculiarly

colonial-era enterprise – an ethnological survey of regions north of Afghanistan about which the British knew little.[7]

Kipling learned rudimentary Russian and had access to newspapers published in Petersburg and Moscow: *Novoye Vremya*, the *Journal de St. Petersburg*, and the *Gazette de Moscow*.[8] Kipling's own writing was well known in fin de siècle and pre-revolutionary Russia and continued to enjoy popularity throughout the Soviet times; one of the early Russian translations of *Kim*, by A.P. Repina, was published in 1915.[9] However, Tynianov could have also read the novel in English. Viktor Shklovsky attested that the literary circles of Leningrad that Tynianov frequented in the early 1920s "were captivated with plot verse [*siuzhetnym stikhom*] and Kipling."[10] *The Death of Vazir-Mukhtar*'s similarities with Kipling's famous spy novel surpass experimentation with rhythmical prose. Both novels are set within the historical context of the Great Game, the Russo-British diplomatic rivalry in Iran, Central Asia, and Afghanistan, although the events in *Kim* take place half a century later. Tynianov makes sure that the reader sees the events of 1829 described in his book as the beginning of the protracted imperialistic struggle that unfolds throughout the nineteenth century. While Griboedov is preoccupied with his diplomatic mission in Iran and economic entrepreneurship in Transcaucasia, his Decembrist friends view these regions as stepping stones to expanding the empire in Central Asia, moving to Khiva, Bukhara, and beyond.[11]

When Griboedov arrives at Petersburg to deliver the Turkmenchay peace treaty at the beginning of the novel, his two closest neighbours in the hotel are spies of the Russian and British empires: Lieutenant Vishniakov and Dr. McNeill, a physician who is employed in the harem of the shah and his son-in-law Alayar Khan. Dr. McNeill jokes about being Griboedov's close neighbour, implying the dangerous proximity of the two empires encroaching on each other's interests.[12] Both neighbours visit Griboedov for drinks and conversations, each pursuing his own goal. McNeill is secretly trying to find out whether Griboedov intends to become the head of the Russian mission in Iran and, if so, to dissuade him from accepting that position. To advise Griboedov in a circumventive way that in Iran his life will be in danger, he tells him that the Iranian women whom he attends as a physician are suspicious, and their husbands are unhappy and in search of what causes their unhappiness, that is, looking for a scapegoat. Griboedov asks whose fault it is, implying that diplomatic manipulations of the British influence the attitudes of the Iranians. The doctor argues that his compatriots gain very little from mediating Persia's payments of war reparations to the Russian side. Griboedov cunningly answers that they could gain "red copper ... Khorasan turquoise, sulfur, olive oil," knowing that the goals of the British surpass exploiting the immediate economic advantages of their influence in Iran. Throughout the entire conversation, McNeill maintains that his advice is not an assignment, and he acts out of an obligation of one European to help another when they find themselves among savages.[13]

While Dr. McNeill warns Griboedov, Lieutenant Vishniakov, a Russian spy exposed by the British, asks for his protection. (Ensuring that Vishniakov is dismissed from his position is another purpose of McNeill's visit to Petersburg.)[14] Griboedov's attempt to prevent Vishniakov's discharge fails, and the latter shoots himself after undressing, spitting on his own epaulets, and destroying the hotel room.[15] Both McNeill's warning and Vishniakov's death appear as premonitions of Griboedov's own demise. Even though Griboedov promises himself that he will not be as artless and straightforward as Vishniakov had been, and will not fall victim to diplomatic games, his cause is lost from the very beginning.[16]

Predictably enough, the losing side of the intelligence game in Kipling's *Kim* is also the Russians. The titular character of the book, a boy named Kim, is the son of an Irish father, raised by an Indian prostitute. Having spent most of his childhood on the streets of Lahore,[17] Kim intimately knows Indian cultures in all their diversity. The boy spies for the British Empire while travelling around India as a disciple of a Tibetan lama, to whom he feels deep attachment. The lama, however, does not know about his disciple's intelligence operations. Kim collaborates with a British spy of Indian origin, Hurree Chunder Mookerjee, or Hurree Babu, a comical cowardly character who unexpectedly reveals his skill and courage while duping two Russian spies into unmasking themselves: he pretends to be a secretly rebellious local dissatisfied with British rule, who "confesses" his resentment only after feigning drunkenness.[18] The two Russian spies are eager to swallow the bait because Hurree Babu's "confession" flatters their self-image as benign colonialists who can understand the Orientals because of their unique position between East and West.[19] They call Hurree Babu "the monstrous hybridism of East and West" representing "India in transition" and fully believe he harbours a "complete hatred of his conquerors."[20] The narrative of the novel counters their opinion, representing the British rule as overall benevolent and progressive.

Despite their claim of being cultural mediators between the East and the West, the Russian spies appear to be indifferent and insensitive towards the local cultures. Seeing the lama's depiction of the wheel of life, one of them wants to buy it. His tactless proposition is refused, upon which he gets angry, tears the sacred picture from the lama's hands, and strikes him on the face.[21] As well, in a display of cultural arrogance, Kipling's Russian spies accuse the British of pride and "unbelievable stupidity" while using the "better and safer" British postal service to mail their intelligence correspondence.[22]

In both *The Death of Vazir-Mukhtar* and *Kim* the failure of the Russians stems from their lack of knowledge and of curiosity. Oriental studies and ethnographic research, as well as more intimate private commingling with the locals, appear as prerequisites if not a guarantee of successful colonization. Kipling and Tynianov each outline their respective sets of characters engaged in Oriental studies and ethnography. These sets contain both representatives of the colonizing side and native researchers aspiring to contribute to modern Western scholarship. Another similarity between the two novels is that scholarship, while clearly serving political objectives, in the eyes of the scholars themselves acquires an absolute value; it is a goal in itself rather than a means for advancing their governments' agendas.

Kim uses his experience of growing up in the streets of an Indian city in his work as an intelligence agent. During his training his supervisor, Colonel Creighton, assigns him to conduct an ethnological survey involving measuring and mapping. One writer maintains that this initiation into the profession of ethnography, as well as the study of English literature at the school of St. Xavier, turned him into a sahib, a white British representative of the imperial power.[23] This statement is partially true in that the novel does explicitly connect literature and ethnography to the politics of the empire, and mastering them are important milestones in Kim's maturation. However, the boy was a clever spy even before he met his British teachers and became conscious of being one. He intuitively knew what to do while he was still running errands for the Afghan intelligence agent Mahbub Ali, who spied for the British using his extensive network as a successful horse trader.

At that time, Kim was culturally Indian, and his tanned countenance was indistinguishable from other boys with whom he played in the streets of Lahore; he did not even know about his own Irish and English origin. Yet Kipling apparently ascribes Kim's inquisitiveness and resourcefulness to the innate nature of the white race;[24] after a long day of travelling, the Indians are happy to camp at the resting station but Kim gets up to explore his surroundings, prompting one of his fellow travellers to ask: "But why not sit and rest? … Only the devils and the English walk to and fro without reason."[25] This productive restlessness, according to Kipling – and not certain historical, economic, or geopolitical preconditions – propelled Europeans on their path towards progress, prosperity, and imperial expansion.

Kim is "thrilled with a boy's pure delight in the Game,"[26] which allows him to indulge his insatiable curiosity in meeting new people from diverse ethnic, religious, and social backgrounds and travelling to distant regions of India. The process of his ethnographical inquiry is more important than the goal of winning the Game. To Colonel Creighton, a British intelligence officer who "uses ethnology as a tool to disguise his political power as an agent of the Survey,"[27] research also means much more than just a smokescreen for his spying operations. His most coveted wish is to become a member of the Royal Society, "which he had bombarded for years with monographs on strange Asiatic cults and unknown customs."[28] Because of this, he feels solidarity with his native collaborator, Hurree Babu, whose fondest desire likewise is "to be made a member of the Royal Society by taking ethnological notes."[29]

In *The Death of Vazir-Mukhtar*, both Griboedov and Mirza Yakub, the eunuch of the shah's harem, appear as Orientalists, scholars who study the Orient. Griboedov, the protagonist, feels that his fate does not allow him to realize his passion for knowledge. On the eve of the day when the Russian mission is attacked, he is sitting in his room conversing with his conscience, which asks him why he abandoned his childhood dreams and whatever happened to his science or scholarship (*nauka*).[30]

Tynianov takes the idea that Griboedov's diplomatic career prevented him from realizing his passion for learning from Griboedov's own letters. One in particular, a draft without an addressee, seems to be a request to be dismissed from his position, with the goal of furthering his education.[31] Griboedov starts the letter by declaring that his education consists of knowing several languages – Slavonic and Russian, Latin, French, English, and German. He adds that while in Iran he learned Persian and Arabic. However, he argues, in order to be a useful member of society "it is not enough to have several different words for one idea";[32] the more one knows, the better one can serve one's homeland. To have the opportunity to learn, he is asking to be dismissed and recalled from the "cheerless country, where not only it is impossible to learn anything, but also that one can forget even that which he knew before."[33]

While for Kim, India is an open book ready to reveal its secret knowledge to his inquisitive mind, for Griboedov Iran is an impediment to his ongoing education. Iran is an important playing piece in the Great Game, but Griboedov is more eager to dedicate his studies to the closer-to-home portion of the "nesting Orients,"[34] the newly acquired

Transcaucasia, where he plans to establish his colonial enterprise, the Russian Transcaucasia Company. Reflecting these preferences in his novel, Tynianov makes the fictional Dr. McNeill tease Griboedov by expressing doubt whether Russia will ever have its own East India and musing that perhaps Emperor Paul's suggestion to situate one on Malta, in the Mediterranean, was not a bad idea.[35] Griboedov, who intends to set up his East India in Transcaucasia, accepts McNeill's challenge. During the doctor's next visit Griboedov, wearing a Georgian dress, offers a toast: "And now, dearest Doctor, let us drink to your East India," adding, "What do you think, there cannot be another East India?"[36]

Like Griboedov, Mirza Yakub is also prevented from quenching his thirst for knowledge by being forcefully transplanted to a place he never wanted to be. He studied the ancient Armenian language in the Ejmiatsin monastery and is on his way to Tiflis to further his education when he is kidnapped, castrated, and turned into a eunuch. Griboedov is enamoured with the "Tale of Igor's Campaign" and dreams of creating an ancient Russian song, believing that it is important to read old sacred books and ancient chronicles. In the same way, Mirza Yakub seems to be looking for the keys to understand and transform reality in the lore of ancient religious poetry and the wisdom of theology. In Iran, he also learns Persian and Arabic. The prominent position of shah's treasurer that he soon acquires gives him innermost knowledge of the culture and politics of the court. Thus, both Mirza Yakub and Griboedov unwillingly become "scholars" of the Orient, Orientalists.

In this capacity, Griboedov is invited to join the examination committee at the School of Oriental Languages in Petersburg. Interestingly, Dr. McNeill also receives but declines their invitation, preferring to attend a military inspection instead, even though he also positions himself as a person compelled to leave for the Orient because of his inquisitiveness.[37] Tynianov portrays the other Orientalists examining the students as eccentric amateurs, a "casual intermixture of Europe and Asia."[38] One of the prominent Orientalist scholars of the time, Osip Senkovsky, appears in the novel as an obnoxious young man shouting that Queen Semiramis was a "velikaia sterva" (great stinker) in a loud argument he started over being allowed to take his dog into the examination room. This remark about Semiramis, in Senkovsky's view, qualifies him as a freethinker, since in making it he intentionally disregards an allusion to the Northern Semiramis, Catherine the Great, that the academician Adelung makes in an attempt to prevent the dog's admission.[39]

During the examination, Senkovsky asks the students trick questions, such as "What are the criteria Bedouin poets use to evaluate the quality of their poems?" When a student answers that a good poem in their view should be concise and memorable, Senkovsky tells him that is wrong; in his opinion, Bedouins believe that their poetry is good because they never have snuffles.[40] Senkovsky, with his "despotic" style, and the rest of the "multi-ethnic gang of teachers and students" fill the classroom "air with murder and the Orient." In this parody of a scholarly quest, "camels roamed the hall of the ministry." To provoke Griboedov, Senkovsky asks one of the examinees to read and translate a passage from the Gulistan, the book of the thirteenth-century Persian poet Saadi, who is very influential both in Europe and in the Middle East. The passage, which contains the advice to be on good terms not only with important people but also with their doorkeepers, janitors, and dogs, is almost word for word repeated in Griboedov's poem *Woe from Wit*.[41] Magnanimously forgiving the provocation, Griboedov gently suggests that Senkovsky is too strict, after which the tension de-escalates and the "battle cry" in the classroom gives way "to cooing." Now the students, prompted by their examiner, read love poems, filling the room with erotic Orientalist images.[42] Griboedov the Orientalist succeeds in manipulating knowledge by diplomatically steering it into a new direction.

The Orientalist ethnographic studies in *Kim* similarly exoticize the cultures they observe. Both Colonel Creighton and Hurree Babu study "Asiatic cults and unknown customs." The latter, however, is not able to overcome the influence of his native culture to the degree necessary to achieve "scholarly objectivity." When Kim, after spending years in St. Xavier school, becomes white (both because his tan fades and because he discovers his Britishness), his supervisor Mahbub Ali brings him to a sorceress who will dye his skin a darker hue, not only to disguise him for an intelligence operation, but also to "fortify" him "against the chances of the Road."[43] As the sorceress drives herself into a frenzy in order to give Kim "the full protection," the reader becomes aware of a concealed observer taking notes from the balcony. This is Hurree Babu, who advises Mahbub Ali not to interrupt "this ventriloquial necromanciss" even though these rituals "must be very disturbing" to Mahbub Ali, for "no enlightened observer is jolly-well upset."[44] As the magic ritual progresses, however, Hurree Babu becomes anxious and, "talking English to reassure himself," wonders how he can "fear the absolutely non-existent." The narrator of the novel explicates: "It is an awful thing still to dread the magic that you contemptuously investigate – to collect folklore for the Royal Society with a lively belief in all Powers of Darkness."[45] While Colonel Creighton's irrational desire to belong to the Royal Society infantilizes him,[46] it is the similarly infantilized colonized who falls short of becoming the "enlightened observer" he claims himself to be. Steeped in the superstitious subjectivity of his own culture, as Kipling wants us to believe, Hurree Babu is unable to achieve an "objective" scholarly point of view. Both novels explore the alleged grey areas between the lack of insight that disadvantages an outsider and the subjectivity that haunts the insider.

The Death of Vazir-Mukhtar reveals the self-doubt of Griboedov, the historical figure, in his knowledge of the Orient and his ability to tease out confidential information that would help his country to win the imperialist competition. Although Griboedov's contemporaries considered him an expert in Oriental studies, he judged his own knowledge with scepticism. Thus, according to Begichev's memoir, serving in Iran "greatly benefited" Griboedov:

> His strong will had been strengthened, his perpetual inquisitiveness had no more obstacles or distractions. He read much on all subjects of science and studied a lot. His ability to learn languages was extraordinary: he learned the Persian language to perfection, read all Persian poets, and was able to write poems in that language.[47]

Interestingly, in one of his letters to Begichev, Griboedov complains that his "paucity of knowledge" about Transcaucasia and Iran "infuriates" him "at every turn." He cannot forgive himself for ignorantly taking scraps of cotton left on prickly bushes by trading caravans for actual growing cotton plants.[48] Neither does Griboedov consider himself an insider who knows the secret motives and hidden interests of the Iranians. In his opinion, only representatives of medical professions forge truly close connections with the Persians, who welcome their help, opening their homes and harems "otherwise unavailable to anyone." [49] In his letter to Konstantin Rodofinikin, director of the Asian Department of the Russian Ministry of Foreign Affairs, Griboedov stresses the importance of including a qualified doctor within the personnel of the Russian mission in Iran. In order to win the Great Game the Russian Empire should not fall behind Great Britain, whose physicians exert their influence across Iran; a Dr. Cormick "decisively owns" the "mind" and "all intentions" of the shah's heir, Abbas-Mirza, in Tabriz, and Dr. McNeill enjoys the similar confidence of the shah himself in Teheran.[50]

During his conversation with Dr. McNeill, Griboedov marvelled at his deep knowledge of "the slightest interests and relations of the state, in which he has been serving for several years as a doctor of the English mission and court doctor of his majesty the shah." Griboedov believes that "no diplomat can achieve this by ordinary means without the help of the useful science that procures Mr. McNeill unobstructed entry everywhere in Persia." For this reason, Griboedov recommends Dr. Alexander Semashko, whose practice in Astrakhan taught him how to cure "illnesses in hot climates" and gained him the trust of the city's "Asiatic residents," as a useful addition to the newly formed Russian mission.[51]

Tynianov reflects in his novel on Griboedov's antagonism towards the sly undercover British agent Dr. McNeill, who "loafed about" the shah's and his son-in-law Alayar Khan's harems "with his clysters, poultices, and powder" and "rubbed and fed laxatives to all those countless wives."[52] The narrator, whose point of view in this scene meshes with that of his protagonist, further explains that while "Russia was conquering the East with Cossack lance, England [did it] with medicinal pills and money."[53] He even claims that "an obscure doctor of the Gujarat company, having successfully cured one of the Hindustan sovereigns, delivered to England those domains that later grew into the East Indies."[54] Tynianov takes the latter historical hypothesis from Griboedov's above-cited letter to the director of the Asian Department of the Russian Ministry of Foreign Affairs.

On a similar note, when in Kipling's novel the teenage Kim acts on a lucky guess and cures a little boy by giving his father a quinine pill for his son,[55] the lama sees him as "no longer a child, but a man, ripened in wisdom, walking as a physician."[56] Kim enjoys his new identity as a physician and the trust of the local people it confers. Hurree Babu also assumes the identity of a "courteous physician":[57] chasing down the Russian spies in the Himalayas, "the courteous Dacca physician … paid for his food in ointments good for goitre and counsels that restore peace between men and women."[58] He arranges secret intelligence exchange meetings with Kim in the woods where he collects medicinal herbs, suggesting that "Kim, as budding physician, must accompany him."[59] While possessing or pretending to possess medical skills is in *Kim* an important method of disguise and of collecting information, ethnography or Oriental studies have greater prominence in the novel as a cover and a tool for gathering intelligence.

In *The Death of Vazir-Mukhtar*, Tynianov creates a character who combines the qualities of a physician and ethnographer, reflecting Griboedov's search for a skilful Russian physician who would use his profession to gain the confidence of the "Asiatics" and a deeper knowledge of the "Orient" and its politics. Tynianov's protagonist finds such a person during the examination at the School of Oriental Languages in Petersburg and immediately invites him to join his mission in Iran.

Tynianov's fictional character of a perfect doctor, scholar, and spy combines the features and professional qualities of the mission's physician with those of its second secretary Karl Fedorovich Adelung, the son of the academician Fedor Adelung (Friedrich von Adelung), a prominent historian, philosopher, and linguist. The fictional Dr. Adelung is passionately interested in both natural and cultural phenomena and, like many other characters in the novel, represents the historical reality of the nineteenth century as well as the fascination of the 1920s with multifaceted, protean personalities. At the same time, for Tynianov he is the perfect character to represent the voyeuristic nature of Orientalism, with its insatiable curiosity and lack of intercultural and interpersonal sensitivity. Thus, at the infamous audience during which Griboedov silently sat in front of the shah for a prolonged period of time in order to intimidate him, "Dr. Adelung, standing behind him and looking in his uniform like a round and short hookah, was inspecting the eunuchs. Eunuchs interested him as a natural phenomenon, a physical one."[60]

As elsewhere in the novel, the original Orientalist text of Tynianov's parody is Pushkin's *Journey to Arzrum*. In chapter four of his *Journey*, Pushkin recounts how, upon learning that among the prisoners of the war there was a hermaphrodite, he asked that the prisoner be brought in for examination; he describes the prisoner's body in Latin, masking callous voyeurism as scientific curiosity.[61] In chapter five he speaks of a Russian officer who was captured and castrated at the age of eighteen, serving afterward for more than twenty years in the harem of one of the shah's sons. Pushkin is condescendingly sympathetic towards this person, who tells the story of "his misfortune, his stay in Persia with touching simplicity," yet stresses the man's importance primarily as a source of knowledge, adding, "In a physiological sense his testimony was precious."[62]

In Tynianov's parodic interpretation, the Russian Orientalists, such as Griboedov and Adelung, treat the eunuch Mirza Yakub as an object of study. However, their attitudes change once they get to know him better, when he moves to the building of the Russian mission after asking for asylum. In his conversation with Adelung, Mirza Yakub is described as "becoming a man of letters, an associate of Senkovsky,"[63] who shares his expertise on different aspects of Persian culture. Adelung is impatiently awaiting the arrival of Mirza Yakub's library and manuscripts. "You are an educated man," he says, "you will write a memoir, we will translate your manuscripts together, and Mr. Senkovsky will publish them in Petersburg. The success will be loud."[64]

Mirza Yakub, in the novel exemplifying an Orientalist with a different point of view, dispels the idea of the Orient as an immutable stagnating entity, a place of strict social hierarchy and despotism, where those who do not belong to the nobility are stripped of dignity. Thus, when Adelung asks if it is "true that, when a harem leaves the city, gunshot signals are given, and everyone runs away from the road and those who don't are subjected to imprisonment," Mirza Yakub replies that it is untrue, and when his harem visits "Negaristan for festivities, there is no end to beggars and onlookers."[65] When Adelung refers to a conflicting description by the seventeenth-century jeweller, traveller, and writer Jean Chardin, whom he considers "a reliable source,"[66] Mirza Yakub reminds Adelung that "Chardin lived when knights existed in France and Russia, it seems, did not have even emperors."[67]

Thus, Mirza Yakub becomes Tynianov's mouthpiece for advocating cultural incommensurability that the author formulates elsewhere, calling Persia "an old country unaware of its age because there were people living there."[68] The parallel between Persia, Russia, and France that Mirza Yakub draws in his argument puts the three countries on equal footing, suggesting that each goes through its own cultural changes and historical development. In contrast, Griboedov's parallels between Persia and pre-Petrine Russia, which Tynianov parodies in his novel, imply that the Orient is a few steps behind his own country, which is trying to catch up with the West.[69]

On the one hand, the character of Mirza Yakub defies the Orientalist outlook by refusing to be an object of scholarly inquiry. On the other hand, he himself is an Orientalist studying Persian society, to which, because of his national origin and social status, he does not quite belong. He and Griboedov are similar in their position of not being quite aligned with either the East or the West, which reflects the complex interrelations that Milica Bakić-Hayden calls "nesting Orientalisms."[70] The hierarchical gradation of othering and of Orientalizing one's neighbour that she discovers between Western and Eastern Europe, the Balkans, and the Near East is applicable to the relationships between the West, Russia, Transcaucasia, and Iran in the nineteenth century. In the same way as Russians, Orientalized by the West, as a form of compensation viewed Transcaucasia as an Oriental and backward land, the residents of that region in their turn Orientalized Iran and despised its political domination. Writings of such representatives of Transcaucasia as the Armenian pedagogue Khachatur Abovian and the poet and military and public figure Alexander Chavchavadze, Griboedov's father-in-law, suggest that they also detested the condescending attitudes of the Russian administrative elites and bypassed Russian mediation to establish cultural connections with Europe. They frame their own attempts at resisting colonization within the colonialist discourse and unwillingly rearticulate many of its underlying assumptions.

Tynianov intuitively grasps these complex relationships and reflects them in his novelistic study, without defining them precisely. Through his parody of the Orientalist scholarship of Griboedov's time, he reveals the idea of knowledge as power. He also shows that in the 1820s Oriental studies in Russia were still amateur and far from the concerted and rigorous efforts of the late nineteenth century. To articulate his anti-imperialist sentiment and quest for authenticity, Tynianov chooses as his mouthpiece the eunuch Mirza Yakub, who is a marginalized minority in both the Russian and the Persian empires and an incomplete man within the framework of patriarchal hierarchy.

To restore the eunuch's dignity, Tynianov portrays him as equal to Griboedov in every aspect: his intellect, knowledge, and courage. He also matches Griboedov in physical stature and the attractiveness of his "passionless face."[71] In Kipling's novel, however, the native ethnographer Hurree Babu cannot compete with the youthful attractiveness of Kim, a chaste teenager whose looks captivate women but who is indifferent to them, instead being captivated by his travels and participation in the Great Game. The Indian intelligence agent is described as "a hulking, obese Babu whose stockinged legs shook with fat" and who walked "with the gait of a bogged cow."[72] He talks with a funny accent in a Babu English, an artificial bookish language that lacks idiomatic expressions.[73] His appearance disqualifies him from being the true hero of the spy novel despite his inventiveness and fearlessness, which strangely enough coexist with episodes of helpless cowardice. While Hurree Babu's character elicits admiration and sympathy from the reader, he remains an endearing native sidekick of the genuine hero of British ancestry.

Unlike *The Death of Vazir-Mukhtar*, which contraposes the understanding of an inquisitive local with a colonizer's awkward attempts to penetrate the mysteries of a colonized culture, Kipling's novel combines the features of both in the person of Kim. A local boy who grew up on the streets of an Indian city, Kim delights in the sights, smells, and sounds of his bountiful country and relishes every opportunity to chat with its diverse inhabitants. It is evident that Kipling has infused his novel with nostalgia for his own early childhood and late adolescence in India. The boy's first unpleasant encounters with the sahibs, the British colonizers, undoubtedly reflect the author's unhappy years in a boarding school in England. However, Kim very soon discovers the advantages of being a sahib. Similarly, his creator professes his loyalty to the British Empire in a personal letter to George F. Beams, stating,

"I am a colonial in that I was born in Bombay but it has never occurred to me to say that I am 'loyal,' because, like you, I am a white man and – one can't step out of one's skin."[74]

It seems that Kim's love and intimate knowledge of India justify his ownership of the country, while not belonging to any of the native ethnic or religious groups gives him a superior ability to "enter" the "souls" of the representatives of these diverse communities. Thus, as part of his training as a spy, Kim participates in a "dressing-up" game to learn "how such and such a caste talked, or walked, or coughed, or spat, or sneezed."[75] The Indian boy trained alongside Kim is less successful: "The Hindu child played this game clumsily. That little mind, keen as an icicle where tally of jewels was concerned, could not temper itself to enter another's soul; but a demon in Kim woke up and sang with joy as he put on the changing dresses, and changed speech and gesture therewith."[76] Kipling here employs the same justification of imperialism that he satirizes in the characters of the Russian spies, who think that they are the more benevolent colonizers because they can better understand the Orientals. The protagonist of Tynianov's novel, Griboedov, similarly validates his claim to ownership of Transcaucasia, where he is planning to establish his new East India by virtue of his love for that country, to which he dedicated eight years of his life, and where he made meaningful personal connections. Just as Kipling lyrically writes of Kim's attachment to India, Tynianov relates Griboedov's joy in seeing people who brought on their faces "that Tiflis air, on their clothes that Tiflis dust."[77]

While Griboedov knows a great deal about the geographic features and the economic potential of the future site of his colonial enterprise, he is less knowledgeable and less curious about Persia. Tynianov endows his native scholar and court administrator Mirza Yakub with better political insight than his protagonist. During Griboedov's audience with the shah, Mirza Yakub, as he looks at him, thinks, "his power is great, but he lacks a lot: knowledge," and he mentally enumerates Griboedov's diplomatic mistakes that forebode the demise of the Russian mission in Teheran, among which was relying on Dr. McNeill's mediation in securing timely payments of the war indemnity.[78] Ironically, it is the eunuch's knowledge of the innermost secrets of the court that makes him a target of the British conspiracy, bringing about his own death and that of Griboedov after the latter gave him political asylum in the Russian mission. He knows too much about the personal life of the shah's harem as well as the diplomatic games the British are playing in order to strengthen their political influence in Persia. The British spy Dr. McNeill visits the shah and his son-in-law, Alayar Khan, and together they plot to destroy Mirza Yakub.[79] McNeill is pale and panicky, because "the English state was changing during those days: its Eastern politics was in the hands which were white, unmanly, covered with rings, disgraced human hands."[80] In one sentence, Tynianov not only explicated the diplomatic intrigue but also summarized the eunuch's traumatic past, and he places his human right to return home above any political affiliations. The personal belongings that Mirza Yakub had packed to take home with him are ransacked. Among the items that disappeared are "the receipts for things bought by the eunuch for the harem," taken in order to accuse him of embezzlement, and manuscripts, notes, "the letters of various persons … including Dr. McNeill," and "that female Koran, which so much interested Dr. Adelung, who wanted to publish it under the editorship of Senkovsky."[81] Here secret political documents such as Mirza Yakub's correspondence with Dr. McNeill are of the same value as the culturally sensitive materials of his Orientalist research.

Tynianov illustrates in his novel how the imperialists use cultural and religious sensitivity to attain their political goals. When attempts to lure Mirza Yakub out of his plan to leave for Transcaucasia fail, a holy war is declared to incite the common people to storm the Russian mission.[82] The night before McNeill, "with all his people," prudently leaves the city "in order to rest, unwind, breathe some fresh air. Only for a day."[83] Tynianov chooses an unconfirmed and debated theory of British conspiracy, which also implicates the Iranian government in inflaming the residents of Teheran and channelling their anger towards destruction of the Russian mission and the deaths of Griboedov and Mirza Yakub among many others. Unlike the somewhat comical development of the Great Game competition in Kipling's novel, this is a deadly confrontation causing misfortune for many people. It seems that the British outsmart the Russians as they do in *Kim*, but it is an illusory victory within Tynianov's Marxist-Leninist rejection of imperialism as a morally sound political system. Channelling the anger of the impoverished residents of Teheran towards expressions of religious intolerance cannot completely mask its real economic and political cause. According to Tynianov, the tragedy in the Russian mission is not entirely an outcome of cunning British intelligence and diplomacy. Rather, it stems from the resentment of Persians impoverished by the war and the constant meddling of the British and Russian empires, as well as economically exploited by their own elites. The demand for costly war reparations is the last straw that, when added to their current economic burden, results in a violent outburst.

To stress the oppressive nature of imperialism, Tynianov throughout his novel insistently reminds his reader about the rebellions of residents of the newly acquired Transcaucasian territories, noting that even Griboedov's own father-in-law, Alexander Chavchavadze, was involved more than once in such resistance.[84] Kipling, conversely, downplays the importance of resistance to British rule in India, making the locals themselves characterize mutinies as "madness."[85] Kim's sincere love for his "Mother India"[86] and his fascination with travelling along the Grand Trunk Road, an ancient arterial road renovated by the British, does not preclude but only reinforces the legitimacy of his and other sahibs' presence and good stewardship. It is true that after obtaining important documents from the Russian spies and carrying them secretly on his body, Kim becomes sick,[87] or goes through an "existential breakdown," which Lizzy Welby interprets as a result of his inability "to dodge the totalitarian colonial patriarchy."[88] It is also true that Kim's friendship with the Tibetan lama is more important to him than his loyalty to the British sahibs. However, it is wrong to interpret Kim's healing as achieving freedom from the wheel of life and escaping totalitarian colonial patriarchy together with the vanity of political competition[89] that the lama believes to have secured for himself and his disciple through meditation and enlightenment.[90] For Mahbub Ali, Kim's intelligence work supervisor, the boy's recovery means that he is back in the Great Game, as he reveals in his conversation with the lama: "but now I understand that the boy, sure of Paradise, can yet enter Government service, my mind is easier."[91] Kipling reconciles these differing opinions through an interpretation of Buddhism according to which one should strive to achieve spiritual liberation not by avoiding life but by living it to its fullest. If Kim's destiny is to be a spy, he will be the best spy possible. Recovering Kim is able to see that "roads were meant to be walked upon, houses to be lived in, cattle to be driven, fields to be tilled, and men and women to be talked to."[92] This affirmation of life also means acceptance of the existing relations of imperial dominance between Britain and India.

Tynianov's novel ends on a less life-affirming note, and the wheel of life he depicts is more sinister. His wheel represents the historic recurrence of autocracy tied together with imperialistic expansionism. He draws parallels between the epochs of Peter the Great, Nicholas I, and his own time when Stalinist ideology was strengthening its grip. His protagonist Griboedov, as well as his "doubles," such as Mirza Yakub and Dr. Adelung, also have a zest for life and a thirst for knowledge, as well as a desire to excel in performing their civic duties, but are ground up by the ruthless wheel of history. They lose the Great Game and their lives not because they are not skilful players, but because there are no winners in a game that is immoral and inhumane.

In Lieu of a Conclusion: Tynianov's Anti-imperialist Legacy and the 2010 Television Adaptation of His Novel

Tynianov's novelistic study of nineteenth-century colonial practices and attitudes had contemporary implications. The failure of the protagonist Griboedov's imperialist ambitions was a cautionary tale for the increasingly imperial Stalinist ideology. Tynianov's criticism of romantic nationalism and its support of imperial expansion was in tune with the anti-imperialist tendencies of the 1920s; however, "by the 1930s such ideas were distinctly out of favor in the Stalinist academic establishment."[1] Literary figures like Pushkin and Griboedov were placed on a pedestal for the rest of the Soviet period, although after de-Stalinization tsarist imperialist practices were again criticized, especially by historians of the Caucasus and Central Asia.[2] Soviet academic studies of the Orient continued to differ from Saidian Orientalism in one important aspect – they did not essentialize the notions of the Orient and the Occident.[3] However, using the Marxist idea of historical stages, they continued to justify the civilizing mission of the more "advanced" Russia towards the "backward" peoples of the East.[4]

During late perestroika and throughout post-Soviet times, essentialist and racialized ideas of the Orient resurfaced in literature, film, media, and popular discourse. Historiography began to view Russia's imperial past "with a mixture of nostalgia, self-righteousness and outright jingoism," and brutal conquerors such as Ermolov were commemorated with new statues.[5] The resurgence of imperial ideology in the 2000s sparked renewed interest in Tynianov's novel, which in 2010 was adapted into a popular television series, *Smert' Vazir-Mukhtara. Liubov' i zhizn' Griboedova* (*The Death of Vazir-Mukhtar: Love and Life of Griboedov*).[6] It is instructive to ask whether the adaptation retains Tynianov's anti-imperialist stance, or if it undergoes Bakhtinian reaccentuation, losing its elements of irony and parody and becoming an Orientalist work of art.

Reaccentuation in the television series affects the portrayal of Iran and Iranians most. While in the novel we see Iran Orientalized by the imagination of its protagonist Griboedov, whose critical remarks about this country and its inhabitants appear in a parodic form throughout the book, awareness of Tynianov's parody is absent from the television series. The visual representations of Iran are Orientalized through gaudy interior decoration and clothing, as well as such Orientalist clichés as belly dancing and hookah smoking. Persian men in the television series behave in an arrogant way and are rude to and dismissive of women, for example in a scene where crown prince Abbas Mirza removes jewellery worn by his wives in order to be able to pay the war reparations.[7]

The interpretation of the eunuch Mirza Yakub's character in the television series starkly deviates from the novel, revelling in Orientalist clichés. Mirza Yakub is portrayed as the epitome of an "Oriental slave," weak, cowardly, and servile. His reason for seeking asylum in the Russian mission has nothing to do with his search for authenticity or his longing to recover his identity; it is based in his passion for Dil Firuz, who in this cinematic interpretation is a young woman of German origin from the harem of the shah's son-in-law Alayar Khan. Unlike the eunuch in the novel, this Mirza Yakub does not carry himself with dignity or address Griboedov as an equal. Instead, he kneels before him and flatters him by praising the power he has over the Iranian monarch.[8] He is terrified and hides when the angry mob starts storming the mission. When found, he tries to run, then screams and falls down under the blows of his killers. In contrast, Griboedov in the television series dies as a hero, fighting and falling back gracefully in slow motion.[9] Both deaths are represented very differently from their depiction in the novel, where Mirza Yakub bravely faces his killers and Griboedov's death is described as almost an accident.[10] Mirza Yakub's disgraceful behaviour in the television series reflects Russian men's fear of emasculation due to the loss of imperial power after the collapse of the Soviet Union.[11] This fear, together with a return to pronatalist patriarchal ideology that reflects the economic and demographic crises of the post-Soviet period,[12] make a non-Russian man who lost his physical virility a poor candidate for the role of a hero. Defying Tynianov's unconventional narrative, the filmmakers give this role back to the main protagonist, the straight heterosexual Russian man Griboedov.

The adaptation faithfully reproduces the scenes from the novel that confirm Griboedov's imperial ambitions without, however, the critical point of view added by Tynianov's irony. To highlight the scope of these ambitions, Tynianov frequently compares his protagonist to

Napoleon,[13] another allusion to Pushkin's *Journey*.[14] In the adaptation, Griboedov's identification with Napoleon is alluded to through the bicorn hat he wears when he visits the Russian court and high officials to discuss his project in Transcaucasia.[15] The television series also portrays him as a successor to Peter the Great's empire-building project by literally positioning him behind the Bronze Horseman, the most famous sculture of the emperor, in one of its shots.

Griboedov's project of establishing a Russian Transcaucasian agricultural manufacturing and trading company occupies a central position both in Tynianov's novel and in its television adaptation. The television series faithfully renders the dialogue from the novel in which Griboedov explains to the Russian foreign minister and the superintendent of the Asiatic Department the significance of the company he is planning to establish. Griboedov argues in favour of the development of Transcaucasia as a profitable colony, rather than as a province similar to those inhabited by ethnic Russians. His patriotic goal is to compete with the British in their ability to produce everything, including products of the warmer regions within one's own empire, rather than buying them from other countries.[16]

There is one important aspect of Griboedov's project that the television series interprets differently from the novel. Griboedov's contemporaries harshly criticized the project as an oppressive and imperialistic attempt to exploit both the local population of Transcaucasia and Russian peasants, whom the project's authors planned to buy from serf owners in Russia proper and resettle on the company's lands. The former serfs would be bound to work for the company for fifty years, after which they would be granted freedom. Tynianov reveals this criticism in his novel, but in the television series Griboedov's attempts to resettle peasants were portrayed as saving them from the bonds of forced servitude.[17]

In his novel, Tynianov underlines the inseparability between Griboedov's marriage to Nina Chavchavadze and his political and economic activity in Georgia. The television series alludes to this connection in a scene in which, within one and the same shot, the viewer can see Nina playing with her siblings and neighbours' children during a party while Griboedov talks to the guests about his plans to bring about the economic development of Transcaucasia, and then in the middle of his speech the running Nina bumps into him.[18]

The adaptation, however, positions the relationship between Griboedov and Nina in a more romantic light. Maria Abramishvili, performing the role of Nina, conveys youthful romantic curiosity about and childlike trust in Griboedov, who is both a family friend and her piano teacher. As the television series progresses, her feelings evolve into true attachment and loyalty. The adaptation stresses the age difference between the two and Nina's complete dependence on her husband, but both are justified by her love. In Tynianov's novel, frequent references to the age difference between Griboedov and Nina are another way of underscoring the unbalanced relationship of colonial domination between their lands. As mentioned above, Nina's character alludes to the myth of an "infantile native" whom Griboedov wants to civilize in a "humane" way, as suggested by French Enlightenment thinker Diderot, through intermarriage between colonizer and colonized.

It is interesting that the adaptation of Tynianov's novel, while preserving the idea of a marriage of convenience, makes Nina its main beneficiary. Here Nina is not only a provincial maiden, but also a maiden "without a dowry [*bespridannitsa*]." The television series twists Tynianov's initial motif of a marriage of convenience in two particular scenes. In the first scene, General Sipiagin points at Griboedov and Nina at a ball and begins to gossip about them. In the novel, he says that their union is a marriage of convenience from Griboedov's side, since he has designs for Georgia.[19] In the television series, Sipiagin says it is a marriage of convenience because Nina's mother is completely impoverished.[20] The television adaptation takes Nina's father, Prince Alexander Chavchavadze, out of the picture altogether to underscore her status as a maiden without a dowry.

The second scene is a conversation between Nina's mother, Princess Salome, and a family friend, Praskovia Akhverdova. In the novel, Princess Salome muses about asking Griboedov for the favour of allowing two young relatives to join his mission in Iran. In the television series, she is thinking about borrowing money from Griboedov.[21] Since the marriage between Griboedov and Nina Chavchavadze represents the union between Russia and Georgia, the filmmakers imply that Nina and her country had no other choice than to seek protection from their more powerful patron.

The visual representation of Tiflis in the television series suggests its partial transformation into a Russian provincial town, where people in European and Georgian "national" attires mingle, and European dances alternate with Georgian ones. Those who read Tynianov's novel closely see the scenes of mingling as the writer's parody of imperial attempts to create a rapprochement between Russian and Georgian people, as well as of Soviet policies of nativization and of endorsement of the "friendship of peoples." Thus, Tynianov describes a cotillion at General Sipiagin's ball "in which, together with Russian maidens, Georgian ones in national costumes splashed."[22] The same ball featured an ensemble of musicians that includes five people from the general's house serfs, five vagabonds, and one "amanat from the princes," a hostage from one of the Caucasian tribes held to guarantee its loyalty to the Russians. The general was proud of the presence of the *amanat* in his music band, considering it a sign of the "rapprochement of two nationalities," and hoping the *amanat* would become "some kind of native genius [*tuzemnyi genii kakoi-nibud'*]."[23]

While Tiflis is a hybrid of a Russian provincial city with local exoticism, Griboedov's companion doctor, Adelung, unequivocally defines the Caucasus in the television series as "not Russia" when he first sees the mountains. In this scene the television adaptation departs from the novel, in which Doctor Adelung, seeing the mountains, suggests that in one hundred years post-coaches will connect them with Vladikavkaz in the same way that they connect Petersburg with Tsarskoe Selo.[24] This parodic equation between the Caucasus and the suburbs of Petersburg might have seemed inappropriate to the filmmakers after the recent Chechen (1994–6 and 1999–2009) and Russo-Georgian (2008) wars. To a certain degree, the television series reflects the "colonizer's guilt" that permeates Tynianov's novel, showing as problematic the views of the Caucasus as either a Russian province or its colony. However, no matter how problematic it is, imperialism in the adaptation appears as destiny rather than an ethical choice.

This televised interpretation reflects the ideology of post-Soviet authenticity that invokes the "shared historical experience" of "the former Soviet Union as a whole: the shared values of the former Soviet states and its peoples – shaped and transmitted during centuries of imperial Russian and Soviet rule."[25] Within that "shared authenticity," the Caucasus and Central Asia are still "crudely Orientalized" and denied "independent agency," while Georgia's pro-Western orientation is viewed as a betrayal.[26] This ideology in its turn is engendered by the continual Orientalization of Russia and its anxiety about political ostracization by the West.

While Tynianov in his novel undermines the myth of the "voluntary and mutually benefiting … happy marital union" between Russia and Georgia – refusing to end his novel with the image of Griboedov's grieving and loyal widow, which became the norm for Griboedov's biographies – the television series ends precisely like that, evoking nostalgia for lost unity. The filmmakers resurrect the spirit of nineteenth-century romanticism with its essentializing views of empire, nationhood, and cultural dichotomies,[27] the spirit that Tynianov exposes through parody and judges from the position of moral universalism and anti-imperialist Enlightenment.

Notes

Introduction

1 Iurii Tynianov, *Smert' Vazir-Mukhtara* (*The Death of Vazir-Mukhtar*) (Leningrad: Priboi, 1929).
2 Aleksandr Sergeevich Griboedov, *Gore ot uma* (*Woe from Wit*), in *Polnoe sobranie sochinenii v trekh tomakh* (St. Petersburg: Notabene, 1995), 1:9–122.
3 Eduard Volodarskii, *Smert' Vazir-Mukhtara. Liubov' i zhizn' Griboedova*, dir. Sergei Vinokurov (Russia: Avrora Films, 2010).
4 Laurence Kelly, *Diplomacy and Murder in Tehran: Alexander Griboyedov and Imperial Russia's Mission to the Shah of Persia* (London: I.B. Tauris, 2002).
5 Sergei Aleksandrovich Fomichev, *Griboedov. Entsiklopediia* (St. Petersburg: Nestor-Istoriia, 2007), 189.
6 Tynianov, *Smert' Vazir-Mukhtara* (1929); see also Yuri Tynyanov, *The Death of Vazir-Mukhtar* (1927), trans. Susan Causey, trans. ed. Vera Tsareva-Brauner (London: Look Media, 2018).
7 Angela Brintlinger, *Writing a Usable Past: Russian Literary Culture, 1917–1937* (Evanston: Northwestern University Press, 2008); Brintlinger, "Griboedov u Tynianova: Biografiia ili mif?" in *A.S. Griboedov: Khmelitskii sbornik* (Smolensk: SGU, 1998), 384–96.
8 N.Ya. Berkovsky, "O Griboedove i o romane Tynianova," in *Mir sozdavaemyi literaturoi* (Moscow: Sovetskii pisatel', 1989), 230–45; G.A. Levinton, "Istochniki i podteksty romana 'Smert' Vazir-Mukhtara,'" in *Tynianovskii sbornik. Tret'i tynianovskie chteniia* (Riga: Zinatne, 1988), 6–14; Arkadiy Viktorovich [A.V.] Belinkov, *Iurii Tynianov* (Moscow: Sovetskii pisatel', 1965).
9 Dimitri N. Breschinsky and Zinaida A. Breschinsky, "On Tynjanov the Writer and His Use of Cinematic Technique in *The Death of the Wazir Mukhtar*," *Slavic and East European Journal* 29, no. 1 (1985): 1–17, https://www.jstor.org/stable/307921; Michael A. Denner, "Dusting Off the

Couch (and Discovering the Tolstoy Connection in Shklovsky's 'Art as Device')," *Slavic and East European Journal* 52, no. 3 (2008): 370–88, https://www.jstor.org/stable/40650988; Ilya Kalinin, "Istoriya kak iskusstvo chlenorazdel'nosti," *Novoe literaturnoe obozrenie* 71 (2005): 103–31.

10 See the following non-exhaustive list of some of the major works on Russian imperialism and Orientalism: Monika Greenleaf, *Pushkin and Romantic Fashion: Fragment, Elegy, Orient, Irony* (Stanford: Stanford University Press, 1994); Susan Layton, *Russian Literature and Empire* (Cambridge: Cambridge University Press, 1994); Katya Hokanson, "Literary Imperialism, *Narodnost'*, and Pushkin's Invention of the Caucasus," *Russian Review* 53, no. 3 (1994): 336–52; Ewa M. Thompson, *Imperial Knowledge: Russian Literature and Colonialism* (Westport: Greenwood, 2000); Harsha Ram, *Imperial Sublime: A Russian Poetics of Empire* (London: University of Wisconsin Press, 2003); David Schimmelpenninck van der Oye, *Russian Orientalism: Asia in the Russian Mind from Peter the Great to the Emigration* (New Haven: Yale University Press, 2010); Vera Tolz, *Russia's Own Orient: The Politics of Identity and Oriental Studies in the Late Imperial and Early Soviet Periods* (Oxford: Oxford University Press, 2011).

11 Vladimir Il'ich Lenin, *Imperializm, kak vysshaia stadiia kapitalizma: populiarnyi ocherk* (Moscow: Kniga, 1986).

12 Tolz, *Russia's Own Orient*, 50–101.

13 Tolz, 51, 81–2.

14 Tolz, 82. See also Terry Martin, *The Affirmative Action Empire: Nations and Nationalism in the Soviet Union, 1923–1939* (London: Cornell University Press, 2001); Francine Hirsch, *Empire of Nations: Ethnographic Knowledge and the Making of the Soviet Union* (London: Cornell University Press, 2005); Yuri Slezkine, "The USSR as a Communal Apartment, or How a Socialist State Promoted Ethnic Particularism," *Slavic Review* 53, no. 2 (1994): 414–52.

15 Tolz, *Russia's Own Orient*, 96.

16 Tolz, 100–1.

17 Tolz, 50.

18 Muriel Atkin, *Russia and Iran: 1780–1828* (Minneapolis: University of Minnesota Press, 1980), 27.

19 Iurii Tynianov, "Promezhutok," in *Literaturnyi fakt* (Moscow: Vysshaia shkola, 1993), 272.

20 Katerina Clark, *Petersburg: Crucible of Cultural Revolution* (Cambridge, MA: Harvard University Press, 1995), 242.

21 Lynne Viola, *Peasant Rebels under Stalin: Collectivization and the Culture of Peasant Resistance* (New York: Oxford University Press, 1999), 24.

1 Colonial Management of Transcaucasia

1 Militsa Vasil'evna Nechkina, *A.S. Griboedov i dekabristy* (Moscow: Izdatel'stvo Akademii nauk SSSR, 1951), 537–45; Aleksandr Aleksandrovič Lebedev, *Griboedov: Fakty i Gipotezy* (Moscow: Iskusstvo, 1980), 270–4.

2 Nikolai Piksanov, *Griboedov. Issledovaniia i kharakteristiki* (Leningrad: Izdatel'stvo pisatelei v Leningrade, 1934), 148.

3 Maria Konstantinovna Rozhkova, *Ekonomicheskaia politika tsarskogo pravitel'stva na srednem vostoke vo vtoroi chetverti XIX veka i russkaia burzhuaziia* (Moscow: Izdatel'stvo akademii nauk SSSR, 1949), 55.

4 Natan Eidelman, *Byt' mozhet za khrebtom Kavkaza* (Moscow: Nauka, 1990), 129–49.

5 Elena Andreeva, *Russia and Iran in the Great Game: Travelogues and Orientalism* (London: Routledge, 2007); Alexander Etkind, *Internal Colonization: The Russian Imperial Experience* (Cambridge: Polity, 2011); Rudi Matthee and Elena Andreeva, eds., *Russians in Iran: Diplomacy and Power in the Qajar Era and Beyond* (London: I.B. Tauris, 2019); David Schimmelpenninck van der Oye, *Russian Orientalism: Asia in the Russian Mind from Peter the Great to the Emigration* (New Haven: Yale University Press, 2010); Vera Tolz, *Russia's Own Orient: The Politics of Identity and Oriental Studies in the Late Imperial and Early Soviet Periods* (Oxford: Oxford University Press, 2011); Ewa M. Thompson, *Imperial Knowledge: Russian Literature and Colonialism* (Westport: Greenwood, 2000).

6 Iurii Tynianov, *Smert' Vazir-Mukhtara* (*The Death of Vazir-Mukhtar*), in *Sochineniia v dvukh tomakh* (Leningrad: Khudozhestvennaia literatura, 1985), 2:85; Yuri Tynyanov, *The Death of Vazir-Mukhtar* (1927), trans. Susan Causey, trans. ed. Vera Tsareva-Brauner (London: Look Media, 2018). Unless otherwise noted, all Russian translations are mine.

7 Aleksandr Sergeevich Griboedov, *Polnoe sobranie sochinenii v trekh tomakh* (St. Petersburg: Dmitrii Bulanin, 2006), 3:325–44, 561–75.

8 Mikhail Zhukovskii, "Zamechaniia na zapisku ob ustroistve zemledel'cheskoi, manufakturnoi i torgovoi kompanii," appendix to I.K. Enikolopov, *Griboedov v Gruzii* (Tbilisi: Zaria Vostoka, 1954), 130–57.

9 Adam Smith, *An Inquiry into the Nature and Causes of the Wealth of Nations* (Edinburgh: Printed for S. Doig and A. Stirling, 1817), vol. 2 (hereafter cited as Smith, *Wealth of Nations*).

10 Abbé Guillaume-Thomas-François Raynal, *A History of the Two Indies*, trans. and ed. Peter Jimack (Aldershot: Ashgate, 2006) (hereafter referred to as *History*); Raynal, *A Philosophical and Political History of the Settlements*

and Trade of the Europeans in the East and West Indies, trans. J.O. Justamond, rev. ed. in 10 vols. (London: Printed for W. Strahan and T. Cadell, 1783) (hereafter cited as Raynal, *Europeans in the East and West Indies*).

11 Muriel Atkin, *Russia and Iran: 1780–1828* (Minneapolis: University of Minnesota Press, 1980), 27.

12 Raynal, *Europeans in the East and West Indies*, 2:192.

13 Griboedov, *Polnoe sobranie sochinenii*, 3:334–9.

14 Tynianov, *Smert' Vazir-Mukhtara* (1985), 179–80.

15 Griboedov, *Polnoe sobranie sochinenii*, 3:339.

16 Griboedov, 3:328.

17 Raynal, *History*, 7.

18 Thomas Flanagan, "The Agricultural Argument and Original Appropriation: Indian Lands and Political Philosophy," *Canadian Journal of Political Science* 22, no. 3 (1989): 589–602.

19 Iakov Gordin, *Kavkaz: Zemlia i krov'* (St. Petersburg: Zhurnal "Zvezda," 2000), 8–9.

20 Pavel Pestel, *Russkaia pravda* (St. Petersburg: Kul'tura, 1906), 47.

21 Smith, *Wealth of Nations*, 2:410.

22 Griboedov, *Polnoe sobranie sochinenii*, 3:328.

23 Zhukovskii, 137.

24 Zhukovskii, 130.

25 Denis Diderot, *Political Writings*, trans. and ed. John Hope Mason and Robert Wokler (Cambridge: Cambridge University Press, 1992), 180.

26 Griboedov, *Polnoe sobranie sochinenii*, 3:341.

27 Raynal, *History*, 112.

28 Raynal, 267–8.

29 Raynal, 268.

30 Raynal, 268.

31 Griboedov, *Polnoe sobranie sochinenii*, 3:326.

32 Ronald Grigor Suny, *The Making of the Georgian Nation* (Bloomington: Indiana University Press, 1988), 70.

33 Griboedov, *Polnoe sobranie sochinenii*, 3:326.

34 Smith, *Wealth of Nations*, 2:484.

35 Smith, 2:475–6.

36 Griboedov, *Polnoe sobranie sochinenii*, 3:338–9.

37 Griboedov, 3:338–9.

38 Raynal, *History*, 274.

39 Raynal, 274–5.

40 Raynal, *Europeans in the East and West Indies*, 3:125.

41 Raynal, 3:125.

42 Pestel, *Russkaia pravda*, 13.

43 Pestel, 48.

44 Boris Tomashevskii, *Pushkin: Book 1, 1813–1824* (Moscow-Leningrad: Akademiia Nauk SSSR, 1956), 1:407–8.
45 Aleksandr Sergeevich Griboedov, *Polnoe sobranie sochinenii v trekh tomakh* (St. Petersburg: Notabene, 1999), 2:339, 608.
46 Griboedov, *Polnoe sobranie sochinenii*, 3:344.
47 Zhukovskii, 140.
48 Zhukovskii, 140.
49 Smith, *Wealth of Nations*, 2:472.
50 Raynal, *History*, 277.
51 Raynal, 145–6.
52 Griboedov, *Polnoe sobranie sochinenii*, 3:297, 321–4.
53 Piksanov, *Griboedov*, 177.
54 Piksanov, 181.
55 Peter Jimack, "Introduction,"in Raynal, *History*, xxvii.
56 John Hope Mason and Robert Wokler, eds., "Introduction," in Denis Diderot, *Political Writings* (Cambridge: Cambridge University Press, 1992), xxvii.
57 This statement is from a passage that Diderot added to Raynal's book in 1780. Raynal, *History*, 112; Jimack, "Introduction," xxiii–iv.
58 Raynal, *History*, 123–4.
59 Raynal, 123.
60 Raynal, 123.
61 Griboedov, *Polnoe sobranie sochinenii*, 3:338–9.
62 Griboedov, 3:334.
63 Griboedov, 3:339.
64 Griboedov, 3:339.
65 Susan Layton, *Russian Literature and Empire* (Cambridge: Cambridge University Press, 1994), 209.
66 Smith, *Wealth of Nations*, 2:489.
67 Smith, 2:489.
68 Smith, 2:489.
69 Smith, 2:489.
70 Tynianov, *Smert' Vazir-Mukhtara* (1985), 85.
71 Raynal, *Europeans in the East and West Indies*, 8:184–5.
72 Raynal, 8:192.
73 Raynal, 8:185.
74 Raynal, 8:185.
75 Zhukovskii, 136.
76 H.V. [Huw Vaughan] Bowen, "'No Longer Mere Traders': Continuities and Change in the Metropolitan Development of the East India Company, 1600–1834," in *The Worlds of the East India Company*, ed. H.V. Bowen, Margarette Lincoln, and Nigel Rigby (Rochester: Boydell, 2002), 19.

77 Philip Lawson, *The East India Company: A History* (London: Longman, 1993), 126–43.
78 Griboedov, *Polnoe sobranie sochinenii*, 3:327.
79 Griboedov, 3:328, 333–4.
80 Griboedov, 3:328.
81 Griboedov, 3:334.
82 Harsha Ram, *Imperial Sublime: A Russian Poetics of Empire* (London: University of Wisconsin Press, 2003), 134.
83 Robert B. Ekelund and Robert F. Hébert, *A History of Economic Theory and Method* (New York: McGraw-Hill, 1975), 31.
84 Raynal, *Europeans in the East and West Indies*, 2:221.
85 Maxine Berg, "From Imitation to Invention: Creating Commodities in Eighteenth-Century Britain," *Economic History Review* 55, no. 1 (2002): 16.
86 Griboedov, *Polnoe sobranie sochinenii*, 3:334.
87 Griboedov, 3:325.
88 Griboedov, 3:325–6.
89 Griboedov, 3:336.
90 Griboedov, 3:325.
91 Griboedov, 3:327.
92 Griboedov, 3:328.
93 Berg, "From Imitation to Invention," 1–2, 7, 15.
94 Berg, 16.
95 Raynal, *Europeans in the East and West Indies*, 8:186.
96 Zhukovskii, 151.
97 Zhukovskii, 151–2.
98 Smith, *Wealth of Nations*, 2:243.
99 Smith, 2:243.
100 Smith, 2:258–60.
101 Raynal, *Europeans in the East and West Indies*, 8:214.
102 Raynal, *History*, 205.
103 Griboedov, *Polnoe sobranie sochinenii*, 3:337.
104 Griboedov, 3:335.
105 O.F. Akimushkin et al., "Comments," in Griboedov, *Polnoe sobranie sochinenii v trekh tomakh* (St. Petersburg: Dmitrii Bulanin, 2006), 3:574–5.
106 Griboedov, *Polnoe sobranie sochinenii*, 3:338.
107 Zhukovskii, 139.
108 Smith, *Wealth of Nations*, 2:507.
109 Griboedov, *Polnoe sobranie sochinenii*, 3:333.
110 Zhukovskii, 156.
111 Zhukovskii, 131.

112 Raynal, *Europeans in the East and West Indies*, 2:186–7.
113 Mike Davis, *Late Victorian Holocausts: El Niño Famines and the Making of the Third World* (London: Verso, 2001), 31–3.
114 Zhukovskii, 133.
115 Zhukovskii, 137.
116 Zhukovskii, 140–1.
117 Smith, *Wealth of Nations*, 3:246–7.
118 Zhukovskii, 135.
119 Zhukovskii, 135.
120 Lawson, *The East India Company*, 152.
121 H.V. [Huw Vaughan] Bowen, *The Business of Empire: The East India Company and Imperial Britain, 1756–1833* (Cambridge: Cambridge University Press, 2006), 53–83.
122 Bowen, *Business of Empire*, 83; Bowen, "No Longer Mere Traders," 28.
123 Lawson, *The East India Company*, 156–9.
124 Griboedov, *Polnoe sobranie sochinenii*, 3:331–2.
125 Kondraty Ryleev, *Stikhotvoreniia. Stat'i. Ocherki. Dokladnye Zapiski. Pis'ma.* (Moscow: Khudozhestvennaia Literatura, 1956), 292–4.
126 Mikhail Lunin, *Sochineniia i pis'ma* (Petersburg: Vsemirnaia Literatura, 1923), 75.
127 Pestel, *Russkaia pravda*, 72–3.
128 Pestel, 50.
129 Pestel, 50.
130 Zhukovskii, 141.
131 Zhukovskii, 153.
132 Zhukovskii, 153.
133 Zhukovskii, 137.
134 Lawson, *The East India Company*, 159–62.
135 Pestel, *Russkaia pravda*, 14.
136 Zhukovskii, 137.
137 Zhukovskii, 137.
138 Sergei Chernov, *Pavel Pestel: Izbrannye stat'i po istorii dekabrizma* (St. Petersburg: Liki Rossii, 2004), 159–60.
139 Zhukovskii, 137.
140 Pestel, *Russkaia pravda*, 40.
141 Zhukovskii, 136.
142 Smith, *Wealth of Nations*, 2:507–8.
143 Kh. Abovian, *Verk' Hayastani*, in *Erkeri liakatar zhoghovatsu ut' hatorov* (Erevan: Haikakan SSR GA Hratarakchutiun, 1961), vol. 3.
144 Kh. Abovian, "Parskastani ev Rusastani mijev tsagats paterazmi nakhorein, mot 1825 t'vakanin," in *Erkeri liakatar zhoghovatsu ut' hatorov* (Erevan: Haikakan SSR GA Hratarakchutiun, 1958), 8:56–9.

145 Piona Akopian, "Khachatur Abovian i ego 'Rany Armenii,'" in Khachatur Abovian, *Rany Armenii* (Erevan: Sovetakan grogh, 1977), 5–20.
146 Leah Feldman, *On the Threshold of Eurasia: Revolutionary Poetics in the Caucasus* (Ithaca: Cornell University Press, 2018), 96.
147 A. Blavatskii, "Po pis'mu erivanskogo uezdnogo nachal'nika ob obide prichinennoi emu ispravliaiushchim dolzhnost' smotritelia erivanskogo uezdnogo uchilishcha tituliarnym sovetnikom Abovianom pri vstreche patriarkha Nersesa," National Archives of Georgia, Ministry of Justice, Tbilisi, Georgia, 9 May 1846, F 4, Op. 3, N 631.
148 Akopian, "Khachatur Abovian," 5.
149 Abovian, *Verk' Hayastani.*
150 Abovian, "Ameriku lis k'tsily," in *Erkeri liakatar zhoghovatsu ut' hatorov* (Erevan: Haikakan SSR GA Hratarakchutiun, 1955), 5:234, 247, 257.
151 Abovian, "Ameriku lis k'tsily," 254.
152 Abovian, 244–5.
153 Abovian, 244.
154 Abovian, 261.
155 Abovian, "Hayastani u hay zhoghovrdi tntesakan u kulturakan vichaki barelavelu ughineri masin," in *Erkeri liakatar zhoghovatsu ut' hatorov* (Erevan: Haikakan SSR GA Hratarakchutiun, 1958), 8:89.
156 Eka Lekashvili, Lia Lursmanashvili, and Ekaterine Tukhashvili, "Silk Production in Georgia: History and Development Opportunities," paper presented at the conference "Fashion through History: Costumes, Symbols, Communication," Sapienza University of Rome, Italy, 2015, https://www.researchgate.net/publication/276061374_Silk_Production_in_Georgia_History_and_Development_Opportunities.
157 Abovian, "Hayastani u hay zhoghovrdi tntesakan u kulturakan," 90.
158 Abovian, 89.
159 Abovian, 90.
160 Abovian, 90–1.
161 Abovian, 87.
162 Abovian, 82–3.
163 Abovian, 94.
164 Abovian, 94–5.

2 The "Oriental Journeys" in *The Death of Vazir-Mukhtar*

1 The novel first appeared in the 1927–8 issues of the journal *Zvezda*, and was published as a book in 1929.
2 Monika Greenleaf, *Pushkin and Romantic Fashion: Fragment, Elegy, Orient, Irony* (Stanford: Stanford University Press, 1994); Susan Layton, *Russian*

Literature and Empire (Cambridge: Cambridge University Press, 1994); Harsha Ram, *Imperial Sublime: A Russian Poetics of Empire* (London: University of Wisconsin Press, 2003).

3 Iurii Tynianov, "Literaturnoe segodnia," in *Literaturnyi fakt* (Moscow: Vysshaia shkola, 1993), 263–4.

4 Boris Eichenbaum, "Tvorchestvo Iu. Tynianova," in *O proze* (Leningrad: Khudozhestvennaia literatura, 1969), 419.

5 Eichenbaum, "Tvorchestvo Iu. Tynianova," 381.

6 Eichenbaum, 420.

7 Iurii Tynianov, "O Khlebnikove," in *Literaturnyi fakt* (Moscow: Vysshaia shkola, 1993), 237.

8 Viktor Shklovsky, "O teorii prozy: 1929g," in *O teorii prozy* (Moscow: Sovetskii pisatel', 1983), 32.

9 Mikhail Bakhtin, "Slovo v romane," in *Vorposy literatury i estetiki* (Moscow: Khudozhestvennaia literatura, 1975), 134.

10 Bakhtin, "Slovo v romane," 82.

11 Bakhtin, 185–6, 230–1.

12 Hans Robert Jauss, *Toward an Aesthetic of Reception*, trans. Timothy Bahti (Minneapolis: University of Minnesota Press, 1982), 17–18.

13 Jauss, *Toward an Aesthetic of Reception*, 18.

14 Iurii Tynianov, "O literaturnoi evolutsii," in *Literaturnyi fakt* (Moscow: Vysshaia shkola, 1993), 146.

15 Iurii Tynianov, *Smert' Vazir-Mukhtara* (*The Death of Vazir-Mukhtar*) (Leningrad: Priboi, 1929), 321–2.

16 Steven Lovell, "Tynianov as Sociologist of Literature," *Slavonic and East European Review* 79, no. 3 (2001): 419–20.

17 Eichenbaum, "Tvorchestvo Iu. Tynianova," 408.

18 Neil Harding, *Leninism* (Durham: Duke University Press, 1996), 113–41, 197–218, 243–63.

19 Iurii Tynianov, "O 'Puteshestvii v Arzrum,'" in *Pushkin i ego sovremenniki* (Moscow: Nauka, 1969), 200, 207–8.

20 Tynianov, "O 'Puteshestvii v Arzrum,'" 195.

21 Tynianov, *Smert' Vazir-Mukhtara* (1929), 508.

22 Aleksandr Sergeevich Pushkin, "Puteshestvie v Arzrum vo vremia pokhoda 1829 goda," in *Sobranie sochinenii v desiati tomakh* (Moscow: Gosudarstvennoe izdatel'stvo khudozhestvennoi literatury, 1959–62), 5:435.

23 Sergei Aleksandrovich Fomichev, "'Griboedovskii epizod' v 'Puteshestvii v Arzrum' Pushkina," in *A.S. Griboedov: Khmelitskii sbornik* (Smolensk: SGU, 1998), 378.

24 Tynianov, "O 'Puteshestvii v Arzrum,'" 198.

25 Tynianov, 207. See also Ian Helfant's article on how Pushkin reshaped his travel notes to create *Journey to Arzrum* ("Sculpting a Persona: The Path from Pushkin's Caucasian Journal to Puteshestvie v Arzrum," *Russian Review* 56, no. 3 [1997]: 366–82).

26 Tynianov, "O 'Puteshestvii v Arzrum,'" 208.

27 K.A. Borozdin, "Nina Aleksandrovna Griboedova," in *A.S. Griboedov v vospominaniiakh sovremennikov*, ed. Nikolai Piksanov (Moscow: Federatsiia, 1929), 302–3.

28 Tynianov, *Smert' Vazir-Mukhtara* (1929), 221.

29 Pushkin, "Puteshestvie v Arzrum," 420.

30 Pushkin, 460.

31 Tynianov, *Smert' Vazir-Mukhtara* (1929), 550.

32 Monika Frenkel Greenleaf, "Pushkin's 'Journey to Arzrum': The Poet at the Border," *Slavic Review* 50, no. 4 (1991): 953.

33 Tynianov, "O 'Puteshestvii v Arzrum,'" 208.

34 Tynianov, 204

35 Tynianov, 203.

36 M.F. Greenleaf, "Pushkin's 'Journey to Arzrum,'" 949.

37 Vladimir Gippius, *Pushkin i khristianstvo* (Petrograd: Sirius, 1915).

38 Evgeny Dobrenko, "Pushkin in Soviet and Post-Soviet Culture," in *The Cambridge Companion to Pushkin*, ed. Andrew Kahn (Cambridge: Cambridge University Press, 2006), 204–5, 207–8.

39 Linda Hutcheon, *A Theory of Parody: The Teachings of Twentieth-Century Art Forms* (New York: Methuen, 1985), 20.

40 Adam Smith, *The Theory of Moral Sentiments* (Oxford: Clarendon, 1976), 47.

41 Viktor Shklovsky, *'Tristram Shendi' Sterna i teoriia romana* (Petrograd: OPOIAZ, 1921), 22–3.

42 Douglas Robinson, *Estrangement and the Somatics of Literature* (Baltimore: Johns Hopkins University Press, 2008), 120–1.

43 Robinson, *Estrangement*, 23.

44 Viktor Shklovsky, "Vyshla kniga Maiakovskogo 'Oblako v shtanakh,'" in *Gamburgskii schet* (Moscow: Sovetskii pisatel', 1990), 58–72.

45 Shklovsky, "Vyshla kniga Maiakovskogo 'Oblako v shtanakh,'" 43.

46 Smith, *Theory of Moral Sentiments*, 47.

47 Michael A. Denner, "Dusting Off the Couch (and Discovering the Tolstoy Connection in Shklovsky's 'Art as Device')," *Slavic and East European Journal* 52, no. 3 (2008): 386.

48 Viktor Shklovsky, *Sentimental'noe puteshestvie* (Moscow: Novosti, 1990), 138.

49 Tynianov, *Smert' Vazir-Mukhtara* (1929), 546.

50 Ilya Kalinin, "Istoriya kak iskusstvo chlenorazdel'nosti," *Novoe literaturnoe obozrenie* 71 (2005): 120–3.

51 Pushkin, "Puteshestvie v Arzrum," 454–5.
52 Shklovsky, *Sentimental'noe puteshestvie*, 92.
53 Shklovsky, 93.
54 Mohammad Gholi Majd, *The Great Famine and Genocide in Persia, 1917–1919* (Lanham: University Press of America, 2013).
55 Shklovsky, *Sentimental'noe puteshestvie*, 128.
56 Majd, *The Great Famine*, 143–57.
57 Tynianov, *Smert' Vazir-Mukhtara* (1929), 508.
58 Shklovsky, *Sentimental'noe puteshestvie*, 83.
59 Shklovsky, 194.
60 M.F. Greenleaf, "Pushkin's 'Journey to Arzrum,'" 959.
61 Shklovsky, *Sentimental'noe puteshestvie*, 116.
62 Tynianov, *Smert' Vazir-Mukhtara* (1929), 489.
63 Olga Ivanovna Popova, *A.S. Griboedov v Persii* (Moscow: Zhizn' i znanie, 1929), 12.
64 Shklovsky, *Sentimental'noe puteshestvie*, 115.
65 Eichenbaum, "Tvorchestvo Iu. Tynianova," 414.
66 Dobrenko, "Pushkin in Soviet and Post-Soviet Culture," 204–5.
67 Sankar Muthu, *Enlightenment against Empire* (Princeton: Princeton University Press, 2003).
68 Angela Brintlinger, "Griboedov u Tynianova: Biografiia ili mif?" in *A.S. Griboedov: Khmelitskii sbornik* (Smolensk: SGU, 1998), 385.
69 Boris Eichenbaum, "Kak sdelana 'Shinel'' Gogolia," in *O proze* (Leningrad: Khudozhestvennaia literatura, 1969), 319.
70 Tynianov, "Literaturnoe segodnia," 264.
71 Shklovsky, *Sentimental'noe puteshestvie*, 283.
72 Shklovsky, 283.
73 Smith, *Theory of Moral Sentiments*, 67.
74 Bakhtin, "Slovo v romane," 209–10.
75 Andreas Schönle, *Authenticity and Fiction in the Russian Literary Journey, 1790–1840* (Cambridge, MA: Harvard University Press, 2000), 33.
76 Tynianov, *Smert' Vazir-Mukhtara* (1929), 241–4.
77 Aleksandr Nikolaevich Radishchev, *Puteshestvie iz Peterburga v Moskvu*, in *Polnoe sobranie sochinenii* (Moscow: Izdatel'stvo Akademii nauk SSSR, 1938), 1:263.
78 Radishchev, *Puteshestvie iz Peterburga v Moskvu*, 1:263.
79 Radishchev, 1:264.
80 Richard Tuck, *The Rights of War and Peace: Political Thought and the International Order from Grotius to Kant* (New York: Oxford University Press, 1999), 197–225.
81 Z. Avalov and J.E.S. Cooper, "The Caucasus since 1918," *Slavonic Review* 3, no. 8 (1924): 331, https://www.jstor.org/stable/4201858.

82 Immanuel Kant, *Ethical Philosophy: The Complete Text of Grounding for the Metaphysics of Morals and Metaphysical Principles of Virtue (Part II of the Metaphysics of Morals)*, trans. James W. Ellington (Indianapolis: Hackett, 1993), 36.
83 Iurii Lotman, "Ideinoe soderzhanie Puteshestviia iz Peterburga v Moskvu," in *Russkaia literatura i kul'tura prosveshcheniia* (Moscow: Ob"edinennoe gumanitarnoe izdatel'stvo, 1998), 390.
84 Shklovsky, *Sentimental'noe puteshestvie*, 196.
85 Shklovsky, 196.
86 Viktor Shklovskii, "Ob istoricheskom romane i o Iurii Tynianove," *Zvezda* 4 (1933): 167–75.
87 Shklovsky, *Sentimental'noe puteshestvie*, 90.
88 Muthu, *Enlightenment against Empire*, 199.
89 Schönle, *Authenticity and Fiction*, 42.
90 Schönle, 42.
91 Harhsa Ram, "Pushkin and the Caucasus," in *The Pushkin Handbook*, ed. David M. Bethea (Madison: University of Wisconsin Press, 2005), 399.
92 Iurii Tynianov, "Promezhutok," in *Literaturnyi fakt* (Moscow: Vysshaia shkola, 1993), 272.

3 A Novelistic Outline of Orientalism

1 Tynianov, *Smert' Vazir-Mukhtara* (1985), 239.
2 To avoid confusion with the general-quartermaster of the Caucasian corps Mikhail Zhukovsky, whose comments on Griboedov and Zaveleisky's proposal I discussed in previous chapters, I will refer to Vasily Zhukovsky as "the poet Zhukovsky."
3 Tynianov, *Smert' Vazir-Mukhtara* (1985), 178–81.
4 Tynianov, *Smert' Vazir-Mukhtara* (1985), 181–3.
5 Tynianov, *Smert' Vazir-Mukhtara* (1985), 179.
6 Harsha Ram, *Imperial Sublime: A Russian Poetics of Empire* (London: University of Wisconsin Press, 2003), 25.
7 Susan Layton, *Russian Literature and Empire* (Cambridge: Cambridge University Press, 1994), 36–53.
8 Tynianov, *Smert' Vazir-Mukhtara* (1985), 179–80.
9 Tynianov, *Smert' Vazir-Mukhtara* (1985), 180.
10 Tynianov, *Smert' Vazir-Mukhtara* (1985), 60.
11 Vera Tolz, *Russia's Own Orient: The Politics of Identity and Oriental Studies in the Late Imperial and Early Soviet Periods* (Oxford: Oxford University Press, 2011), 7–9.
12 Tynianov, *Smert' Vazir-Mukhtara* (1985), 181.

13 Aleksandr Sergeevich Pushkin, "Kavkazskii plennik," in *Sobranie sochinenii v desiati tomakh* (Moscow: Gosudarstvennoe izdatel'stvo khudozhestvennoi literatury, 1959–62), 3:117.
14 P.A. Viazemskii, *Estetika i literaturnaia kritika* (Moscow: Iskusstvo, 1984), 393.
15 Ram, *Imperial Sublime*, 192–3.
16 Ram, 193.
17 Kevork K. Oskanian, "A Very Ambiguous Empire: Russia's Hybrid Exceptionalism," *Europe-Asia Studies* 70, no. 1 (2018): 37.
18 Iurii Tynianov, "O 'Puteshestvii v Arzrum,'" in *Pushkin i ego sovremenniki* (Moscow: Nauka, 1969), 195.
19 Pushkin, "Kavkazskii plennik," 3:117.
20 Iakov Gordin, *Kavkaz: Zemlia i krov'* (St. Petersburg: Zhurnal "Zvezda," 2000), 28.
21 Tynianov, *Smert' Vazir-Mukhtara* (1985), 181.
22 Tynianov, *Smert' Vazir-Mukhtara* (1985), 181.
23 Tynianov, *Smert' Vazir-Mukhtara* (1985), 181.
24 Tynianov, *Smert' Vazir-Mukhtara* (1985), 181–2.
25 Tynianov, *Smert' Vazir-Mukhtara* (1929), 246.
26 Gordin, *Kavkaz*, 23.
27 Andrei Evgen'evich Rozen, *Zapiski dekabrista* (Irkutsk: Vostochno-Sibirskoe knizhnoe izdatel'stvo, 1984), 390.
28 Rozen, *Zapiski dekabrista*, 390.
29 Tynianov, *Smert' Vazir-Mukhtara* (1985), 183.
30 Ram, *Imperial Sublime*, 24.
31 Tynianov, *Smert' Vazir-Mukhtara* (1985), 85.
32 Tolz, *Russia's Own Orient*, 27.
33 Tynianov, *Smert' Vazir-Mukhtara* (1985), 84.
34 Philip Lawson, *The East India Company: A History* (London: Longman, 1993), 58, 138, 157.
35 Aleksandr Sergeevich Pushkin, *Evgenii Onegin*, in *Sobranie sochinenii v desiati tomakh* (Moscow: Gosudarstvennoe izdatel'stvo khudozhestvennoi literatury, 1959–62), 4:14.
36 Tynianov, *Smert' Vazir-Mukhtara* (1985), 183.
37 Dimitri N. and Zinaida A. Breschinsky, "On Tynjanov the Writer and His Use of Cinematic Technique in *The Death of the Wazir Mukhtar*," *Slavic and East European Journal* 29, no. 1 (1985): 6, https://www.jstor.org/stable/307921."
38 Mikhail Zhukovsky, "Zamechaniia na zapisku ob ustroistve zemledel'cheskoi, manufakturnoi i torgovoi kompanii," appendix to I.K. Enikolopov, *Griboedov v Gruzii* (Tbilisi: Zaria Vostoka, 1954)," 148.
39 Angela Brintlinger, "Griboedov u Tynianova: Biografiia ili mif?" in *A.S. Griboedov: Khmelitskii sbornik* (Smolensk: SGU, 1998), 386.

40 Tynianov, *Smert' Vazir-Mukhtara* (1985), 182–3.
41 Tynianov, *Smert' Vazir-Mukhtara* (1985), 181.
42 Tynianov, *Smert' Vazir-Mukhtara* (1985), 242.
43 Tynianov, *Smert' Vazir-Mukhtara* (1985), 242.
44 Aleksandr Aleksandrovič Lebedev, *Griboedov: Fakty i Gipotezy* (Moscow: Iskusstvo, 1980), 273.
45 Tynianov, *Smert' Vazir-Mukhtara* (1985), 242.
46 Tynianov, *Smert' Vazir-Mukhtara* (1985), 243.
47 Pavel Pestel, *Russkaia pravda* (St. Petersburg: Kul'tura, 1906), 58–9.
48 Jean-Charles-Léonard Simonde de Sismondi, *New Principles of Political Economy, or, Of Wealth in Its Relation to Population*, trans. Richard Hyse (London: Transaction, 1991), 53.
49 Simonde de Sismondi, *New Principles*, 53.
50 Tynianov, *Smert' Vazir-Mukhtara* (1985), 244.
51 Natan Eidelman, *Byt' mozhet za khrebtom Kavkaza* (Moscow: Nauka, 1990), 130.
52 Sheila Fitzpatrick, *Stalin's Peasants: Resistance and Survival in the Russian Village after Collectivisation* (New York: Oxford University Press, 1994), 129, 148–9.
53 Tynianov, *Smert' Vazir-Mukhtara* (1985), 7.
54 Walter D. Mignolo, *The Darker Side of Western Modernity: Global Futures, Decolonial Options* (Durham: Duke University Press, 2011), 2–3.
55 Tynianov, *Smert' Vazir-Mukhtara* (1985), 184.
56 Eidelman, *Byt' mozhet za khrebtom Kabkaza*, 162–3.
57 Aleksandr Sergeevich Griboedov, *Polnoe sobranie sochinenii v trekh tomakh* (St. Petersburg: Dmitrii Bulanin, 2006), 3:118.
58 Angela Brintlinger, *Writing a Usable Past: Russian Literary Culture, 1917–1937* (Evanston: Northwestern University Press, 2008), 43.
59 Tynianov, *Smert' Vazir-Mukhtara* (1985), 45, 46.
60 Dmitri Pisarev, *Pushkin i Belinskii* (Moscow-Petrograd: Gosudarstvennoe izdatel'stvo, 1923), 160. Utilitarianism in arts is the main theme of another of Pisarev's articles, "Razrushenie estetiki," in *Sochineniia v chetyrekh tomakh* (Moscow: Gosudarstvennoe izdatel'stvo khudozhestvennoi literatury, 1955), 3:418–511.
61 Tynianov, *Smert' Vazir-Mukhtara* (1929), 245.
62 Lawson, *The East India Company*, 152.

4 "The Fountain of Bakhchisaray"

1 Tynianov, *Smert' Vazir-Mukhtara* (1985), 240.
2 Aleksandr Sergeevich Pushkin, "Bakhchisaraiskii fontan," in *Sobranie sochinenii v desiati tomakh* (Moscow: Gosudarstvennoe izdatel'stvo khudozhestvennoi literatury, 1959–62), 3:143–58.

3 Susan Layton, *Russian Literature and Empire* (Cambridge: Cambridge University Press, 1994), 196–8.
4 I.M. Murav'ev-Apostol, "Vypiska iz puteshestviia po Tavride," in Pushkin, *Polnoe sobranie sochinenii v desiati tomakh* (Leningrad: Nauka, 1977), 4:150.
5 Mikhail Kizilov, "Slave Trade in the Early Modern Crimea from the Perspective of Christian, Jewish and Muslim Sources," *Journal of Early Modern History* 11, no. 1–2 (2007): 11.
6 Leonid Grossman, *Pushkin* (Moscow: Molodaia gvardiia, 1958).
7 L.N. Malinovskaia, "Semanticheskoe pole Bakhchisaraiskogo fontana ("slioz") v kontekste islamskoi traditsii," in *Istoriia i arkheologiia Iugo-Zapadnogo Kryma* (Simferopol: Tavriia, 1993), 185–6.
8 "Durbe Diliary Bikech," *Bakhchisaraiskii istoriko-kul'turnyi i arkheologicheskii muzei-zapovednik* (2015), http://handvorec.ru/pamyatniki/hanskij-dvorets/historymus/dyurbe-dilyary-bikech/(accessed 24 July 2020).
9 Suriving project documents co-authored by Griboedov and Zaveleisky, "Zapiska ob uchrezhdenii rossiiskoi zakavkazskoi kompanii" (A note on the founding of the Russian Transcaucasian Company), and "Vstuplenie k proektu ustava" (Introduction to the project of the charter) of the Russian Transcaucasian Company (1828), in Aleksandr Sergeevich Griboedov, *Polnoe sobranie sochinenii v trekh tomakh* (St. Petersburg: Dmitrii Bulanin, 2006), 3:325–44, 561–75.
10 Tynianov, *Smert' Vazir-Mukhtara* (1985), 182.
11 Pavel Pestel, *Russkaia pravda* (St. Petersburg: Kul'tura, 1906); Sergei, *Pavel Pestel: Izbrannye stat'i po istorii dekabrizma* (St. Petersburg: Liki Rossii, 2004), 159–60.
12 Layton, *Russian Literature and Empire*, 209
13 Tynianov, *Smert' Vazir-Mukhtara* (1985), 90.
14 Tynianov, *Smert' Vazir-Mukhtara* (1929).
15 K.F. Adelung, K.K. Bode, and D.F. Kharlamova, "Memoirs and Letters," in *A.S. Griboedov v vospominaniiakh sovremennikov* (Moscow: Khudozhestvennaia literatura, 1980), 170–97, 201–5; V.S. Shaduri, "Kak sooruzhalsia pamiatnik Griboedovu na gore Mtatsminda," in *Tam gde v'etsia Alazan'* (Tbilisi: Merani, 1977), 64–8.
16 Tynianov, *Smert' Vazir-Mukhtara* (1985), 390.
17 Iu. M. Lotmàn, *Besedy o russkoi kul'ture: Byt i traditsii russkogo dvorianstva, XVIII–nachalo XIX veka* (St. Petersburg: Iskusstvo–SPB, 1994), 59.
18 Tynianov, *Smert' Vazir-Mukhtara* (1985), 128.
19 K.A. Polevoi, "Iz stat'i 'O zhizni i sochineniiakh A.S. Griboedova,'" in *A.S. Griboedov v vospominaniiakh sovremennikov* (Moscow: Khudozhestvennaia literatura, 1980), 161.

20 Aleksandr Sergeevich Pushkin, "Otryvki iz pisem, mysli i zamechaniia," in *Sobranie sochinenii v desiati tomakh* (Moscow: Gosudarstvennoe izdatel'stvo khudozhestvennoi literatury, 1959–62), 6:16–17.
21 Aleksandr Sergeevich Pushkin, "Al'bom Onegina," in *Sobranie sochinenii v desiati tomakh* (Moscow: Gosudarstvennoe izdatel'stvo khudozhestvennoi literatury, 1959–62), 4:479.
22 Vissarion Belinsky, "Sochineniia Aleksandra Pushkina," in *Sobranie sochinenii v trekh tomakh*, 3:419 (Moscow: Gosudarstvennoe izdatel'stvo khudozhestvennoi literatury, 1948).
23 A.A. Bestuzhev, "Znakomstvo moe s A.S. Griboedovym," in *A.S. Griboedov v vospominaniiakh sovremennikov* (Moscow: Khudozhestvennaia literatura, 1980), 102.
24 Bestuzhev, "Znakomstvo moe s A.S. Griboedovym," 102.
25 Layton, *Russian Literature and Empire*, 175.
26 Tynianov, *Smert' Vazir-Mukhtara* (1985), 365.
27 Tynianov, *Smert' Vazir-Mukhtara* (1985), 90.
28 Belinsky, "Sochineniia Aleksandra Pushkina," 422.
29 Aleksandr Sergeevich Pushkin, "Uchast' moia reshena. Ia zhenius' …," in *Sobranie sochinenii v desiati tomakh* (Moscow: Gosudarstvennoe izdatel'stvo khudozhestvennoi literatury, 1959–62), 5:501.
30 Tynianov, *Smert' Vazir-Mukhtara* (1985), 329.
31 Pushkin, "Bakhchisaraiskii fontan," 147–8.
32 Tynianov, *Smert' Vazir-Mukhtara* (1985), 281–3.
33 I. Babel, *Odesskie rasskazy* (Letchworth: Prideaux, 1924), 31–9.
34 Tynianov, *Smert' Vazir-Mukhtara* (1985), 281.
35 Pushkin, "Bakhchisaraiskii fontan," 148.
36 Tynianov, *Smert' Vazir-Mukhtara* (1985), 281.
37 Tynianov, *Smert' Vazir-Mukhtara* (1985), 281.
38 Tynianov, *Smert' Vazir-Mukhtara* (1985), 282.
39 Babel, *Odesskie rasskazy*, 33.
40 Pushkin, *Evgenii Onegin*, 23–4.
41 Regan Treewater, *Isaak Babel's Image of the Humanized Jew in the* Odesskie rasskazy (Ottawa: Library and Archives Canada, 2008), 35–72.
42 Layton, *Russian Literature and Empire*, 175.
43 Rebecca Gould, *Writers and Rebels: The Literature of Insurgency in the Caucasus* (New Haven: Yale University Press, 2016), 189.
44 M.Ia. Alaverdiants, *Test' A.S. Griboedova – Kniaz' Aleksandr Chavchavadze v kharakteristike armianskogo istorika* (St. Petersburg: Elektro-Tipografiia N. Ia. Stoikovoi, 1910), 5–6.
45 Harsha Ram and Zaza Shatirishvili, "Romantic Topography and the Dilemma of Empire: The Caucasus in the Dialogue of Georgian and Russian Poetry," *Russian Review* 63 (January 2004): 3.

46 Alaverdiants, *Test' A.S. Griboedova – Kniaz' Aleksandr Chavchavadze*, 8.
47 Alaverdiants, 8.
48 See Ram and Shatirishvili, "Romantic Topography."
49 A. Chavchavadze, "Kratkii istoricheskii ocherk Gruzii i ee polozheniia s 1801 po 1831," in V.S. Shaduri, *Letopis' druzhby gruzinskogo i russkogo narodov s drevnikh vremen do nashikh dnei* (Tbilisi: Literatura da Khelovneb'a, 1967), 1:104–5.
50 Ram and Shatirishvili, "Romantic Topography," 17.
51 Liubov Kurtynova-D'Herlugnan, *The Tsar's Abolitionists: The Slave Trade in the Caucasus and Its Suppression* (Leiden: Brill, 2010).
52 Nicholas Griffin, *Caucasus: A Journey to the Land between Christianity and Islam* (Chicago: University of Chicago Press, 2004), 110–55.
53 Chavchavadze, "Kratkii istoricheskii ocherk Gruzii," 143.
54 Chavchavadze, 141.
55 Ram and Shatirishvili, "Romantic Topography," 2.
56 Ram and Shatirishvili, 2.
57 Igor' Bogomolov, *Aleksandr Chavchavadze i russkaia kul'tura Tbilisi* (Tbilisi: Metsniereba, 1964), 12; V.S. Shaduri, *Letopis' druzhby gruzinskogo i russkogo narodov s drevnikh vremen do nashikh dnei* (Tbilisi: Literatura da Khelovneb'a, 1967), 1:141–3.
58 Bogomolov, *Aleksandr Chavchavadze*, 14.
59 Bogomolov, 28–9.
60 Bogomolov, 28–9.
61 Tynianov, *Smert' Vazir-Mukhtara* (1985), 188.
62 Tynianov, *Smert' Vazir-Mukhtara* (1985), 188.
63 Tynianov, *Smert' Vazir-Mukhtara* (1985), 163.
64 Tynianov, *Smert' Vazir-Mukhtara* (1985), 169.

5 Persia in the Works of the Soviet Avant-Garde

1 Tynianov, *Smert' Vazir-Mukhtara* (1985), 52.
2 Tynianov, *Smert' Vazir-Mukhtara* (1985), 217.
3 K.A. Borozdin, "Nina Aleksandrovna Griboedova," in *A.S. Griboedov v vospominaniiakh sovremennikov*, ed. Nikolai Piksanov (Moscow: Federatsiia, 1929), 304.
4 Iurii Tynianov, "Pushkin," in *Literaturnyi fakt* (Moscow: Vysshaia shkola, 1993), 179.
5 Tynianov, *Smert' Vazir-Mukhtara* (1985), 275, 344.
6 Susan Layton, *Russian Literature and Empire* (Cambridge: Cambridge University Press, 1994), 197–8.
7 Tynianov, *Smert' Vazir-Mukhtara* (1985), 180.

8 Tynianov, *Smert' Vazir-Mukhtara* (1985), 51, 93, 320.
9 Vasilii Kamenskii, "Zhongler," *LEF: Zhurnal levogo fronta iskusstv*, no. 1 (Moscow and Petersburg: Gosudarstvennoe izdatel'stvo, 1923), 45–7.
10 David Gillespie, *Russian Cinema* (Harlow: Pearson Education, 2003), 60.
11 Leon I. Twarog, "Changing Patterns of a Revolutionary Hero," *Slavonic and East European Review* 32, no. 79 (1954): 367.
12 Michael Khodarkovsky, "The Stepan Razin Uprising: Was It a 'Peasant War'?" *Jahrbücher für Geschichte Osteuropas* 42, no. 1 (1994): 7–10.
13 V.N. Korolev, "Utopil li Sten'ka Razin kniazhnu?" *Istoricheskie issledovaniia o kazachestve*, Razdorskii etnograficheskii muzei-zapovednik, http://www.razdory-museum.ru/c_razin-1.html (accessed 24 July 2020).
14 Korolev, "Utopil li Sten'ka Razin kniazhnu?"
15 Aleksis Rannit, "Iran in Russian Poetry," *Slavic and East European Journal* 17, no. 3 (1973): 266.
16 Tynianov, *Smert' Vazir-Mukhtara* (1985), 139.
17 Tynianov, *Smert' Vazir-Mukhtara* (1985), 139.
18 Tynianov, *Smert' Vazir-Mukhtara* (1985), 139.
19 Aleksandr Sergeevich Griboedov, "Zagorodnaya poezdka," 277.
20 Griboedov, 277.
21 Khodarkovsky, "The Stepan Razin Uprising" 5.
22 Khodarkovsky, 10–19.
23 V.I. Lenin, "Rech' s Lobnogo mesta na otkrytii pamiatnika Stepanu Razinu," in *Sochineniia* (Moscow: Gosudarstvennoe izdatel'stvo politicheskoi literatury, 1950), 304.
24 Paul Avrich, *Russian Rebels, 1600–1800* (New York: Schocken, 1976), 72.
25 Tynianov, *Smert' Vazir-Mukhtara* (1985), 244.
26 Tynianov, *Smert' Vazir-Mukhtara* (1985), 304.
27 Tynianov, *Smert' Vazir-Mukhtara* (1929), 446–7.
28 Viktor Shklovsky, *Sentimental'noe puteshestvie* (Moscow: Novosti, 1990), 108.
29 Shklovsky, *Sentimental'noe puteshestvie*, 115.
30 Aleksandr Blok, *Dvenadtsat'* (Petersburg: Alkonost", 1918), 38–42.
31 Maksimilian Voloshin, "Sten'kin sud," in *Stikhotvoreniia i poemy* (St. Petersburg: Nauka, 1995), 231.
32 Vasilii Kamenskii, "Stepan Razin," in *Poemy* (Moscow: Khudozhestvennaia literatura, 1961), 59–100.
33 Kamenskii, "Stepan Razin," 75.
34 Kamenskii, 79–80.
35 Kamenskii, 78.
36 Kamenskii, 81–3.
37 Kamenskii, 83.
38 Kamenskii, 84–7.
39 Vasilii Kamenskii, *Proza poeta* (Moscow: Vagrius, 2001), 95.
40 Kamenskii, *Proza poeta*, 111.

41 Kamenskii, 117.
42 Kamenskii, 139.
43 Tynianov, *Smert' Vazir-Mukhtara* (1985), 139.
44 Marina Tsvetaeva, *Izbrannye sochineniia* (Minsk: Mastatskaia literature, 1984), 63.
45 Tynianov, *Smert' Vazir-Mukhtara* (1985), 56.
46 Layton, *Russian Literature and Empire*, 175.
47 Griboedov, "Zagorodnaya poezdka," 277.
48 Tynianov, *Smert' Vazir-Mukhtara* (1985), 277.
49 Tynianov, *Smert' Vazir-Mukhtara* (1985), 351.
50 Iurii Tynianov, "O Khlebnikove," in *Sobranie proizvedenii* (Munich: Wilhelm Fink, 1968; repr., Leningrad: Izdatel'stvo pisatelei, 1928–33), 1:27.
51 Iurii Tynianov, "Promezhutok," in *Literaturnyi fakt* (Moscow: Vysshaia shkola, 1993), 272.
52 Tynianov, "Promezhutok," 278.
53 Tynianov, "O Khlebnikove," in *Sobranie proizvedenii* (1968), 1:29.
54 Tynianov, "O Khlebnikove," 1:28.
55 Tynianov, 1:29.
56 Tynianov, "Promezhutok," 272.
57 Velimir Khlebnikov, "Voina v myshelovke," in *Sobranie sochinenii v shesti tomakh*, (Moscow: IMLI RAN, 2002), 3:175.
58 Erich Maria Remarque, *All Quiet on the Western Front* (New York: Ballantine Books, 1987), 11–22.
59 Velimir Khlebnikov, "Pis'mo dvum iapontsam," in *Sobranie sochinenii v shesti tomakh* (Moscow: IMLI RAN, 2006), 6.1:252–6; Khlebnikov, "Voina v myshelovke," 177.
60 Velimir Khlebnikov, "Truba Gul'-mully," in *Sobranie sochinenii v shesti tomakh* (Moscow: IMLI RAN, 2002), 3:301.
61 Aleksandr Sergeevich Pushkin, "Puteshestvie v Arzrum vo vremia pokhoda 1829 goda," in *Sobranie sochinenii v desiati tomakh* (Moscow: Gosudarstvennoe izdatel'stvo khudozhestvennoi literatury, 1959–62), 454–5.
62 Velimir Khlebnikov, "Pisma," in *Sobranie sochinenii v shesti tomakh* (Moscow: IMLI RAN, 2006), 6.2:208.
63 Pushkin, "Puteshestvie v Arzrum," 454.
64 Pushkin, 454.
65 Khlebnikov, "Truba Gul'-mully," 317.
66 A. Kosterin, "Russkie dervishi," *Moskva* 9 (1966): 216–21.
67 Khlebnikov, "Pis'ma," 209.
68 Khlebnikov, "Voina v myshelovke," 182.
69 N. Gumilev, "Kapitany," in *Sobranie sochinenii* (Moscow: Terra, 1991), 1:144.
70 Khlebnikov, "Voina v myshelovke," 184.
71 N. Gumilev, "K. Bal'mont. Tol'ko liubov'," *Sobranie sochinenii*, vol. 4 (Moscow: Terra, 1991), 203.

72 Khlebnikov, "Truba Gul'-mully," 310.
73 Velimir Khlebnikov, "Navruz truda," in *Sobranie sochinenii v shesti tomakh* (Moscow: IMLI RAN, Nasledie, 2001), 2:191.
74 Khlebnikov, "Truba Gul'-mully," 302-3.
75 Khlebnikov, "Navruz truda," 192.
76 Khlebnikov, "Truba Gul'-mully," 306–7.
77 Khlebnikov, 307.
78 Khlebnikov, "Navruz truda," 192.
79 Khlebnikov, "Truba Gul'-mully," 306.
80 Khlebnikov, "Navruz truda," 192.
81 Tynianov, *Smert' Vazir-Mukhtara* (1929), 446–7.
82 Velimir Khlebnikov, "I vot zelenoe ushchelie Zorgama …," *in Sobranie sochinenii v shesti tomakh* (Moscow: IMLI RAN, 2002), 3:294.
83 Ronald Vroon, "Velimir Khlebnikov's 'Razin: Two Trinities': A Reconstruction," *Slavic Review* 39, no. 1 (1980): 70–84.
84 Khlebnikov, "I vot zelenoe ushchelie Zorgama …," 296.
85 Khlebnikov, "Pis'mo dvum iapontsam," 256.
86 Khlebnikov, "I vot zelenoe ushchelie Zorgama …," 296.
87 Khlebnikov, 297.
88 Khlebnikov, 298.
89 Khlebnikov, 295–6.
90 Khlebnikov, 295–6.
91 Khlebnikov, 295.
92 Khlebnikov, "Vidite, persy, vot ia idu …," in *Sobranie sochinenii v shesti tomakh* (Moscow: IMLI RAN, Nasledie, 2001), 2:132.
93 Blok, *Dvenadtsat'*, 88.
94 Abbas Amanat, *Resurrection and Renewal: The Making of the Babi Movement in Iran, 1844–1850* (Ithaca: Cornell University Press, 1989), 303.
95 Amanat, *Resurrection and Renewal*, 330.
96 Amanat, 304–7.
97 Amanat, 330–1.
98 Amanat, 329–30.
99 Khlebnikov, "Truba Gul'-mully," 304.
100 Khlebnikov, "Pisma," 207.
101 Khlebnikov, "Truba Gul'-mully," 304.
102 Tynianov, *Smert' Vazir-Mukhtara* (1985), 365.

6 The "Treacherous Eunuch"

1 Tynianov, *Smert' Vazir-Mukhtara* (1985), 257–75.
2 Charles de Secondat, Baron de Montesquieu, *Lettres Persanes* (Paris: Garnier-Flammarion, 1964).

3 Tynianov, *Smert' Vazir-Mukhtara* (1985), 313.
4 L.N. Tolstoi, "Kholstomer," in *Sobranie sochinenii v dvenadtsati tomakh* (Moscow: Khudozhestvennaia literatura, 1958), 10:111.
5 Tynianov, *Smert' Vazir-Mukhtara* (1985), 313.
6 Tynianov, *Smert' Vazir-Mukhtara* (1985), 313–14.
7 Tynianov, *Smert' Vazir-Mukhtara* (1985), 158–60.
8 Tynianov, *Smert' Vazir-Mukhtara* (1985), 42, 47, 113–14.
9 Tynianov, *Smert' Vazir-Mukhtara* (1985), 48–9.
10 Aleksandr Blok, *Katilina* (Petersburg: Alkonost", 1919).
11 Tynianov, *Smert' Vazir-Mukhtara* (1985), 312.
12 Aleksandr Sergeevich Pushkin, "Bakhchisaraiskii fontan," in *Sobranie sochinenii v desiati tomakh* (Moscow: Gosudarstvennoe izdatel'stvo khudozhestvennoi literatury, 1959–62), 144–5.
13 Tynianov, *Smert' Vazir-Mukhtara* (1985), 313, 316.
14 Pushkin, "Bakhchisaraiskii fontan," 145.
15 Montesquieu, *Lettres Persanes*, 33, 79.
16 Montesquieu, 45.
17 Corey Robin, "Reflections on Fear: Montesquieu in Retrieval," *American Political Science Review* 94, no. 2 (2000): 353.
18 Tynianov, *Smert' Vazir-Mukhtara* (1985), 7.
19 Katerina Clark, *Petersburg: Crucible of Cultural Revolution* (Cambridge, MA: Harvard University Press, 1995), 242.
20 Tynianov, *Smert' Vazir-Mukhtara* (1985), 315.
21 Tynianov, *Smert' Vazir-Mukhtara* (1985), 307, 326.
22 Tynianov, *Smert' Vazir-Mukhtara* (1985), 328.
23 Tynianov, *Smert' Vazir-Mukhtara* (1985), 355.
24 Tynianov, *Smert' Vazir-Mukhtara* (1985), 270, 313.
25 Tynianov, *Smert' Vazir-Mukhtara* (1985), 313.
26 Tynianov, *Smert' Vazir-Mukhtara* (1985), 316.
27 Tynianov, *Smert' Vazir-Mukhtara* (1985), 329.
28 A.P. Chekhov, "Kashtanka," in *Sochineniia* (Moscow: Nauka, 1985), 4:448.
29 Chekhov, "Kashtanka," 4:449.
30 Tynianov, *Smert' Vazir-Mukhtara* (1985), 313.
31 Chekhov, "Kashtanka," 4:439–40.
32 Tynianov, *Smert' Vazir-Mukhtara* (1985), 328.
33 Tynianov, *Smert' Vazir-Mukhtara* (1985), 356.
34 Tynianov, *Smert' Vazir-Mukhtara* (1985), 356.
35 Tynianov, *Smert' Vazir-Mukhtara* (1985), 356.
36 Montesquieu, *Lettres Persanes*, 252–3.
37 Tynianov, *Smert' Vazir-Mukhtara* (1985), 356, 344.
38 Tynianov, *Smert' Vazir-Mukhtara* (1985), 313.
39 Tynianov, *Smert' Vazir-Mukhtara* (1985), 15.

40 Aleksandr Sergeevich Griboedov, *Polnoe sobranie sochinenii v trekh tomakh* (St. Petersburg: Dmitrii Bulanin, 2006), 3:19.
41 Tynianov, *Smert' Vazir-Mukhtara* (1985), 12–14.
42 Griboedov, *Polnoe sobranie sochinenii*, 3:16, 19.
43 Elena Andreeva, "Diplomacy and Murder in Tehran: Alexander Griboyedov and Imperial Russia's Mission to the Shah of Persia by Laurence Kelly," *Iranian Studies* 36, no. 3 (2003): 416.
44 Tynianov, *Smert' Vazir-Mukhtara* (1985), 264.
45 Tynianov, *Smert' Vazir-Mukhtara* (1985), 356.
46 Tynianov, *Smert' Vazir-Mukhtara* (1985), 10.
47 Aleksandr Sergeevich Pushkin, "Puteshestvie v Arzrum vo vremia pokhoda 1829 goda," in *Sobranie sochinenii v desiati tomakh* (Moscow: Gosudarstvennoe izdatel'stvo khudozhestvennoi literatury, 1959–62), 420.
48 Tynianov, *Smert' Vazir-Mukhtara* (1985), 72.
49 Nikolai Piksanov, *Griboedov. Issledovaniia i kharakteristiki* (Leningrad: Izdatel'stvo pisatelei v Leningrade, 1934), 89.
50 Piksanov, *Griboedov*, 119.
51 Piksanov, 146.
52 Tynianov, *Smert' Vazir-Mukhtara* (1985), 332.
53 Tynianov, *Smert' Vazir-Mukhtara* (1985), 332.
54 Aleksandr Sergeevich Griboedov, "Putevye pisma k S.N. Begichevu," in *Sochineniia* (Goslitizdat, 1959), 405.
55 Griboedov, *Polnoe sobranie sochinenii*, 3:175.
56 Maxim von Vock, "Iz donesenii M. Ya. Fon Foka," in *A.S. Griboedov v vospominaniiakh sovremennikov* (Moscow: Khudozhestvennaia literatura, 1980), 290.
57 Tynianov, *Smert' Vazir-Mukhtara* (1985), 305.
58 Tynianov, *Smert' Vazir-Mukhtara* (1985), 333.
59 Tynianov, *Smert' Vazir-Mukhtara* (1985), 333.
60 Griboedov, *Polnoe sobranie sochinenii*, 3:175.
61 Tynianov, *Smert' Vazir-Mukhtara* (1985), 334.
62 Griboedov, *Polnoe sobranie sochinenii*, 3:118.
63 Griboedov, 3:98.
64 Aleksandr Sergeevich Pushkin, "Pora, moi drug, pora! pokoia serdtse prosit…," in *Sobranie sochinenii v desiati tomakh* (Moscow: Gosudarstvennoe izdatel'stvo khudozhestvennoi literatury, 1959–62), 2:387.
65 Pushkin, "Pora, moi drug, pora!" 2:387.
66 Tynianov, *Smert' Vazir-Mukhtara* (1985), 356.
67 Tynianov, *Smert' Vazir-Mukhtara* (1985), 379.
68 Pushkin, "Puteshestvie v Arzrum," 436.
69 Tynianov, *Smert' Vazir-Mukhtara* (1985), 379.
70 Tynianov, *Smert' Vazir-Mukhtara* (1985), 375.
71 Tynianov, *Smert' Vazir-Mukhtara* (1985), 376.

7 An Iranian Delegation's Visit to Petersburg

1 George A. Bournoutian, *From Tabriz to St. Petersburg: Iran's Mission of Apology to Russia in 1829* (Costa Mesa: Mazda, 2014), xvii.
2 Mirza Mostafa Afshar, *Safarname-ye Khosrow Mirza be qalam-e Mirza Mostafa Afshar* [*Travelogue of Khosrow Mirza Penned by Mirza Mostafa Afshar*] (Teheran: Chapkhane-ye Ettehad: 1349/1970). All translations from Persian are mine.
3 Anatolii Nikiforov and Aleksandr Sokurov, *Russkii kovcheg*, directed by Aleksandr Sokurov (Russia/Germany: Hermitage Bridge Studio/Egoli Tossell Film/Fora-film, 2002).
4 Tynianov, *Smert' Vazir-Mukhtara* (1985), 40–3, 400–2.
5 For an overview of the prince's visit, its purpose, and historical context, see Firuza I. Melville, "Khosrow Mirza's Mission to St Petersburg in 1829," in *Iranian-Russian Encounters: Empires and Revolutions since 1800*, ed. Stephanie Cronin (Abingdon: Routledge, 2013), 69–94.
6 Tynianov, *Smert' Vazir-Mukhtara* (1985), 40.
7 Tynianov, *Smert' Vazir-Mukhtara* (1985), 255.
8 Tynianov, *Smert' Vazir-Mukhtara* (1985), 42.
9 Tynianov, *Smert' Vazir-Mukhtara* (1985), 50.
10 Tynianov, *Smert' Vazir-Mukhtara* (1985), 407.
11 Tynianov, *Smert' Vazir-Mukhtara* (1985), 50.
12 Tynianov, *Smert' Vazir-Mukhtara* (1985), 40.
13 Tynianov, *Smert' Vazir-Mukhtara* (1985), 411.
14 Tynianov, *Smert' Vazir-Mukhtara* (1985), 411–12.
15 Tynianov, *Smert' Vazir-Mukhtara* (1985), 40.
16 Bournoutian, *From Tabriz to St. Petersburg*, 84.
17 Afshar, *Safarname-ye Khosrow Mirza*, 207–13.
18 Afshar, 211.
19 Afshar, 212.
20 Afshar, 213.
21 Afshar, 238–42.
22 Monica Ringer, "The Quest for the Secret of Strength in Iranian Nineteenth-Century Travel Literature: Rethinking Tradition in the Safarnameh," in *Iran and the Surrounding World: Interactions in Culture and Cultural Politics*, ed. Nikki R. Keedie and Rudolph P. Matthee (Seattle: University of Washington Press, 2002), 146–61.
23 Tynianov, *Smert' Vazir-Mukhtara* (1985), 43.
24 Tynianov, *Smert' Vazir-Mukhtara* (1985), 402.
25 Aleksandr Sergeevich Griboedov, *Gore ot uma* (*Woe from Wit*), in *Polnoe sobranie sochinenii v trekh tomakh* (St. Petersburg: Notabene, 1995), 48.
26 Griboedov, *Gore ot uma*, 61.

27 Katerina Clark, *Petersburg: Crucible of Cultural Revolution* (Cambridge, MA: Harvard University Press, 1995), 242–83.
28 Clark, *Petersburg*, 242.
29 Tynianov, *Smert' Vazir-Mukhtara* (1985), 7.
30 Clark, *Petersburg*, 243.
31 Tynianov, *Smert' Vazir-Mukhtara* (1985), 407. Tynianov is citing a description of a waltz in *Literaturnaia gazeta*, St. Petersburg, 1841, no. 96; see P. Stolpianskii, *Muzyka i muzitsirovanie v starom Peterburge* (Leningrad: Muzyka, 1989), 92.
32 Aleksandr Sergeevich Pushkin, *Evgenii Onegin*, in *Sobranie sochinenii v desiati tomakh* (Moscow: Gosudarstvennoe izdatel'stvo khudozhestvennoi literatury, 1959–62), 19.
33 Tynianov, *Smert' Vazir-Mukhtara* (1985), 407.
34 Sergei Aleksandrovich Fomichev, "'Griboedovskii epizod' v 'Puteshestvii v Arzrum' Pushkina," in *A.S. Griboedov: Khmelitskii sbornik* (Smolensk: SGU, 1998), 381–3.
35 Aleksandr Pushkin, *Polnoe sobranie sochinenii A.S. Pushkina v shesti tomakh* (Berlin: Slovo, 1921), 4:473.
36 Clark, *Petersburg*, 263, 282.
37 Pushkin, *Polnoe sobranie sochinenii*, 1:500.
38 Susan Layton, *Russian Literature and Empire* (Cambridge: Cambridge University Press, 1994), 266.
39 Angela Brintlinger, *Writing a Usable Past: Russian Literary Culture, 1917–1937* (Evanston: Northwestern University Press, 2008).
40 Iurii Tynianov, "O literaturnoi evolutsii," in *Literaturnyi fakt* (Moscow: Vysshaia shkola, 1993), 146.
41 Mel Gordon, "Meyerhold's Biomechanics," *Drama Review* 18, no. 3 (1974): 78.
42 See a detailed description of this étude in Gordon, "Meyerhold's Biomechanics," 86–7.
43 Tynianov, *Smert' Vazir-Mukhtara* (1985), 407.
44 Pendulum and cyclical movement in Tynianov's novel have been convincingly interpreted both as oscillation between myth and fact in Tynianov's construction of Griboedov's character that reveals Novyi LEF's preoccupation with literature of fact (see Angela Brintlinger, "Griboedov u Tynianova: Biografiia ili mif?" in *A.S. Griboedov: Khmelitskii sbornik* [Smolensk: SGU, 1998], 384–96), and as a symbol of cyclical return of history (see Dragan Kujundžić, *The Return of History: Russian Nietzscheans after Modernity* [Albany: State University of New York Press, 1997]).
45 Tynianov, *Smert' Vazir-Mukhtara* (1985), 17.
46 Tynianov, *Smert' Vazir-Mukhtara* (1985), 16.
47 Tynianov, *Smert' Vazir-Mukhtara* (1985), 8.
48 Tynianov, *Smert' Vazir-Mukhtara* (1985), 7.

49 Yevgeny Zamyatin, *My* (New York: Mezdunarodnoe Literaturnoe Sodruzhestvo, 1967), 7.
50 Zamyatin, *My*, 5.
51 Julia Vaingurt, "Poetry of Labor and Labor of Poetry: The Universal Language of Gastev's Biomechanics," *Russian Review* 67, no. 2 (2008): 220–3.
52 Vaingurt, "Poetry of Labor," 218–20.
53 Aleksandr Blok, *Stikhotvoreniia* (Moscow: Musaget, 1916), 3:136.
54 Jean-Louis Cohen, "America: A Soviet Ideal," *AA Files* 5 (1984): 32–40.
55 Kondraty Ryleev, *Stikhotvoreniia. Stat'i. Ocherki. Dokladnye Zapiski. Pis'ma* (Moscow: Khudozhestvennaia Literatura, 1956), 292–4; Dmitrii Zavalishin, "Zapiska o kolonii Ross," in *Rossiia v Kalifornii: Russkie dokumenty o kolonii Ross i rossiisko-kaliforniiskikh sviaziakh, 1803–1850*, ed. A.A. Istomin, J.R. Gibson, and V.A. Tishkov (Moscow: Nauka, 2005), 1:555–7.
56 Vaingurt, "Poetry of Labor," 225.
57 Vladimir Maiakovskii, *Izbrannye proizvedeniia* (Moscow-Leningrad: Sovetskii pisatel', 1963), 2:180–5.
58 Griboedov, *Gore ot uma*, 95–7.
59 Tynianov, *Smert' Vazir-Mukhtara* (1985), 163, 388.
60 A.V. Arkhipova, "Chatskii v interpretatsii russkikh pisatelei XIX veka," in *A.S. Griboedov: Khmelitskii sbornik* (Smolensk: SGU, 1998), 209–10.
61 Aleksandr Sergeevich Griboedov, "Putevye pis'ma k S.N. Begichevu," in *Sochineniia* (Goslitizdat, 1959), 407.
62 Griboedov, *Gore ot uma*, 47.
63 Afshar, *Safarname-ye Khosrow Mirza*, 200.
64 Griboedov, *Polnoe sobranie sochinenii*, 3:339.
65 Griboedov, "Putevye pisma k S.N. Begichevu," in *Sochineniia* (Goslitizdat, 1959), 2:303.
66 Griboedov, *Polnoe sobranie sochinenii*, 3:407–8.
67 In reality, Griboedov and Zaveleisky were never prevented from establishing their company, but were only denied the special privileges they had requested. The company was established shortly after Griboedov's death *na obshchikh osnovaniiakh*, that is, it had the same rights as other enterprises in Transcaucasia.
68 Tynianov, *Smert' Vazir-Mukhtara* (1985), 7.
69 Tynianov, *Smert' Vazir-Mukhtara* (1985), 45.
70 Firuza I. Melville, "Khosrow Mirza's Mission to St Petersburg in 1829," in *Iranian-Russian Encounters: Empires and Revolutions since 1800*, ed. Stephanie Cronin (Abingdon: Routledge, 2013), 70; Rudi Matthee, "Between Sympathy and Enmity: Nineteenth-Century Iranian Views of the British and the Russian," in *Looking at the Colonizer: Cross-Cultural Perceptions in central Asia and the Caucasus, Bengal and Related Areas*, ed. Beate Eschment and Hans Harder (Würzburg: Ergon, 2004), 311–38.

71 Stephanie Cronin, "Importing Modernity: European Military Mission to Qajar Iran," *Comparative Studies in Society and History* 50, no. 1 (2008): 200.
72 Cronin, "Importing Modernity," 207.
73 Cronin, 197.
74 Afshar, *Safarname-ye Khosrow Mirza*, 219.
75 Afshar, 222, 243–4.
76 Afshar, 222, 225.
77 Afshar, 226.
78 Nikolai Gogol, *Polnoe sobranie sochinenii* (Moscow: T.I. Gagen, 1880), 2:83.
79 Mirza Afshar apparently relies on the equivalency between civil, military, and court rank in the table of rank introduced by Peter the Great.
80 Afshar, *Safarname-ye Khosrow Mirza*, 245.
81 Afshar, 244.
82 Count Paul Sukhtelen, "Persidskoe posol'stvo v Rossii, 1829 goda (po bumagam Grafa P.P. Sukhtelena)." *Russkii arkhiv* 27, no. 1, edited by M.G. Rozanov (Moscow, 1889), 248.
83 Bournoutian, *From Tabriz to St. Petersburg*, 194.
84 Afshar, *Safarname-ye Khosrow Mirza*, 267.
85 Afshar, 244.
86 Afshar, 235–7.
87 Iurii Tynianov, "Voskovaia persona," in *Sochineniia v dvukh tomakh* (Leningrad: Khudozhestvennaia literatura, 1985), 1:353–457.
88 Afshar, *Safarname-ye Khosrow Mirza*, 236.
89 Berzhe, "Khosrov-Mirza, 1813–1875," 341.
90 Maryam Ekhtiar, "An Encounter with the Russian Czar: The Image of Peter the Great in Early Qajar Historical Writings," *Iranian Studies* 29, no. 1–2 (1996): 62, https://www.jstor.org/stable/4310969.
91 Afshar, *Safarname-ye Khosrow Mirza*, 236.
92 Ekhtiar, "An Encounter," 68.
93 Tynianov, *Smert' Vazir-Mukhtara* (1985), 257.
94 Adeeb Khalid, "Russian History and the Debate over Orientalism," *Kritika: Explorations in Russian and Eurasian History* 1, no. 4 (2000): 696.
95 Tynianov, *Smert' Vazir-Mukhtara* (1985), 257.
96 L. Trotskii, *Literatura i revoliutsiia* (Moscow: Politizdat, 1991).
97 Tynianov, *Smert' Vazir-Mukhtara* (1985), 17.
98 Tynianov, *Smert' Vazir-Mukhtara* (1985), 16.
99 Tynianov, *Smert' Vazir-Mukhtara* (1985), 160–1.
100 L.N. Tolstoi, "Rubka lesa," in *Sobranie sochinenii v dvenadtsati tomakh* (Moscow: Khudozhestvennaia literatura, 1958), 2:34–70.
101 L.N. Tolstoi, "Khadzhi-Murat," in *Sobranie sochinenii v dvenadtsati tomakh* (Moscow: Khudozhestvennaia literatura, 1958), 12:234–351.

102 Andrei Bely, *Petersburg* (Moscow: Eksmo, 2007), 18–22.
103 Tynianov, *Smert' Vazir-Mukhtara* (1985), 161; Bely, *Petersburg*, 22.
104 Zamyatin, *My*, 9, 24–30.
105 For this interpretation of "Wax Effigy" see Kevin Platt, "Antichrist Enthroned: Demonic Visions of Russian Rulers," in *Russian Literature and Its Demons*, ed. Pamela Davidson (New York: Berghahn, 2000), 87–124. On the manifestions of the myth of Peter the Great throughout Russian history, see Kevin Platt, *Terror and Greatness: Ivan and Peter as Russian Myths* (Ithaca: Cornell University Press, 2011).
106 Clark, *Petersburg*, 13.
107 Tolstoy was writing the novella during the Anglo-Boer war (1898–1902), which he took to heart. See Layton, *Russian Literature and Empire*, 263.
108 Layton, *Russian Literature and Empire*, 263–87.
109 Griboedov mentions kaleidoscopes as appropriate gifts to present to Persians in his letter to Begichev: "Putevye pisma k S.N. Begichevu," in *Sochineniia* (Goslitizdat, 1959), 406.
110 Velimir Khlebnikov, "Kave-kuznets," in *Sobranie sochinenii v shesti tomakh* (Moscow: IMLI RAN, Nasledie, 2001), 2:197.
111 Tynianov, *Smert' Vazir-Mukhtara* (1985), 298.

8 *Vazir-Mukhtar* as a Parody of a Spy Novel

1 James Fenimore Cooper, *The Prairie* (Oxford: Oxford University Press, 1999 [1827]).
2 Angela Brintlinger, "The Persian Frontier: Griboedov as Orientalist and Literary Hero Author," *Canadian Slavonic Papers/Revue Canadienne des Slavistes* 45, no. 3/4 (2003): 373.
3 Rudyard Kipling, *Kim* (New York: Open Road Integrated Media, 2015 [1901]).
4 "The Nobel Prize in Literature 1907," *NobelPrize.org*, https://www.nobelprize.org/prizes/literature/1907/summary/ (accessed 6 October 2020).
5 Mukund Belliappa, "The Unsentimental Education of Rudyard Kipling," *Antioch Review* 73, no. 2 (2015): 209.
6 Belliappa, "Unsentimental Education," 217.
7 Belliappa, 217.
8 Belliappa, 217.
9 FantLab.ru, online translator at https://fantlab.ru/translator3384.
10 Viktor Shklovskii, "O Maiakovskom," in *Sobranie sochinenii v trekh tomakh* (Moscow: Khudozhestvennaia literatura, 1974), 3:107.
11 Tynianov, *Smert' Vazir-Mukhtara* (1985), 240.

12 Tynianov, *Smert' Vazir-Mukhtara* (1985), 58.
13 Tynianov, *Smert' Vazir-Mukhtara* (1985), 61–2.
14 Tynianov, *Smert' Vazir-Mukhtara* (1985), 109, 123.
15 Tynianov, *Smert' Vazir-Mukhtara* (1985), 120–1.
16 Tynianov, *Smert' Vazir-Mukhtara* (1985), 125.
17 Currently the capital of the province of Punjab in Pakistan.
18 Kipling, *Kim*, 394–5.
19 Kipling, 397.
20 Kipling, 397.
21 Kipling, 399–402.
22 Kipling, 395.
23 Juniper Ellis, "Writing Race: Education and Ethnography in Kipling's 'Kim,'" *Centennial Review* 39, no. 2 (1995): 315–29, https://www.jstor.org/stable/23739159.
24 On Kipling's view of race and Orientalism, see David Scott, "Kipling, the Orient, and Orientals: 'Orientalism' Reoriented?" *Journal of World History* 22, no. 2 (2011): 299–328, https://www.jstor.org/stable/23011713.
25 Kipling, *Kim*, 132.
26 Kipling, 341.
27 Matthew Fellion, "Knowing Kim, Knowing in *Kim*," *Studies in English Literature, 1500–1900* 53, no. 4 (2013): 898, https://doi.org/10.1353/sel.2013.0038.
28 Kipling, *Kim*, 293.
29 Kipling, 291.
30 Tynianov, *Smert' Vazir-Mukhtara* (1985), 365.
31 A.S. Griboedov, *Polnoe sobranie sochinenii v trekh tomakh* (St. Petersburg: Dmitrii Bulanin, 2006), 3:54.
32 Griboedov, *Polnoe sobranie sochinenii v trekh tomakh*, 54.
33 Griboedov, 54.
34 Milica Bakić-Hayden, "Nesting Orientalisms: The Case of Former Yugoslavia," *Slavic Review* 54, no. 4 (1995), 917–31, https://www.jstor.org/stable/2501399.
35 Tynianov, *Smert' Vazir-Mukhtara* (1985), 62.
36 Tynianov, *Smert' Vazir-Mukhtara* (1985), 89.
37 Tynianov, *Smert' Vazir-Mukhtara* (1985), 60–3.
38 Tynianov, *Smert' Vazir-Mukhtara* (1985), 65.
39 Tynianov, *Smert' Vazir-Mukhtara* (1985), 63–4.
40 Tynianov, *Smert' Vazir-Mukhtara* (1985), 65.
41 Tynianov, *Smert' Vazir-Mukhtara* (1985), 67; Aleksandr Griboedov, *Gore ot uma* (*Woe from Wit*), in *Polnoe sobranie sochinenii v trekh tomakh* (St. Petersburg: Notabene, 1995), 116.
42 Tynianov, *Smert' Vazir-Mukhtara* (1985), 68.

43 Kipling, *Kim*, 298.
44 Kipling, 300–1.
45 Kipling, 302.
46 Fellion, "Knowing Kim," 900.
47 S.N. Begichev, "Zapiska ob A.S. Griboedove," in *A.S. Griboedov v vospominaniiakh sovremennikov*, ed. V.E. Vatsuro (Moscow: Khudozhestvennaia literatura, 1980), 20.
48 Aleksandr Sergeevich Griboedov, "Putevye pisma k S.N. Begichevu," in *Sochineniia* (Goslitizdat, 1959), 401.
49 Aleksandr Sergeevich Griboedov, *Izbrannye pis'ma* (Moscow-Leningrad: Khudozhestvennaia literatura, 1959), 82.
50 Griboedov, *Izbrannye pis'ma*, 82.
51 Griboedov, 82.
52 Tynianov, *Smert' Vazir-Mukhtara* (1985), 59–60.
53 Tynianov, *Smert' Vazir-Mukhtara* (1985), 60.
54 Tynianov, *Smert' Vazir-Mukhtara* (1985), 60.
55 Kipling, *Kim*, 316.
56 Kipling, 318.
57 Kipling, 377.
58 Kipling, 388.
59 Kipling, 388.
60 Tynianov, *Smert' Vazir-Mukhtara* (1985), 334–5.
61 A.S. Pushkin, *Sobranie sochinenii v desiati tomakh* (Moscow: Khudozhestvennaia literatura, 1960), 5:448–9.
62 Pushkin, *Sobranie sochinenii v desiati tomakh*, 5:448–9.
63 Tynianov, *Smert' Vazir-Mukhtara* (1985), 359.
64 Tynianov, *Smert' Vazir-Mukhtara* (1985), 358.
65 Tynianov, *Smert' Vazir-Mukhtara* (1985), 357.
66 Tynianov, *Smert' Vazir-Mukhtara* (1985), 357.
67 Tynianov, *Smert' Vazir-Mukhtara* (1985), 357–8.
68 Tynianov, *Smert' Vazir-Mukhtara* (1985), 257.
69 Tynianov, *Smert' Vazir-Mukhtara* (1985), 257.
70 Bakić-Hayden, "Nesting Orientalisms," 917–31.
71 Tynianov, *Smert' Vazir-Mukhtara* (1985), 356.
72 Kipling, *Kim*, 268.
73 Ellis, "Writing Race," 327.
74 Ellis, 326.
75 Kipling, *Kim*, 267.
76 Kipling, 267–8.
77 Tynianov, *Smert' Vazir-Mukhtara* (1985), 155.
78 Tynianov, *Smert' Vazir-Mukhtara* (1985), 355.
79 Tynianov, *Smert' Vazir-Mukhtara* (1985), 359–60.

80 Tynianov, *Smert' Vazir-Mukhtara* (1985), 359.
81 Tynianov, *Smert' Vazir-Mukhtara* (1985), 359.
82 Tynianov, *Smert' Vazir-Mukhtara* (1985), 361.
83 Tynianov, *Smert' Vazir-Mukhtara* (1985), 361.
84 Tynianov, *Smert' Vazir-Mukhtara* (1985), 84, 163, 388.
85 Kipling, *Kim*, 90–1.
86 Lizzy Welby, *Rudyard Kipling's Fiction: Mapping Psychic Spaces* (Edinburgh: Edinburgh University Press, 2015), 100–33.
87 Kipling, *Kim*, 456–9.
88 Welby, *Rudyard Kipling's Fiction*, 101.
89 Matthew Fellion is also sceptical of such interpretation; see Fellion, "Knowing Kim," 909.
90 Kipling, *Kim*, 473–6.
91 Kipling, 474.
92 Kipling, 469.

In Lieu of a Conclusion

1 David Schimmelpenninck van der Oye, "The Curious Fate of Edward Said in Russia," *Etudes de lettres*, no. 2–3 (2014): 89.
2 Kevork K. Oskanian, "A Very Ambiguous Empire: Russia's Hybrid Exceptionalism," *Europe-Asia Studies* 70, no. 1 (2018): 38.
3 Stephanie Cronin, "Introduction: Edward Said, Russian Orientalism and Soviet Iranology," *Iranian Studies* 48, no. 5 (2015): 656–7.
4 Oskanian, "A Very Ambiguous Empire," 35.
5 Alexander Morrison, "The Russian Empire and the Soviet Union: Too Soon to Talk of Echoes?" in *Echoes of Empire: Memory, Identity and the Legacy of Imperialism*, ed. Kalypso Nicolaidis, Berny Sèbe, and Gabrielle Maas (London: I.B. Tauris, 2015), 7–8.
6 Eduard Volodarskii, *Smert' Vazir-Mukhtara. Liubov' i zhizn' Griboedova*, dir. Sergei Vinokurov (Russia: Avrora Films, 2010).
7 Volodarskii, *Smert' Vazir-Mukhtara*, episode 8.
8 Volodarskii, episode 9.
9 Volodarskii, episode 10.
10 Tynianov, *Smert' Vazir-Mukhtara* (1985), 376, 379.
11 Rosalind Marsh, "The Concepts of Gender, Citizenship, and Empire and Their Reflection in Post-Soviet Culture," *Russian Review* 72, no. 2 (2013): 200.
12 Stehn A. Mortensen, "Discursive Propagation in Putin's Russia: Prohibiting 'Propaganda of Non-Traditional Sexual Relations,'" *Zeitschrift für Slavische Philologie* 72, no. 2 (2016): 350.
13 Tynianov, *Smert' Vazir-Mukhtara* (1985), 19, 31, 71, 76, 417.

14 Aleksandr Sergeevich Pushkin, "Puteshestvie v Arzrum vo vremia pokhoda 1829 goda," in *Sobranie sochinenii v desiati tomakh* (Moscow: Gosudarstvennoe izdatel'stvo khudozhestvennoi literatury, 1959–62), 435.
15 Volodarskii, *Smert' Vazir-Mukhtara*, episode 1.
16 Tynianov, *Smert' Vazir-Mukhtara* (1985), 84.
17 Volodarskii, *Smert' Vazir-Mukhtara*, episode 5.
18 Volodarskii, episode 5.
19 Tynianov, *Smert' Vazir-Mukhtara* (1985), 187.
20 Volodarskii, *Smert' Vazir-Mukhtara*, episode 5.
21 Volodarskii, episode 5.
22 Tynianov, *Smert' Vazir-Mukhtara* (1985), 188.
23 Tynianov, *Smert' Vazir-Mukhtara* (1985), 187–8.
24 Tynianov, *Smert' Vazir-Mukhtara* (1985), 153.
25 Oskanian, "A Very Ambiguous Empire," 43.
26 Oskanian, 44–5.
27 Adeeb Khalid, "Russian History and the Debate over Orientalism," *Kritika: Explorations in Russian and Eurasian History* 1, no. 4 (2000): 693.

Bibliography

ARCHIVE

National Archives of Georgia, Ministry of Justice, Tbilisi, Georgia

SOURCES

Abovian, Kh. "Ameriku lis k'tsily." In *Erkeri liakatar zhoghovatsu ut' hatorov,* 5:234–61. Erevan: Haikakan SSR GA Hratarakchutiun, 1955.

– "Hayastani u hay zhoghovrdi tntesakan u kulturakan vichaki barelavelu ughineri masin." In *Erkeri liakatar zhoghovatsu ut' hatorov,* 8:82–95. Erevan: Haikakan SSR GA Hratarakchutiun, 1958.

– "Parskastani ev Rusastani mijev tsagats paterazmi nakhorein, mot 1825 t'vakanin." In *Erkeri liakatar zhoghovatsu ut' hatorov,* 8:55–62. Erevan: Haikakan SSR GA Hratarakchutiun, 1958.

– *Verk' Hayastani.* In *Erkeri liakatar zhoghovatsu ut' hatorov,* vol. 3. Erevan: Haikakan SSR GA Hratarakchutiun, 1961.

Adelung, K.F. "Pis'ma k ottsu. 1828 g." In Vatsuro, *A.S. Griboedov v vospominaniiakh sovremennikov,* 170–91.

Afshar, Mirza Mostafa. *Safarname-ye Khosrow Mirza be qalam-e Mirza Mostafa Afshar.* Teheran: Chapkhane-ye Ettehad, 1349/1970.

Akimushkin, O.F., et al. "Comments." In Griboedov, *Polnoe sobranie sochinenii v trekh tomakh,* 3:574–5.

Akopian, Piona. "Khachatur Abovian i ego 'Rany Armenii.'" In Khachatur Abovian, *Rany Armenii,* 5–20. Erevan: Sovetakan grogh, 1977.

Alaverdiants, M.Ia. *Test' A.S. Griboedova – Kniaz' Aleksandr Chavchavadze v kharakteristike armianskogo istorika.* St. Petersburg: Elektro-Tipografiia N. Ia. Stoikovoi, 1910.

Amanat, Abbas. *Resurrection and Renewal: The Making of the Babi Movement in Iran, 1844–1850.* Ithaca: Cornell University Press, 1989.

Andreeva, Elena. "Diplomacy and Murder in Tehran: Alexander Griboyedov and Imperial Russia's Mission to the Shah of Persia by Laurence Kelly." *Iranian Studies* 36, no. 3 (2003): 413–17.

– *Russia and Iran in the Great Game: Travelogues and Orientalism.* London: Routledge, 2007.

Arkhipova, A.V. "Chatskii v interpretatsii russkikh pisatelei XIX veka." In *A.S. Griboedov: Khmelitskii sbornik,* 199–217. Smolensk: SGU, 1998.

Atkin, Muriel. *Russia and Iran: 1780–1828.* Minneapolis: University of Minnesota Press, 1980.

Avalov, Z., and J.E.S. Cooper. "The Caucasus since 1918." *Slavonic Review* 3, no. 8 (1924): 320–36. https://www.jstor.org/stable/4201858.

Avrich, Paul. *Russian Rebels, 1600–1800.* New York: Schocken, 1976.

Babel, I. *Odesskie rasskazy.* Letchworth: Prideaux, 1924.

Bakhtin, Mikhail. "Slovo v romane." In *Vorposy literatury i estetiki,* 72–233. Moscow: Khudozhestvennaia literatura, 1975.

Bakić-Hayden, Milica. "Nesting Orientalisms: The Case of Former Yugoslavia." *Slavic Review* 54, no. 4 (1995): 917–31. https://www.jstor.org/stable/2501399.

Begichev, S.N. "Zapiska ob A.S. Griboedove." In Vatsuro, *A.S. Griboedov v vospominaniiakh sovremennikov,* 23–31.

Belinkov, Arkadiy Viktorovich [A.V]. *Yurii Tynianov.* Moscow: Sovetskii pisatel', 1965.

Belinsky, Vissarion. "Sochineniia Aleksandra Pushkina." In *Sobranie sochinenii v trekh tomakh,* 13:74–492. Moscow: Gosudarstvennoe izdatel'stvo khudozhestvennoi literatury, 1948.

Belliappa, Mukund. "The Unsentimental Education of Rudyard Kipling." *Antioch Review* 73, no. 2 (2015): 209–24.

Bely, Andrei. *Petersburg.* Moscow: Eksmo, 2007.

Berg, Maxine. "From Imitation to Invention: Creating Commodities in Eighteenth-Century Britain." *Economic History Review* 55, no. 1 (2002): 1–30.

Berkovsky, N.Ya. "O Griboedove i o romane Tynianova." In *Mir sozdavaemyi literaturoi,* 230–45. Moscow: Sovetskii pisatel', 1989.

Berzhe, A.P. "Khosrov-Mirza, 1813–1875." In *Russkaia starina,* 25:333–50. St. Petersburg, 1879.

Bestuzhev, A.A. "Znakomstvo moe s A.S. Griboedovym." In Vatsuro, *A.S. Griboedov v vospominaniiakh sovremennikov,* 97–103.

Blavatskii, A. "Po pis'mu erivanskogo uezdnogo nachal'nika ob obide prichinennoi emu ispravliaiushchim dolzhnost' smotritelia erivanskogo uezdnogo uchilishcha tituliarnym sovetnikom Abovianom pri vstreche patriarkha Nersesa." National Archives of Georgia, Ministry of Justice, Tbilisi, 9 May 1846, F 4, Op. 3, N 631.

Blok, Aleksandr. *Dvennadtsat'.* Petersburg: Alkonost", 1918.

– *Katilina*. Petersburg: Alkonost", 1919.

– *Stikhotvoreniia*. 3 vols. Moscow: Musaget, 1916.

Bode, K.K. "Smert' Griboedova." In Vatsuro, *A.S. Griboedov v vospominaniiakh sovremennikov*, 201–5.

Bogomolov, Igor'. *Aleksandr Chavchavadze i russkaia kul'tura Tbilisi*. Tbilisi: Metsniereba, 1964.

Borozdin, K.A. "Nina Aleksandrovna Griboedova." In Vatsuro, *A.S. Griboedov v vospominaniiakh sovremennikov*, 302–14.

Bournoutian, George A. *From Tabriz to St. Petersburg: Iran's Mission of Apology to Russia in 1829*. Costa Mesa: Mazda, 2014.

Bowen, H.V. [Huw Vaughan]. *The Business of Empire: The East India Company and Imperial Britain, 1756–1833*. Cambridge: Cambridge University Press, 2006.

– "'No Longer Mere Traders': Continuities and Change in the Metropolitan Development of the East India Company, 1600–1834." In *The Worlds of the East India Company*, edited by H.V. Bowen, Margarette Lincoln, and Nigel Rigby, 19–32. Rochester: Boydell, 2002.

Breschinsky, Dimitri N., and Zinaida A. Breschinsky. "On Tynjanov the Writer and His Use of Cinematic Technique in *The Death of the Wazir Mukhtar*." *Slavic and East European Journal* 29, no. 1 (1985): 1–17. https://www.jstor.org/stable/307921.

Brintlinger, Angela. "Griboedov u Tynianova: biografiia ili mif?" In *A.S. Griboedov: Khmelitskii sbornik*, 384–96. Smolensk: SGU, 1998.

– "The Persian Frontier: Griboedov as Orientalist and Literary Hero Author." *Canadian Slavonic Papers/Revue Canadienne des Slavistes* 45, no. 3/4 (2003): 371–93.

– *Writing a Usable Past: Russian Literary Culture, 1917–1937*. Evanston: Northwestern University Press, 2008.

Chavchavadze, A. "Kratkii istoricheskii ocherk Gruzii i ee polozheniia s 1801 po 1831." In V. Shaduri, *Letopis' druzhby gruzinskogo i russkogo narodov s drevnikh vremen do nashikh dnei*, 1:104-5. Tbilisi: Literatura da khelovneb'a, 1967.

Chekhov, A.P. "Kashtanka." In *Sochineniia*. Vol. 4. Moscow: Nauka, 1985.

Chernov, Sergei. *Pavel Pestel: Izbrannye stat'i po istorii dekabrizma*. St. Petersburg: Liki Rossii, 2004.

Clark, Katerina. *Petersburg: Crucible of Cultural Revolution*. Cambridge, MA: Harvard University Press, 1995.

Cohen, Jean-Louis. "America: A Soviet Ideal." *AA Files* 5 (1984): 32–40.

Cooper, James Fenimore. *The Prairie*. Oxford: Oxford University Press, 1999 [1827].

Cronin, Stephanie. "Importing Modernity: European Military Mission to Qajar Iran." *Comparative Studies in Society and History* 50, no. 1 (2008): 197–226.

– "Introduction: Edward Said, Russian Orientalism and Soviet Iranology." *Iranian Studies* 48, no. 5 (2015): 647–62.

Davis, Mike. *Late Victorian Holocausts: El Niño Famines and the Making of the Third World*. London: Verso, 2001.

Denner, Michael A. "Dusting Off the Couch (and Discovering the Tolstoy Connection in Shklovsky's 'Art as Device')." *Slavic and East European Journal* 52, no. 3 (2008): 370–88. https://www.jstor.org/stable/40650988.

Diderot, Denis. *Political Writings*. Translated and edited by John Hope Mason and Robert Wokler. Cambridge: Cambridge University Press, 1992.

Dobrenko, Evgeny. "Pushkin in Soviet and Post-Soviet Culture." In *The Cambridge Companion to Pushkin*, edited by Andrew Kahn, 202–20. Cambridge: Cambridge University Press, 2006.

"Durbe Diliary Bikech." *Bakhchisaraiskii istoriko-kul'turnyi i arkheologicheskii muzei-zapovednik*. 2015. http://handvorec.ru/pamyatniki/hanskij-dvorets/historymus/dyurbe-dilyary-bikech/ (accessed July 24, 2020).

Eichenbaum, Boris. "Kak sdelana 'Shinel'' Gogolia." In *O proze*, 306–26. Leningrad: Khudozhestvennaia literatura, 1969.

– "Tvorchestvo Iu. Tynianova." In *O proze*, 380–420. Leningrad: Khudozhestvennaia literatura, 1969.

Eidelman, Natan. *Byt' mozhet za khrebtom Kavkaza*. Moscow: Nauka, 1990.

Ekelund, Robert B., and Robert F. Hébert. *A History of Economic Theory and Method*. New York: McGraw-Hill, 1975.

Ekhtiar, Maryam. "An Encounter with the Russian Czar: The Image of Peter the Great in Early Qajar Historical Writings." *Iranian Studies* 29, no. 1–2 (1996): 57–70. https://www.jstor.org/stable/4310969.

Ellis, Juniper. "Writing Race: Education and Ethnography in Kipling's 'Kim.'" *Centennial Review* 39, no. 2 (1995): 315–29. https://www.jstor.org/stable/23739159.

Enikolopov, I.K. *Griboedov v Gruzii*. Tbilisi: Zaria Vostoka, 1954.

Etkind, Alexander. *Internal Colonization: The Russian Imperial Experience*. Cambridge: Polity, 2011.

Feldman, Leah. *On the Threshold of Eurasia: Revolutionary Poetics in the Caucasus*. Ithaca: Cornell University Press, 2018.

Fellion, Matthew. "Knowing Kim, Knowing in Kim." *Studies in English Literature, 1500–1900* 53, no. 4 (2013): 897–912. https://doi.org/10.1353/sel.2013.0038.

Fitzpatrick, Sheila. *Stalin's Peasants: Resistance and Survival in the Russian Village after Collectivisation*. New York: Oxford University Press, 1994.

Flanagan, Thomas. "The Agricultural Argument and Original Appropriation: Indian Lands and Political Philosophy," *Canadian Jurnal of Political Science* 22, no. 3 (1989): 589–602.

Fomichev, Sergei Aleksandrovich. *Griboedov. Entsiklopediia*. St. Petersburg: Nestor-Istoriia, 2007.

– "'Griboedovskii epizod' v 'Puteshestvii v Arzrum' Pushkina." In *A.S. Griboedov: Khmelitskii sbornik*, 374–83. Smolensk: SGU, 1998.

Gillespie, David. *Russian Cinema*. Harlow: Pearson Education, 2003.

Gippius, Vladimir. *Pushkin i Khristianstvo*. Petrograd: Sirius, 1915.

Gogol, Nikolai. *Polnoe sobranie sochinenii*. 2 vols. Moscow: T.I. Gagen, 1880.

Gordin, Iakov. *Kavkaz: Zemlia i krov'*. St. Petersburg: Zhurnal "Zvezda," 2000.

Gordon, Mel. "Meyerhold's Biomechanics." *Drama Review* 18, no. 3 (1974): 73–88.

Gould, Rebecca. *Writers and Rebels: The Literature of Insurgency in the Caucasus*. New Haven: Yale University Press, 2016.

Greenleaf, Monika. *Pushkin and Romantic Fashion: Fragment, Elegy, Orient, Irony*. Stanford: Stanford University Press, 1994.

Greenleaf, Monika Frenkel. "Pushkin's 'Journey to Arzrum': The Poet at the Border." *Slavic Review* 50, no. 4 (1991): 940–53.

Griboedov, Aleksandr Sergeevich [A.S.]. *Gore ot uma*. In *Polnoe sobranie sochinenii v trekh tomakh*, 1:9–122. St. Petersburg: Notabene, 1995.

– *Izbrannye pis'ma*. Moscow-Leningrad: Khudozhestvennaia literatura, 1959.

– *Polnoe sobranie sochinenii v trekh tomakh*. Vol. 2. St. Petersburg: Notabene, 1999.

– *Polnoe sobranie sochinenii v trekh tomakh*. Vol. 3. St. Petersburg: Dmitrii Bulanin, 2006.

– "Putevye pis'ma k S.N. Begichevu." In *Sochineniia*, 394–413. Moscow-Leningrad: Goslitizdat, 1959.

– "Vstuplenie k proektu ustava." In *Polnoe sobranie sochinenii v trekh tomakh*, 3:561–75.

– "Zagorodnaya poezdka (otryvok iz pis'ma iuzhnogo zhitelia)." In *Polnoe sobranie sochinenii v trekh tomakh*, 2:275–7.

– "Zapiska ob uchrezhdenii rossiiskoi zakavkazskoi kompanii." In *Polnoe sobranie sochinenii v trekh tomakh*, 3:325–44.

Griffin, Nicholas. *Caucasus: A Journey to the Land between Christianity and Islam*. Chicago: University of Chicago Press, 2004.

Grossman, Leonid. *Pushkin*. Moscow: Molodaia gvardiia, 1958.

Gumilev, N. "Kapitany." In *Sobranie sochinenii*, 1:142–7. Washington, DC: Victor Kamkin, 1962.

– "K. Bal'mont. Tol'ko liubov'." In *Sobranie sochinenii*, 4:202–4. Washington, DC: Victor Kamkin, 1968.

Harding, Neil. *Leninism*. Durham: Duke University Press, 1996.

Helfant, Ian. "Sculpting a Persona: The Path from Pushkin's Caucasian Journal to *Puteshestvie v Arzrum*," *Russian Review* 56, no. 3 (1997): 366–82.

Hirsch, Francine. *Empire of Nations: Ethnographic Knowledge and the Making of the Soviet Union*. Ithaca: Cornell University Press, 2005.

Hokanson, Katya. "Literary Imperialism, *Narodnost'*, and Pushkin's Invention of the Caucasus," *Russian Review* 53, no. 3 (1994): 336–52.

Hutcheon, Linda. *A Theory of Parody: The Teachings of Twentieth-Century Art Forms*. New York: Methuen, 1985.

Jauss, Hans Robert. *Toward an Aesthetic of Reception*. Translated by Timothy Bahti. Minneapolis: University of Minnesota Press, 1982.

Jimack, Peter. "Introduction." In Abbé Guillaume-Thomas-François Raynal, *A History of the Two Indies*, translated and edited by Peter Jimack, ix–xxix. Aldershot: Ashgate, 2006.

Kalinin, Ilya. "Istoriya kak iskusstvo chlenorazdel'nosti." *Novoe literaturnoe obozrenie* 71 (2005): 103–31.

Kamenskii, Vasilii. *Proza poeta*. Moscow: Vagrius, 2001.

– "Stepan Razin." In *Poemy*, 59–100. Moscow: Khudozhestvennaia literatura, 1961.

– "Zhongler." In *LEF: Zhurnal levogo fronta iskusstv*, no. 1, 45–7. Moscow and Petersburg: Gosudarstvennoe izdatel'stvo, 1923.

Kant, Immanuel. *Ethical Philosophy: The Complete Text of Grounding for the Metaphysics of Morals and Metaphysical Principles of Virtue (Part II of the Metaphysics of Morals)*. Translated by James W. Ellington. Indianapolis: Hackett, 1993.

Kelly, Laurence. *Diplomacy and Murder in Tehran: Alexander Griboyedov and Imperial Russia's Mission to the Shah of Persia*. London: I.B. Tauris, 2002.

Khalid, Adeeb. "Russian History and the Debate over Orientalism." *Kritika: Explorations in Russian and Eurasian History* 1, no. 4 (2000): 691–9.

Kharlamova, D.F. "Eshche neskol'ko slov o Griboedove." In Vatsuro, *A.S. Griboedov v vospominaniiakh sovremennikov*, 192–7.

Khlebnikov, Velimir. "I vot zelenoe ushchelie Zorgama …" In *Sobranie sochinenii v shesti tomakh*, 3:294–8. Moscow: IMLI RAN, 2002.

– "Kave-kuznets." In *Sobranie sochinenii v shesti tomakh*, 2:197-8. Moscow: IMLI RAN, Nasledie, 2001.

– "Navruz truda." In *Sobranie sochinenii v shesti tomakh*, 2:191–2. Moscow: IMLI RAN, Nasledie, 2001.

– "Pisma." In *Sobranie sochinenii v shesti tomakh*, vol. 6, bk. 2, 105–218. Moscow: IMLI RAN, 2006.

– "Pis'mo dvum iapontsam." In *Sobranie sochinenii v shesti tomakh*, vol. 6, bk. 1, 252–6. Moscow: IMLI RAN, 2006.

– *Sobranie sochinenii v shesti tomakh*. Vol. 3. Moscow: Nasledie, 2000.

– "Truba Gul'-mully." In *Sobranie sochinenii v shesti tomakh*, 3:299–317. Moscow: IMLI RAN, 2002.

– "Vidite, persy, vot ia idu …." In *Sobranie sochinenii v shesti tomakh*, 2:132. Moscow: IMLI RAN, Nasledie, 2001.

– "Voina v myshelovke." In *Sobranie sochinenii v shesti tomakh*, 3:175–91. Moscow: IMLI RAN, 2002.

Khodarkovsky, Michael. "The Stepan Razin Uprising: Was It a 'Peasant War'?" *Jahrbücher für Geschichte Osteuropas* 42, no. 1 (1994): 1–19.

Kipling, Rudyard. *Kim*. New York: Open Road Integrated Media, 2015 [1901].

Kizilov, Mikhail. "Slave Trade in the Early Modern Crimea from the Perspective of Christian, Jewish and Muslim Sources." *Journal of Early Modern History* 11, no. 1–2 (2007): 1–31.

Korolev, V.N. "Utopil li Sten'ka Razin kniazhnu?" *Istoricheskie issledovaniia o kazachestve*. Razdorskii etnograficheskii muzei-zapovednik. http://www.razdory-museum.ru/c_razin-1.html (accessed 24 July 2020).

Kosterin, A. "Russkie dervishi." *Moskva* 9 (1966): 216–21.

Kujundžić, Dragan. *The Return of History: Russian Nietzscheans after Modernity*. Albany: State University of New York Press, 1997.

Kurtynova-D'Herlugnan, Liubov. *The Tsar's Abolitionists: The Slave Trade in the Caucasus and Its Suppression*. Leiden: Brill, 2010.

Lawson, Philip. *The East India Company: A History*. London: Longman, 1993.

Layton, Susan. *Russian Literature and Empire: Conquest of the Caucasus from Pushkin to Tolstoy*. Cambridge: Cambridge University Press, 1994.

Lebedev, Aleksandr Aleksandrovič. *Griboedov: Fakty i Gipotezy*. Moscow: Iskusstvo, 1980.

Lekashvili, Eka, Lia Lursmanashvili, and Ekaterine Tukhashvili. "Silk Production in Georgia: History and Development Opportunities." Paper presented at the conference "Fashion through History: Costumes, Symbols, Communication," Sapienza University of Rome, Italy, 2015. https://www.researchgate.net/publication/276061374_Silk_Production_in_Georgia_History_and_Development_Opportunities (accessed 23 July 2020).

Lenin, V.I. *Imperializm, kak vysshaia stadiia kapitalizma: populiarnyi ocherk*. Moscow: Kniga, 1986.

– "Rech' s Lobnogo mesta na otkrytii pamiatnika Stepanu Razinu." In *Sochineniia*, 304. Moscow: Gosudarstvennoe izdatel'stvo politicheskoi literatury, 1950.

Levinton, G.A. "Istochniki i podteksty romana 'Smert' Vazir-Mukhtara." In *Tynianovskii sbornik. Tret'i tynianovskie chteniia*, 6–14. Riga: Zinatne, 1988.

Lotman, Iu. M. *Besedy o russkoi kul'ture: Byt i traditsii russkogo dvorianstva, XVIII – nachalo XIX veka*. St. Petersburg: Iskusstvo-SPB, 1994.

Lotman, Yurii. "Ideinoe soderzhanie Puteshestviia iz Peterburga v Moskvu." In *Russkaia literatura i kul'tura prosveshcheniia*, 387–409 Moscow: Ob"edinennoe gumanitarnoe izdatel'stvo, 1998.

Lovell, Steven. "Tynianov as Sociologist of Literature." *Slavonic and East European Review* 79, no. 3 (2001): 419–20.

Lunin, Mikhail. *Sochineniia i pis'ma*. Petersburg: Vsemirnaia Literatura, 1923.

Maiakovskii, Vladimir. *Izbrannye proizvedeniia*. 2 vols. Moscow-Leningrad: Sovetskii pisatel', 1963.

Majd, Mohammad Gholi. *The Great Famine and Genocide in Persia, 1917–1919*. Lanham: University Press of America, 2013.

Malinovskaia, L.N. "Semanticheskoe pole Bakhchisaraiskogo fontana ('slioz') v kontekste islamskoi traditsii." In *Istoriia i arkheologiia Iugo-Zapadnogo Kryma*, 174–87. Simferopol: Tavriia, 1993.

Marsh, Rosalind. "The Concepts of Gender, Citizenship, and Empire and Their Reflection in Post-Soviet Culture." *Russian Review* 72, no. 2 (2013): 187–211.

Martin, Terry. *The Affirmative Action Empire: Nations and Nationalism in the Soviet Union, 1923–1939*. Ithaca: Cornell University Press, 2001.

Mason, John Hope, and Robert Wokler, eds. "Introduction." In Denis Diderot, *Political Writings*, ix–xxxv. Cambridge: Cambridge University Press, 1992.

Matthee, Rudi. "Between Sympathy and Enmity: Nineteenth-Century Iranian Views of the British and the Russian." In *Looking at the Colonizer: Cross-Cultural Perceptions in Central Asia and the Caucasus, Bengal and Related Areas*, edited by Beate Eschment and Hans Harder, 311–38. Würzburg: Ergon, 2004.

Matthee, Rudi, and Elena Andreeva, eds. *Russians in Iran: Diplomacy and Power in the Qajar Era and Beyond*. London: I.B. Tauris, 2019.

Melville, Firuza I. "Khosrow Mirza's Mission to St Petersburg in 1829." In *Iranian-Russian Encounters: Empires and Revolutions since 1800*, edited by Stephanie Cronin, 69–94. Abingdon: Routledge, 2013.

Mignolo, Walter D. *The Darker Side of Western Modernity: Global Futures, Decolonial Options*. Durham: Duke University Press, 2011.

Montesquieu. *Lettres Persanes*. Paris: Garnier-Flammarion, 1964.

Morrison, Alexander. "The Russian Empire and the Soviet Union: Too Soon to Talk of Echoes?" In *Echoes of Empire: Memory, Identity and the Legacy of Imperialism*, edited by Kalypso Nicolaidis, Berny Sèbe, and Gabrielle Maas, 155–74. London: I. B. Tauris, 2015.

Mortensen, Stehn A. "Discursive Propagation in Putin's Russia: Prohibiting 'Propaganda of Non-Traditional Sexual Relations.'" *Zeitschrift für Slavische Philologie* 72, no. 2 (2016): 349–81.

Murav'ev-Apostol, I.M. "Vypiska iz putewestviia po Tavride." In Pushkin, *Polnoe sobranie sochinenii v desiati tomakh*, 4:150. Leningrad: Nauka, 1977.

Muthu, Sankar. *Enlightenment against Empire*. Princeton: Princeton University Press, 2003.

Nechkina, Militsa Vasil'evna. *A.S. Griboedov i dekabristy*. Moscow: Izdatel'stvo Akademii nauk SSSR, 1951.

Nikiforov, Anatolii, and Aleksandr Sokurov. *Russkii kovcheg* (film). Directed by Aleksandr Sokurov. Russia/Germany: Hermitage Bridge Studio/Egoli Tossell Film/Fora-film, 2002.

Oskanian, Kevork K. "A Very Ambiguous Empire: Russia's Hybrid Exceptionalism." *Europe-Asia Studies* 70, no. 1, (2018): 26–52.

Pestel, Pavel. *Russkaia pravda*. St. Petersburg: Kul'tura, 1906.

Piksanov, Nikolai. *Griboedov. Issledovaniia i kharakteristiki.* Leningrad: Izdatel'stvo pisatelei v Leningrade, 1934.

Pisarev, Dmitri. *Pushkin i Belinskii.* Moscow-Petrograd: Gosudarstvennoe izdatel'stvo, 1923.

– "Razrushenie estetiki." In *Sochineniia v chetyrekh tomakh,* 3:418–511. Moscow: Gosudarstvennoe izdatel'stvo khudozhestvennoi literatury, 1955.

Platt, Kevin. "Antichrist Enthroned: Demonic Visions of Russian Rulers." In *Russian Literature and Its Demons,* edited by Pamela Davidson, 87–124. New York: Berghahn Books, 2000.

– *Terror and Greatness: Ivan and Peter as Russian Myths.* Ithaca: Cornell University Press, 2011.

Polevoi, K.A. "Iz stat'i 'O zhizni i sochineniiakh A.S. Griboedova.'" In Vatsuro, *A.S. Griboedov v vospominaniiakh sovremennikov,* 160–7.

Popova, Olga Ivanovna. *A.S. Griboedov v Persii.* Moscow: Zhizn' i znanie, 1929.

Pushkin, Aleksandr Sergeevich. "Bakhchisaraiskii fontan." In *Sobranie sochinenii v desiati tomakh,* 3:143–58.

– *Evgenii Onegin.* In *Sobranie sochinenii v desiati tomakh,* 4:5–200.

– "Kavkazskii plennik." In *Sobranie sochinenii v desiati tomakh,* 3:87–120.

– "Al'bom Onegina." In *Sobranie sochinenii v desiati tomakh,* 4:477–81.

– "Otryvki iz pisem, mysli i zamechaniia." In *Sobranie sochinenii v desiati tomakh,* 6:15–24.

– *Polnoe sobranie sochinenii A.S. Pushkina v shesti tomakh.* 6 vols. Berlin: Slovo, 1921–2.

– "Pora, moi drug, pora! pokoia serdtse prosit ..." In *Sobranie sochinenii v desiati tomakh,* 2:387.

– "Puteshestvie v Arzrum vo vremia pokhoda 1829 goda." In *Sobranie sochinenii v desiati tomakh,* 5:412–62.

– *Sobranie sochinenii v desiati tomakh.* 10 vols. Moscow: Gosudarstvennoe izdatel'stvo khudozhestvennoi literatury, 1959–62.

– "Uchast' moia reshena. Ia zhenius' ...." In *Sobranie sochinenii v desiati tomakh,* 5:498–501.

Radishchev, Aleksandr Nikolaevich. "Puteshestvie iz Peterburga v Moskvu." In *Polnoe sobranie sochinenii,* 1:225–392. Moscow: Izdatel'stvo Akademii nauk SSSR, 1938.

Ram, Harsha. *Imperial Sublime: A Russian Poetics of Empire.* Madison: University of Wisconsin Press, 2003.

– "Pushkin and the Caucasus." In *The Pushkin Handbook,* edited by David M. Bethea, 379–402. Madison: University of Wisconsin Press, 2005.

Ram, Harsha, and Zaza Shatirishvili. "Romantic Topography and the Dilemma of Empire: The Caucasus in the Dialogue of Georgian and Russian Poetry." *Russian Review* 63 (January 2004): 1–25.

Rannit, Aleksis. "Iran in Russian Poetry." *Slavic and East European Journal* 17, no. 3 (1973): 265–77.

Raynal, Abbé Guillaume-Thomas-François. *A History of the Two Indies.* Translated and edited by Peter Jimack. Aldershot: Ashgate, 2006.

– *A Philosophical and Political History of the Settlements and Trade of the Europeans in the East and West Indies.* Translated by J.O. Justamond. Revised ed., 10 vols. London: Printed for W. Strahan and T. Cadell, 1783.

Remarque, Erich Maria. *All Quiet on the Western Front.* New York: Ballantine Books, 1987.

Ringer, Monica. "The Quest for the Secret of Strength in Iranian Nineteenth-Century Travel Literature: Rethinking Tradition in the Safarnameh." In *Iran and the Surrounding World: Interactions in Culture and Cultural Politics,* edited by Nikki R. Keedie and Rudolph P. Matthee, 146–61. Seattle: University of Washington Press, 2002.

Robin, Corey. "Reflections on Fear: Montesquieu in Retrieval." *American Political Science Review* 94, no. 2 (2000): 347–60.

Robinson, Douglas. *Estrangement and the Somatics of Literature.* Baltimore: Johns Hopkins University Press, 2008.

Rozen, Andrei Evgen'evich. *Zapiski dekabrista.* Irkutsk: Vostochno-Sibirskoe knizhnoe izdatel'stvo, 1984.

Rozhkova, Maria Konstantinovna. *Ekonomicheskaia politika tsarskogo pravitel'stva na srednem vostoke vo vtoroi chetverti XIX veka i russkaia burzhuaziia.* Moscow and Leningrad: Izdatel'stvo akademii nauk SSSR, 1949.

Ryleev, Kondraty. *Stikhotvoreniia. Stat'i. Ocherki. Dokladnye Zapiski. Pis'ma.* Moscow: Khudozhestvennaia literatura, 1956.

Schimmelpenninck van der Oye, David. *Russian Orientalism: Asia in the Russian Mind from Peter the Great to the Emigration.* New Haven: Yale University Press, 2010.

– "The Curious Fate of Edward Said in Russia." *Etudes de lettres,* no. 2–3 (2014): 81–94.

Schönle, Andreas. *Authenticity and Fiction in the Russian Literary Journey, 1790–1840.* Cambridge, MA: Harvard University Press, 2000.

Scott, David. "Kipling, the Orient, and Orientals: 'Orientalism' Reoriented?" *Journal of World History* 22, no. 2 (2011): 299–328. https://www.jstor.org/stable/23011713.

Shaduri, V.S. "Kak sooruzhalsia pamiatnik Griboedovu na gore Mtatsminda." In *Tam gde v'etsia Alazan',* 64–8. Tbilisi: Merani, 1977.

– *Letopis' druzhby gruzinskogo i russkogo narodov s drevnikh vremen do nashikh dnei.* Tbilisi: Literatura da Khelovneb'a, 1967.

Shklovsky, Viktor. "Ob istoricheskom romane i o Iurii Tynianove." *Zvezda* 4 (1933): 167–75.

– "O Maiakovskom." In *Sobranie sochinenii v trekh tomakh,* 3:7–142. Moscow: Khudozhestvennaia literatura, 1974.

– "O teorii prozy: 1929 g." In *O teorii prozy*, 1–62. Moscow: Sovetskii pisatel', 1983.
– *Sentimental'noe puteshestvie*. Moscow: Novosti, 1990.
– *Tristram Shendi Sterna i teoriia romana*. Petrograd: OPOIAZ, 1921.
– "Vyshla kniga Maiakovskogo 'Oblako v shtanakh.'" In *Gamburgskii schet*, 58–72. Moscow: Sovetskii pisatel', 1990.
Simonde de Sismondi, Jean-Charles-Léonard. *New Principles of Political Economy, or, Of Wealth in Its Relation to Population*. Translated by Richard Hyse. New Brunswick: Transaction, 1991.
Slezkine, Yuri. "The USSR as a Communal Apartment, or How a Socialist State Promoted Ethnic Particularism." *Slavic Review* 53, no. 2 (1994): 414–52.
Smith, Adam. *An Inquiry into the Nature and Causes of the Wealth of Nations*. 3 vols. Edinburgh: Printed for S. Doig and A. Stirling, 1817.
– *The Theory of Moral Sentiments*. Oxford: Clarendon, 1976.
Stolpianskii, P. *Muzyka i muzitsirovanie v starom Peterburge*. Leningrad: Muzyka, 1989.
Sukhtelen, Count Paul. "Persidskoe posol'stvo v Rossii, 1829 goda (po bumagam Grafa P.P. Sukhtelena)." *Russkii arkhiv* 27, no. 1, edited by M.G. Rozanov. Moscow, 1889.
Suny, Ronald Grigor. *The Making of the Georgian Nation*. Bloomington: Indiana University Press, 1988.
Thompson, Ewa M. *Imperial Knowledge: Russian Literature and Colonialism*. Westport: Greenwood, 2000.
Tolstoi, L. N. "Khadzhi-Murat." In *Sobranie sochinenii v dvenadtsati tomakh*, 12:234–351.
– "Kholstomer." In *Sobranie sochinenii v dvenadtsati tomakh*, 10:96–132.
– "Rubka lesa." In *Sobranie sochinenii v dvenadtsati tomakh*, 2:34–70.
– *Sobranie sochinenii v dvenadtsati tomakh*. Moscow: Khudozhestvennaia literatura, 1958.
Tolz, Vera. *Russia's Own Orient: The Politics of Identity and Oriental Studies in the Late Imperial and Early Soviet Periods*. Oxford: Oxford University Press, 2011.
Tomashevskii, Boris. *Pushkin: Book 1, 1813–1824*. Moscow-Leningrad: Akademiia Nauk SSSR, 1956.
Treewater, Regan. *Isaak Babel's Image of the Humanized Jew in the* Odesskie rasskazy. Ottawa: Library and Archives Canada, 2008.
Trotskii, L. *Literatura i revoliutsiia*. Moscow: Politizdat, 1991.
Tsvetaeva, Marina. *Izbrannye sochineniia*. Minsk: Mastatskaia literature, 1984.
Tuck, Richard. *The Rights of War and Peace: Political Thought and the International Order from Grotius to Kant*. Oxford: Oxford University Press, 1999.
Twarog, Leon I. "Changing Patterns of a Revolutionary Hero." *Slavonic and East European Review* 32, no. 79 (1954): 367–84.

Tynyanov, Yury [Tynianov, Yurii]. *The Death of Vazir-Mukhtar* (1927). Translated by Susan Causey. Translation editor Vera Tsareva-Brauner. London: Look Media, 2018.

"Literaturnoe segodnia." In *Literaturnyi fakt*, 247–64.

– *Literaturnyi fakt*. Moscow: Vysshaia shkola, 1993.

– "O Khlebnikove." In *Literaturnyi fakt*, 230–8. Also published in *Sobranie proizvedenii*, vol. 1. Leningrad: Izdatel'stvo pisatelei, 1928–33. Reprint, Munich: Wilhelm Fink, 1968.

– "O literaturnoi evolutsii." In *Literaturnyi fakt*, 137–48.

– "O 'Puteshestvii v Arzrum.'" In *Pushkin i ego sovremenniki*, 192–208. Moscow: Nauka, 1969.

– "Promezhutok." In *Literaturnyi fakt*, 264–91.

– "Pushkin." In *Literaturnyi fakt*, 158–200.

– *Smert' Vazir-Mukhtara*. Leningrad: Priboi, 1929.

– *Smert' Vazir-Mukhtara* (*The Death of Vazir-Mukhtar*). In *Sochineniia v dvukh tomakh*, 2:85. Leningrad: Khudozhestvennaia literatura, 1985.

– "Voskovaia persona." In *Sochineniia v dvukh tomakh*, 1:353–457. Leningrad: Khudozhestvennaia literatura, 1985.

Vaingurt, Julia. "Poetry of Labor and Labor of Poetry: The Universal Language of Gastev's Biomechanics." *Russian Review* 67, no. 2 (2008): 209–29.

Viazemskii, P.A. *Estetika i literaturnaia kritika*. Moscow: Iskusstvo, 1984.

Vatsuro, V.E., ed. *A.S. Griboedov v vospominaniiakh sovremennikov*. Moscow: Khudozhestvennaia literatura, 1980.

Viola, Lynne. *Peasant Rebels under Stalin: Collectivization and the Culture of Peasant Resistance*. Oxford: Oxford University Press, 1999.

Vock, Maxim von. "Iz donesenii M. Ya. Fon Foka." In Vatsuro, *A.S. Griboedov v vospominaniiakh sovremennikov*, 288–91.

Volodarskii, Eduard. *Smert' Vazir-Mukhtara. Liubov' i zhizn' Griboedova* (television series). Directed by Sergei Vinokurov. Russia: Avrora Films, 2010.

Voloshin, Maksimilian. "Sten'kin sud." In *Stikhotvoreniia i poemy*, 231–2. St. Petersburg: Nauka, 1995.

Vroon, Ronald. "Velimir Khlebnikov's 'Razin: Two Trinities': A Reconstruction." *Slavic Review* 39, no. 1 (1980): 70–84.

Welby, Lizzy. *Rudyard Kipling's Fiction: Mapping Psychic Spaces*. Edinburgh: Edinburgh University Press, 2015.

Zamyatin, Yevgeny. *My*. New York: Mezdunarodnoe Literaturnoe Sodruzhestvo, 1967.

Zavalishin, Dmitrii. "Zapiska o kolonii Ross." In *Rossiia v Kalifornii: Russkie dokumenty o kolonii Ross i rossiisko-kaliforniiskikh sviaziakh, 1803–1850,* edited by A.A. Istomin, J.R. Gibson, and V.A. Tishkov, 1:555–7. Moscow: Nauka, 2005.

Zhukovskii, Mikhail. "Zamechaniia na zapisku ob ustroistve zemledel'cheskoi, manufakturnoi i torgovoi kompanii." Appendix to I.K. Enikilopov, *Griboedov v Gruzii,* 130–57. Tbilisi: Zaria Vostoka, 1954.

Index

www.ingramcontent.com/pod-product-compliance
Lightning Source LLC
LaVergne TN
LVHW040149080826
844660LV00014B/899/J

* 9 7 8 1 4 8 7 5 4 3 8 5 3 *